T5-DGK-275

Corporate Medievalism II

Studies in Medievalism XXII

2013

Studies in Medievalism

Founded by Leslie J. Workman

Previously published volumes are listed at the back of this book

Corporate Medievalism II

Edited by
Karl Fugelso

Studies in Medievalism XXII 2013

Cambridge
D. S. Brewer

First published 2013
D. S. Brewer, Cambridge

ISBN 978–1–84384–355–9

ISSN 0738–7164

D. S. Brewer is an imprint of Boydell & Brewer Ltd
PO Box 9, Woodbridge, Suffolk IP12 3DF, UK
and of Boydell & Brewer Inc,
668 Mt Hope Avenue, Rochester, NY 14620–2731, USA
website: www.boydellandbrewer.com

A CIP catalogue record for this book is available
from the British Library

Printed and bound in Great Britain by
CPI Group (UK) Ltd, Croydon, CR0 4YY

Studies in Medievalism

Studies in Medievalism provides an interdisciplinary medium of exchange for scholars in all fields, including the visual and other arts, concerned with any aspect of the post-medieval idea and study of the Middle Ages and the influence, both scholarly and popular, of this study on Western society after 1500.

Studies in Medievalism is published by Boydell & Brewer, Ltd., P.O. Box 9, Woodbridge, Suffolk IP12 3DF, UK; Boydell & Brewer, Inc., 668 Mt. Hope Avenue, Rochester, NY 14620, USA. Orders and inquiries about back issues should be addressed to Boydell & Brewer at the appropriate office.

For a copy of the style sheet and for inquiries about **Studies in Medievalism**, please contact the editor, Karl Fugelso, at the Dept. of Art+Design, Art History, and Art Education, Towson University, 3103 Center for the Arts, 8000 York Rd, Towson, MD 21252–0001, USA, tel. 410–704–2805, fax 410–704–2810 ATTN: Fugelso, e-mail <kfugelso@towson.edu>. All submissions should be sent to him as e-mail attachments in Word.

Acknowledgments

The device on the title page comes from the title page of *Des Knaben Wunderhorn: Alte deutsche Lieder*, edited by L. Achim von Arnim and Clemens Brentano (Heidelberg and Frankfurt, 1806).

The epigraph is from an unpublished paper by Lord Acton, written about 1859 and printed in Herbert Butterfield, *Man on His Past* (Cambridge: Cambridge University Press, 1955), 212.

Studies in Medievalism

I: Corporate Medievalism II: Some Perspective(s)

II: Interpretations

Illustrations

Figures are between pages 138 and 152

Volume XXII 2013

Two great principles divide the world, and contend for the master, antiquity and the middle ages. These are the two civilizations that have preceded us, the two elements of which ours is composed. All political as well as religious questions reduce themselves practically to this. This is the great dualism that runs through our society.

Lord Acton

Editorial Note

In the year since we went to press with *Studies in Medievalism XXI: Corporate Medievalism* global finances have hardly improved. Indeed, in some ways they have declined. By many measures unemployment and consumer confidence in the United States have worsened. Much of Europe is suffering under ever-growing austerity. And the so-called developing world has seen a dramatic slowing, and in some cases even reversal, of its recent gains.

All of which may explain why we received an extraordinary number of emotional responses to *SIM* 21. Already underpaid academics are increasingly experiencing the pinch through not only their students (and perhaps research) but also their wallet. As employer expectations grow, salaries are shrinking, philanthropic organizations are downsizing, publishers are disappearing, and entire departments are being eliminated. This has resulted in the time for the research needed to produce papers being increasingly at a premium.

But several authors managed to fend off other responsibilities long enough to address the ways in which medievalism has been affected by corporations, particularly those of a financial nature. Elizabeth Emery discusses commercial factors behind medieval references in the Woolworth Building, which, upon its completion in 1913, was the tallest and most opulent skyscraper in New York. Amy S. Kaufman examines how the novelists Margaret Atwood, Octavia Butler, and Suzanne Collin refract modern corporations through an imagined and highly dystopic Middle Ages. And Richard Utz observes that Google and other technology companies not only provide tools to refine our study of medievalism, but also advertise their efforts to emulate idealized medieval institutions.

These essays have implications that are often highly relevant to our other papers, but the connection is particularly explicit in Clare Simmons's article, "'Longest, oldest and most popular': Medievalism in the Lord Mayor's Show." The organizers of this annual London pageant claim medieval roots that Simmons shows to be quite false, and in tracking the history of these claims and pointing out their numerous anachronisms, she exposes a textbook example of the ways in which even ostensibly not-for-profit organizations distort the past for their own purposes.

More subtle, but just as powerful, are the corporate influences behind our other seven articles, which address a wide range of other themes more directly. In "Gendering Percy's *Reliques*: *Ancient Ballads* and the Making of Women's

Arthurian Writing," Katie Garner concentrates on the feminist implications of the editing and afterlife of an Arthurian text. In "Romancing the Pre-Reformation: Charles Reade's *The Cloister and the Hearth*," Mark B. Spencer observes the many ways in which a monument of Victorian medievalism has become dated as both history and fiction. In "Renovation and Resurrection in M. R. James's 'An Episode of Cathedral History,'" Patrick J. Murphy and Fred Porcheddu examine the medievalist roots behind a medievalist ghost-story. In "Rodin's *Gates of Hell* and Dante's *Inferno* 7: Fortune, the Avaricious and Prodigal, and the Question of Salvation," Aida Audeh examines how pivotal issues in the *Divine Comedy* are treated in one of the most famous sculptures of the late nineteenth and early twentieth centuries. In "Film Theory, the Sister Arts Tradition, and the Cinematic *Beowulf*," Nickolas Haydock explores how we can productively relate adaptations of medieval texts to scholarly studies of those sources. And in "Red Days, Black Knights: Medieval-themed Comic Books in American Containment Culture," Peter Lee analyzes how the Middle Ages were manipulated to promote patriotic themes in the early days of a popular medium geared toward children.

Thus, thanks to the heterogeneity of our authors' direct subjects and approaches, we offer new insights on many specialties within medievalism. And thanks to the pervasive nature of corporate influence, we offer new perspectives on the foundations, media, and practices of our field as a whole. That is, we offer a starting point for a much-needed and, I hope, enduring discussion of the motives behind medievalism and its study.

The Corporate Gothic of New York's Woolworth Building: Medieval Branding in the Original "Cathedral of Commerce"

Elizabeth Emery

On Broadway, north of Wall Street, the commercial offerings of one storefront blend into the next. Banks, shoe stores, and stationery shops alternate with Duane Reade pharmacies and signs advertising space for rent: "MAGNIFICENT CORNER STORE. 1100 SQ. FT. OF BROADWAY FRONTAGE."[1] From the ground it is difficult to distinguish one skyscraper from the next and to realize that this particular sign graces a window of the famous Woolworth Building, legendary in 1913 as the "cathedral of commerce." The relationships among exterior and interior, reputation and function, spectacle and commerce in New York skyscrapers lie at the heart of this essay, which examines dime-store magnate Frank Woolworth and his architect Cass Gilbert's calculated use of Gothic decorative motifs in the grandest New York skyscraper of their day. The Woolworth Building features a Gothic portal with grotesques symbolizing commerce, a lobby based on a Latin-cross plan, decorated with Byzantine-style mosaics and triptych murals figuring Labor and Commerce, and numerous pinnacles, buttresses, ogive windows, and gargoyles. The effect was so grandiose that an early British visitor declared the skyscraper a "cathedral of commerce" unrivaled by anything in London.[2]

1 This sign figures in a Google Maps picture of The Woolworth Building (June 2012).

2 Alan Francis in "Yours is Land of Contrast," an article in the *New York Times*, 27 April 1913: SM12. The phrase would be widely echoed, most notably by Samuel Parkes Cadman

How could a cathedral, literally the seat of a bishop in a house of worship, be compatible with commerce? The word "cathedral" was often associated with the Gothic style at the end of the nineteenth century,[3] yet it is odd to equate a secular technologically-advanced American office building with old European houses of worship.[4] What were the relationships among American businessmen and architects, international commerce, and European culture at this time? And why would Woolworth Five and Dime stores, which were, as Jean Maddern Pitrone has put it, "as American as apple pie,"[5] have chosen to symbolize their corporate identity with European architecture from the Middle Ages?

The answer derives in great part from the American medievalism of the Gilded Age, a nexus of tensions related to fashion, aesthetics, consumerism, philanthropy, nationalism, and rivalry with Europe.[6] Above all, however, it stems from Woolworth and Gilbert's prescient ability to tap into contemporaries' conflicting beliefs about Gothic architecture and to put them into the service of a corporate venture. In order to explain how medieval forms were ideal for symbolizing modern business, I will first outline Woolworth's vision for his office building. I will then trace the popularity of Gothic architecture in 1911 New York, and examine the ways in which Woolworth and Gilbert's particular blend of flamboyant Gothic led to the Woolworth Building's apotheosis as "the cathedral of commerce."

Commerce was, after all, Woolworth's dominant concern. Gail Fenske has shown that the skyscraper was intended as a trademark: a visual motif that

in his foreword to a guidebook published by Edwin A. Cochran, *The Cathedral of Commerce: The Tallest Building in the World* (New York: Broadway Park Place Company, 1921 [1917]).

3 Alain Erlande-Brandenburg discusses the links between the word *cathedral* and the Gothic style, in *The Cathedral*, trans. Martin Thom (Cambridge: Cambridge University Press, 1989), 1–14.

4 The Woolworth Building was the epitome of modern technology. See *The Cathedral of Commerce* and H. Addington Bruce's *Above the Clouds and Old New York* (New York: Hugh McAtamney, 1913), n.p.

5 Jean Maddern Pitrone, *F. W. Woolworth and the American Five and Dime: A Social History* (Jefferson, NC: McFarland Publishing, 2007), 1.

6 A few recent articles treating medievalism in the early twentieth-century American context include Elizabeth Emery, "Postcolonial Gothic: The Medievalism of America's 'National' Cathedrals," in *Medievalisms in the Postcolonial World*, ed. Kathleen Davis and Nadia Altschul (Baltimore, MD: Johns Hopkins University Press, 2009), 237–64; Laura Morowitz "The Cathedral of Commerce: French Gothic Architecture and Wanamaker's Department Store," in *Medieval Art and Architecture after the Middle Ages*, ed. Janet T. Marquardt and Alyce A. Jordan (Cambridge: Cambridge Scholars Publishing, 2009), 340–62; and Kathleen Davis, "Tycoon Medievalism, Corporate Philanthropy, and American Pedagogy," *American Literary History* 22:4 (Winter 2010): 781–800.

would advertise the Woolworth Company in the United States and abroad.[7] The building was not commissioned because of a need for more space; rather, the rent paid by tenants occupying fifty-five of its floors would finance the entire venture (his company took up only two floors and the storefront).[8] This was a clever idea, as was the use of architecture as branding. Perhaps more importantly, the Woolworth Building's construction was a media event: papers publicized the fact that the $13.5 million for its construction was paid in cash ("A Skyscraper Built by the Nickels of Millions" read a headline in the *New York Times*),[9] and published pictorial updates on the building's progress. Woolworth and his publicist sponsored publicity events and brochures dedicated to the skyscraper's construction and transformed its observation deck into a major tourist attraction.[10]

But Woolworth could have done this without using medieval motifs, as he did in his first flagship building in Lancaster, Pennsylvania (1900–1), modeled after New York department stores (themselves modeled on Parisian counterparts).[11] What commercial advantages could be derived from making references to medieval architectural styles in the Woolworth Building's most accessible public spaces: the Byzantine lobby, the German Rathskeller (its vaulted ceiling featured medieval hunting scenes, castles, ships, minstrels), the Flemish tapestry room, and especially the Observation Deck where, as on the towers of Notre-Dame de Paris, visitors moved in and among gargoyles, statues, pinnacles, and flamboyant arches? After all, most of the working spaces were indistinguishable from those of any other office building.[12]

If it were not for the prevalence of medieval decorative references in the public spaces, one might argue that Woolworth and Cass were simply following a trend now known as "skyscraper Gothic," decoratively referring to the soaring aspirations of Gothic cathedrals, the tallest European buildings before the construction of the Eiffel Tower in 1889. Many of the first skyscraper architects, such as Louis Sullivan in Chicago, explicitly created an architectural vocabulary that referenced Gothic motifs.[13] Debates in

7 Gail Fenske, *The Skyscraper and the City: The Woolworth Building and the Making of Modern New York* (Chicago: University of Chicago Press, 2008), 29.

8 Fenske, *The Skyscraper*, 30, 33, 144.

9 *New York Times* (1 January 1911), SM6.

10 On the publicity campaigns and tourism see Fenske, *The Skyscraper*, 162–64, 210–15, 294, 299–300.

11 Fenske describes this building, modeled on Parisian department stores, in *The Skyscraper*, 30–31.

12 The notable exception was Woolworth's Empire-style office building (he idealized Napoleon).

13 Narciso G. Menocal interprets Sullivan's attraction to the Gothic as an offshoot of his interest in nature. "Louis Sullivan's Use of the Gothic: From Skyscrapers to Banks," in

the popular press drew attention to shared features such as height, weight distribution, and techniques for maximizing natural light.[14] Furthermore, an American Gothic revival in church building, led by the firm of Cram and Goodhue, had similarly inspired enthusiasm for the spiritual aspirations of Gothic cathedrals and for the symbolic importance of their ornamentation. More Gothic cathedrals were being built at the time of the Woolworth Building's construction (including New York's Cathedral of St. John the Divine) than at any time since the fifteenth century: "A Wave of Enthusiasm for Cathedrals Sweeping the Nation" read a headline for the *New York Times* in November 1913, just months after the Woolworth Building's grand opening.[15]

The contemporary American vogue for citing Gothic forms in both skyscrapers and churches certainly played a role in the Woolworth Building's medievalism, as did the fashion for building private homes modeled on medieval and Renaissance models. Woolworth's French Renaissance chateau on the corner of Eightieth Street and Fifth Avenue featured a "medieval German" smoking room, a Louis XIV reception room, and a French eighteenth-century drawing room, among others.[16] In his choice of exterior style he followed a trend set by Alva Vanderbilt, who established medieval and Renaissance architecture as the ultimate visual symbol of American social prestige when she commissioned a medieval mansion from architect Richard Morris Hunt in 1878. He produced a near replica of the fifteenth-century merchant Jacques Coeur's house in Bourges.[17]

Like Vanderbilt, other Americans on "Billionaire's Row" (Fifth Avenue) promoted medieval and Renaissance architecture as a visual marker of their

Medievalism in American Culture, ed. Bernard Rosenthal and Paul E. Szarmach (Binghamton, NY: Medieval and Renaissance Texts and Studies, 1989), 215–50. See Margaret Heilbrun, ed., *Inventing the Skyline: The Architecture of Cass Gilbert* (New York: New York Historical Society, 2000), 250–52, for Gilbert's debt to Sullivan.

14 Mona Domosh shows that comparisons of tall buildings to European structures, particularly cathedrals, were common in the 1890s, "Those 'Sudden Peaks That Scrape the Sky': The Changing Imagery of New York's First Skyscrapers," in *Place Images in Media: Portrayal, Experience, and Meaning*, ed. Leo Zonn (Savage, MD: Rowman & Littlefield Publishers, 1990), 9–30. A 1905 article by Frederic Stymetz Lamb, "Modern Use of the Gothic: The Possibilities of a New Architectural Style," proposing Gothic styles as perfect for skyscrapers, launched a debate in *The Craftsman* 8 (May 1905): 150–70. A. D. F. Hamlin and Bertram Goodhue assessed and Louis Sullivan contested Lamb's ideas in the next issue, 9 (June 1905): 325–38.

15 *New York Times* (24 August 1913), SM11.

16 Fenske describes Woolworth's tours of Europe and his fascination with Parisian architecture in *The Skyscraper*, 34–38. She describes his chateau on pp. 39–40.

17 Wayne Craven, *Gilded Mansions: Grand Architecture and High Society* (New York: W. W. Norton, 2009), 110.

success: "in the noble edifices of the Old World the new aristocrats found suitably grandiose symbols to match their visions of their own place in the social, political, and economic order at the turn of the century – not only in their domestic architecture but also in civic structures."[18] This desire to create a European-style heritage for twentieth-century New York explains many of the stylistic choices evident in the construction of the city's libraries, parks, museums, and opera houses.

Commercial ventures followed this vogue. Department stores such as Macy's and Wanamaker's may have imported the best in modern European fashions, but they also hosted traveling exhibits of old European art and, in their New York and Philadelphia stores, produced grandiose spectacles recreating the naves or rose windows of Gothic cathedrals. Sometimes they even showcased European artisans and their hand-crafted traditional wares.[19] As a result of such conspicuous American consumption, medieval and Renaissance art represented exoticism, wealth, and nostalgia for a pre-industrial past when workers were alleged to have invested themselves spiritually in their labor.[20]

Woolworth's choice of a Gothic style for his office building can thus be read as a response to a social context in which medieval art and architecture had become important cultural signifiers of prestige, ambition, and morality. These were important associations for Woolworth's stores which, in 1911, sold products that cost no more than five or ten cents – cheap, mass-produced items like sewing supplies and hair pins – to a clientele of largely working-class families. As much as he admired the lavish spectacles put on for the bourgeoisie by Parisian department stores and their New York counterparts, Macy's and Wanamaker's, Woolworth could not compete and found himself the target of ridicule.[21] His initial plan was to build a New York version of the Victoria Tower of London's Houses of Parliament (designed in the nineteenth century by the Gothic Revival architects Charles Barry and A. W. N. Pugin), which would enhance the reputation of his brand name by associating it with the powerful British Empire.[22] Like Alva Vanderbilt, he insisted on a medieval form as the perfect expression of commercial and

18 Craven, *Gilded Mansions*, 31.

19 See Laura Morowitz, "The Cathedral of Commerce," 340–62.

20 This stereotype of medieval workers as "primitive" and pure was common in Europe and America. See, for example, Lynda Jessup, *Antimodernism and Artistic Experience: Policing the Boundaries of Modernity* (Toronto: University of Toronto Press, 2001) and Elizabeth Emery and Laura Morowitz, *Consuming the Past: The Medieval Revival in Fin-de-siècle France* (Aldershot: Ashgate Press, 2003).

21 See "Fifth Avenue's 5 and 10 Cent Store De Luxe," *New York Times* (29 July 1917), 32.

22 Fenske, *The Skyscraper*, 123.

social success, and chose an architect, Cass Gilbert, who had already built a critically-acclaimed Gothic-style office building in lower Manhattan (the West Building, 1905–7).[23]

Gilbert's participation brought fifteenth-century European models (rather than nineteenth-century Gothic Revival) into play. Woolworth had seized upon the Victoria Tower largely for the way it looked, while Gilbert's use of medieval forms was intended to add a symbolic dimension to commercial enterprises. Like others influenced by the Ecole des Beaux-Arts, which advocated masking steel-frame architecture with more aesthetically pleasing forms from the past, Gilbert employed historical models to suggest moral qualities. A good example is Pierre Lebrun's design for the Metropolitan Life Building (1909), modeled on the campanile at St. Mark's Place in Venice to associate the speculative activities of an insurance company with a European sense of civic responsibility and pride.[24]

Gilbert had been an enthusiast of Gothic architecture since his days at the Massachusetts Institute of Technology, studying the writings of Viollet-le-Duc and Ruskin, and traveling through Europe.[25] Gail Fenske suggests that by explicitly drawing on secular Gothic models at the West Building – the *hôtels de ville* of free-trading Flemish cities such as Brussels, Middleburg, Audenarde, and Bruges – Gilbert appealed to American nostalgia for the idealized trade practices of the Middle Ages at a time that had come to favor militarization abroad and economic disparity over international free markets. The pictorial pinnacles of his West Street building, its crown, and markedly Gothic lobby, with vaulting, arches, and clerestory windows, linked a New York corporation focused on coal, iron, rail, and maritime activities to Romanticized notions of democratic and productive free trade.[26] Gilbert would do the same with the Woolworth Building.

The choice of secular Gothic styles was thus not arbitrary; they referred specifically to contemporary debates linking American commerce to the medieval past: "The influence of the Feudal Lord has passed into the Merchant's hands," wrote T. W. Higginson in the pages of *Hunt's Merchants' Magazine* in 1853. The difference, he noted, was that:

23 Fenske, *The Skyscraper*, 68.

24 Olivier Zunz discusses the Metropolitan Life Building in *Making America Corporate: 1870–1920* (Chicago: University of Chicago Press, 1990), 114. On the influence of Beaux-Arts aesthetics in the United States, see Sean Dennis Cashman, *America in the Age of the Titans: The Progressive Era and World War I* (New York: New York University Press, 1988), 363–65.

25 Fenske, *The Skyscraper*, 77, 83–84.

26 Fenske, *The Skyscraper*, 107–10. Morowitz exposes the ways in which department-store baron John Wanamaker and his associates similarly exploited medieval themes to align their commercial ventures with pre-industrial and Christian traditions, "The Cathedral of Commerce," 355–66.

> the watchword of Feudalism was *Separation* and *Restriction*; while that of the Money Power is *Union* and *Freedom*. Feudalism built cities with castle and fortress, moat and wall, to keep men asunder; the cities of the Money Power may be known by exchange and market-place, railroad and steamship, to bring men together.[27]

Such idealistic discourse served as a way of justifying – on moral grounds – business practices that led to social inequality. Higginson would conclude his article by encouraging merchants to embrace the *noblesse oblige* of their medieval predecessors, to serve as "Stewards of God" by sharing their wealth with others.[28]

While this article dates from the 1850s, Kathleen Davis has provided a clear example of the persistence into the 1900s of using ideas about the Middle Ages to recast commercial activities as noble pursuits intended to support the common good. Andrew Carnegie's 1901 *Gospel of Wealth: The Problem of the Administration of Wealth*, for example, also emphasized the moral superiority of the wealthy and their obligations to the less fortunate.[29] Seemingly disinterested gifts (like Carnegie's libraries) contributed to the common good, but they served another purpose. Davis, influenced by Pierre Bourdieu, suggests that they were a clever way of perpetuating a brand name under the guise of moral stewardship.[30]

The Woolworth Building can be considered in much the same vein. As we saw above, Woolworth's primary goal was to build a trademark building – advertising – that would create even more business. But both he and Gilbert became so engrossed in making the building the tallest and most splendid in the world that the final product captured the public's imagination in ways they had not expected, thus leading the well-known minister Samuel Parkes Cadman to proclaim it as an act of philanthropy, a splendid "cathedral of commerce" generously gifted to the world:

> The man who proposes and the architect who designs a truly great building confer a lasting favor on the race at large. Our indebtedness to those who constructed the Parthenon, the Coliseum at Rome, St. Peter's Cathedral in that city, St. Paul's in London, St. Mark's in Venice

27 T. W. Higginson, "Conscience in the Counting Room: or the True Interests of the Merchant," *Hunt's Merchants' Magazine* 28:1 (January 1853): 19–40 (24).

28 Higginson, "Conscience," 36.

29 Davis, "Tycoon Medievalism."

30 Davis, "Tycoon Medievalism," 783.

> and the pure Gothic of St. Chapelle [sic] and Notre Dame in Paris is utterly beyond ordinary methods of computation.[31]

Cadman cites the edifice's aesthetic attraction and its cultural excellence, but goes much further, echoing Higginson's and Carnegie's conviction that commerce is morally beneficent. "'The Cathedral of Commerce' – the chosen habitation of that spirit in man which, through means of change and barter, binds alien people into unity and peace, and reduces the hazards of war and bloodshed. [. . .] Just as religion monopolized art and architecture during the Medieval epoch, so commerce has engrossed the United States since 1865."[32] The Gothic style of the Woolworth Building was thus only a part of why New Yorkers understood it as a cathedral; the association between commerce and medieval values also had a great deal to do with it.

Such enthusiastic praise reveals that Woolworth's Cathedral of Commerce was interpreted in terms of Carnegie's *Gospel of Wealth*, in idealized medieval terms that glossed over the period's less than unified and peaceful activities: strike breaking, racial and sexual discrimination, and armed intervention in international trade disputes.[33] Wealthy businessmen may have ennobled themselves with the trappings of feudalism, but there is a reason many industrialists of this period came to be known as "robber barons."

Cadman interpreted the Woolworth Building in grandiose terms, yet neither Woolworth nor Gilbert had intended to build a cathedral.[34] Given the social history I have just traced, it is easy to see why the public interpreted it as such: commercial ambition had so often been expressed as a logical development from medieval traditions that they did not question the association. And most importantly, the building looked like a cathedral. As Gothic churches such as St. Patrick's and St. John the Divine went up all over New York City, Americans knew what a cathedral was. The Woolworth Building's terracotta sheathing echoed the limestone of Gothic cathedrals, its tower "pierced" the heavens, and exterior decoration – gargoyles, ogives, and pinnacles – would not have been out of place on a church.

31 In Cochran, *The Cathedral of Commerce*, 1. Cadman's comments echo word for word the cultural aspirations expressed in the New York press about building a Gothic cathedral for New York City. See Emery, "Postcolonial Gothic," 240–41.

32 In Cochran, *The Cathedral of Commerce*, 1–2.

33 Kathleen Davis notes that tycoons such as Carnegie and Woolworth squeezed the labor force to make ever greater profits. "Tycoon Medievalism," 788, 791–97.

34 Unlike Wanamaker, who actively attempted to fuse commerce and Christian values (see Morowitz, "The Cathedral of Commerce"), both Woolworth and Gilbert denied having done this explicitly. Fenske cites interviews in which they insisted on their secular intent. *The Skyscraper*, 268.

Unlike the West Building, where Gilbert's architectural models were secular *hôtels de ville*, the Woolworth Building featured more ecclesiastical referents, including Antwerp, Reims, and Maline Cathedrals, the crossing tower of the Benedictine Abbey Church of Saint-Ouen in Rouen, the roof of the Guild Hall in Cologne, Jacques Coeur's mansion at Bourges, the Hotel de Cluny in Paris, and the Hotel de Ville in Compiègne, among others.[35]

Furthermore, the building's lobby, its most prominent public space, looked like a cathedral. Visitors entered from a Gothic portal where the statues of saints had been replaced by figures related to commerce. The lobby had the size, shape, and darkness of a nave, and it was covered with stained glass and mosaics, even if these represented labor and commerce rather than biblical prophets and apostles. The iconography referenced Gothic art in a secular and humorous way related to the building's purpose – corbels feature Woolworth counting his nickels, Gilbert holding a model of the Woolworth Building, and squirrels saving their nuts – yet to the visitor entering the building the effect was that of a Gothic cathedral. In fact, the Gothic style in America had become so synonymous with church architecture by 1913 that the public might not, as Gilbert suggested, have recognized the secular motifs.[36]

Regardless of intentions, the expression, "the cathedral of commerce," became the perfect vehicle for publicizing this grandiose building. The tagline, along with "the tallest building in the world," became indistinguishable from the trademark image of the building's silhouette on the skyline. The words and image would be reproduced on the hundreds of postcards, souvenir booklets, tickets, spoons, sewing cards, dominoes, and other collectibles still circulating on eBay.

Woolworth and Gilbert's brilliant use of medieval branding to pique the public's imagination, to draw visitors, and to create "buzz" was new in 1913, but it was also the beginning of the end of dressing up steel-frame construction skyscrapers with styles from the past. After the two world wars, as the United States increasingly asserted itself on the international stage, most architects no longer looked to European monuments from the past – London's Victoria Tower, Belgian *hôtels de ville*, or French cathedrals – to project moral messages about skyscrapers' identities. The Gothic style, so pervasive in the years from 1880 to 1914 as a way of grafting American iden-

35 Fenske identifies these sources from Gilbert's papers and notebooks. *The Skyscraper*, 155–58.

36 Cited in Fenske, *The Skyscraper*, 268.

tity to old European roots, made way for steel-and-glass skyscrapers, which mirrored a new American self-confidence.[37]

Exactly one hundred years later, a time when "medieval bloodletting" has become the most predominant reference to European economic practices, it is striking to revisit the Woolworth Building's history and to realize that corporate America once expressed its goals in terms of the commercial and aesthetic practices of the European Middle Ages. In 2012 one might ask whether the United States has swung too far in the opposite direction, its financial and political leaders criticized for looking so far forward that they have failed to address the responsibilities and dangers that accompany great wealth.

Today's most visible symbol of international trade, the "Freedom Tower" rising only a few blocks south of the Woolworth Building, is a case in point. Looking resolutely to the future, it was designed as a response to the terrorist attacks of 11 September 2001, an expression of indomitable American spirit rising from the footprint of disaster. Yet such symbolism seems to have overlooked a reality critical for commercial success: tenants. A skyscraper may take on a symbolic function as a landmark or a trademark, but it is first and foremost a corporate office building filled with workers, one of the primary reasons why the Woolworth Building is not open to tourists today. The Freedom Tower's managers have now recognized some of the incompatibilities between patriotic symbolism and practical functionality. They have begun rebranding the site as the "One World Trade Center," its street address.[38] Unlike the Woolworth Building, which used a flamboyant Gothic moniker – "the cathedral of commerce" – to attract clients, "One World Trade Center" must downplay its historical significance to do so, insisting, instead, on a more neutral corporate identity that reflects the commercial character of its neighborhood.

37 For a discussion of the shift from historical styles to more "impersonal statements" of the corporate ethos, see Cashman, *America*, 374–82. See Emery, "Postcolonial Gothic," for theories about "grafting" of American identity on European history.

38 Rick Hamson, "Rising at Ground Zero, a Symbol of Resilience." *USA Today* (10 May 2009). Accessed 12 July 2012, www.usatoday.com/news/nation/2009–05–10-tower_N.htm.

Our Future is Our Past: Corporate Medievalism in Dystopian Fiction

Amy S. Kaufman

> When next you eat a golden Peach
> And lightly throw away the pit,
> Consider how it shines with Life –
> God dwelling in the midst of it.
>
> "The God's Gardeners Oral Hymnbook,"
> Margaret Atwood, *The Year of the Flood*

When economists and political scientists warn of the "new medievalism," they are referring to a new feudalism governed by a corporate-government hybrid to which the whole world is doomed to be enslaved.[1] Companies like Google create "villages" for their employees while banks indenture us through escalating interest rates on credit cards, mortgages, and loans. Monsanto's iron-fisted control of land, water, and seed echoes injunctions against hunting on the king's land.[2] As corporations consolidate power at an alarming rate, the onset of a new Middle Ages seems all but inevitable.

1 Examples are too numerous to list but representative analyses include Stephen J. Kobrin, "Back to the Future: Neomedievalism and the Postmodern Digital World Economy," *Journal of International Affairs* 51.2 (1998): 361–86; Tim Duvall, "The New Feudalism: Globalization, the Market, and the Great Chain of Consumption," *New Political Science* 25.1 (2003): 81–97; John Rapley, "The New Middle Ages," *Foreign Affairs* 85.3 (2006): 95–103; Phil Williams, *From the New Middle Ages to a New Dark Age: The Decline of the State and US Strategy* (Carlisle, PA: Strategic Studies Institute, U.S. Army War College, June 2008); Parag Khanna, "Neomedievalism," *Foreign Policy* (May 2009): 91; Jerry West, "The New Feudalism," *OpEd-News.com* (29 January 2010), www.opednews.com; Jack Clark, "Facebook, Google: Welcome to the New Feudalism," *ZDNet* (10 September 2011), www.zdnet.com; Bob Johnson, "The New Feudalism," *Daily Kos* (16 April 2011), www.dailykos.com.

2 See Ashlee Vance, "Google and Mountain View Recast Company-Town Model," *The*

Predictions of a return to the past have also inspired the dystopian visions of Octavia Butler's *Earthseed* duology, Margaret Atwood's *Oryx and Crake* duology, and Suzanne Collins's *Hunger Games* trilogy, all of which predict dark worlds where corporation, state, and church have merged into ideological, financial, and agricultural conglomerates, manipulative institutions whose power structures mimic medieval feudalism and whose abuses of power have created neomedieval societies. The novels also critique the myth that free-market capitalism is permanently sustainable and self-regulating, suggesting instead that feudalism is capitalism's logical conclusion. Each author offers us a highly plausible scenario in which water, food, medicine, and jobs are scarce, owned by corporations that have subsumed government. The people of the future are obliged to barter their autonomy for survival. Elites consolidate within walled, wealthy capitols to which the peasants (aptly named "pleebs" in Atwood's novels) have no access. Medieval economic and transportation systems abound: most people walk because only the wealthy have cars or fuel; people trade goods and services because currency is devalued; and peasants survive by farming, hunting, foraging, or stealing. Vengeance has replaced law, since corporate authorities are ineffectual unless their own interests are at stake. Inquisitions and torture, distinctly medieval in inspiration, are prevalent in each dystopian world but are also distinctly *neo*medieval: totalizing power structures utilize contemporary information systems to enforce ideological homogeneity and quell resistance.[3] The world outside corporate-protected walls seems brutal and lawless, and yet the neomedieval corporate political structure remains panoptical, able to exercise seemingly limitless power against those who transgress borders or whisper blasphemies.

Each author works from the assumption that such omnipotent ideological, economic, and political structures are medieval in nature, and they pit their heroines against a medieval worldview. The dystopian heroine embodies values like socialism, religious liberty, environmentalism, and feminism. Yet

New York Times (18 February 2010): A19A; CBS News, "Agricultural Giant Battles Small Farmers," *CBSNews.com* (4 January 2011): www.cbsnews.com/2100–18563_162–4048288; Randeep Ramesh, "Monsanto's Chapati Patent Raises Indian Ire," *The Guardian* (31 January 2004): www.guardian.co.uk; Bernard Simon, "Monsanto Wins Patent Case on Plant Genes," *The New York Times* (22 May 2004): www.nytimes.com.

3 I use the term "neomedieval" as I argued for its definition in "Medieval Unmoored," *Studies in Medievalism XIX: Defining Neomedievalism(s)*, ed. Karl Fugelso (Cambridge: D. S. Brewer, 2010), 1–11 (3), as a mode of representation that "consumes the Middle Ages in fragmented, repetitive tropes" in which "futurity is foreclosed, for the future leads only to the past." See also Carol L. Robinson and Pamela Clements, "Living with Neomedievalism," *Studies in Medievalism XVIII: Defining Medievalism(s)*, ed. Karl Fugelso (Cambridge: D. S. Brewer, 2009), 55–75.

ironically, the modes of resistance she employs turn out to be very medieval after all.

Octavia Butler's *Parable of the Sower* (1993) and *Parable of the Talents* (1998) follow Lauren Oya Olamina's journey from her impoverished childhood in a twenty-first-century Los Angeles suburb to her leadership of a new religion, Earthseed.[4] Just as today's political scientists and financial analysts warn, in Butler's dystopian United States, feudal arrangements are becoming the only means of employment. President Donner institutes an economic plan that will "suspend 'overly restrictive' minimum wage, environmental, and worker protection laws for those employers willing to take on homeless employees and provide them with training and adequate room and board."[5] Companies soon take over cities and control all of their resources, providing salaries so low that workers become trapped.[6] Slavery is also a central motif in Butler's future: factories have "drivers" to get people to work harder.[7] The second book shifts from suggesting antebellum slavery to evoking neomedievalism, indicating that the two socioeconomic modes are aligned (and indeed, the feudal Middle Ages were part of the inspiration for plantations in the antebellum South).[8] Gangs of "Crusaders" wearing black tunics with giant white crosses raid communities, burn crops, and round up heretics to reeducate them through rape, torture, slavery, and biblical recitation – they even hold witch burnings.[9] Butler drives home the medievalism of the Crusaders whenever she can: "They were so certain they were right that, like medieval inquisitors, they would kill you, even torture you to death, to save your soul."[10] But what Butler's Crusaders have that medieval crusaders lacked is decimating firepower (tanks and machine guns) and slave collars, which allow them to monitor and control their captives, choking slaves who disobey.[11]

Despite invoking the obviously terrifying prospect of a return to the past, Butler's narrative also draws on the Middle Ages for hope. At one point in *Parable of the Sower*, Lauren points out that after the medieval plague, "there

4 Octavia E. Butler, *Parable of the Sower* (New York: Warner Books, 1993); and *Parable of the Talents* (New York: Aspect, 1998).

5 Butler, *Sower*, 27.

6 Butler, *Sower*, 119.

7 Butler, *Sower*, 323.

8 See Eugene D. Genovese, "The Southern Slaveholders' View of the Middle Ages," in *Medievalism in American Culture: Papers of the 18th Annual Conference of the Center for Medieval and Early Renaissance Studies* (Binghamton, NY: SUNY Center for Medieval and Renaissance Texts and Studies, 1989), 31–52.

9 Butler, *Talents*, 19–20.

10 Butler, *Talents*, 305.

11 Butler, *Talents*, 141–42.

was a lot of vacant land for the taking, and if [the survivors] had a trade, they realized they could demand better pay for their work."[12] Such "peasant revolt" stories, it turns out, are integral to all three dystopian visions, which find medieval modes of resistance the most effective means of overcoming the encroaching past.

In Atwood's *Oryx and Crake* (2004) and *The Year of the Flood* (2010), the reigning neomedieval corporate-government structure is called CorpSeCorps, which "started as a private security firm for the Corporations, but then they'd taken over when the local police forces collapsed for lack of funding," eventually subsuming the army and the government.[13] Atwood, like Butler, is intentional about her allusions to the medieval past: CorpSeCorps compounds are compared to castles more than once, and as one character's father explains to him:

> Long ago, in the days of knights and dragons, the king and dukes had lived in castles, with high walls and drawbridges and slots on the ramparts so you could pour hot pitch on your enemies [. . .] and the Compounds were the same idea. Castles were for keeping you and your buddies nice and safe inside, and for keeping everybody else outside.[14]

Resisters are subject to public executions neomedieval-style, combining "medieval" brutality with panoptical publicity. Websites such as *hedsoff.com* and *deathrowlive.com* feature twenty-four-hour executions.[15] The luckiest of the accused are given a slim chance at survival through televised trial by combat in the Painball Arena.[16] But just as in Butler's dystopia, hope also takes medieval form, this time through The Gardeners, a vegetarian community that governs itself "as ruthlessly as medieval monks" and eventually destroys CorpSeCorps by releasing a plague.[17] The Gardeners honor a neomedieval cocktail of saints known for ecologically friendly views, celebrating saints' days for both Dian Fossey and Julian of Norwich. They even eschew modern healing techniques in favor of maggots and leeches.[18]

Collins's *Hunger Games* trilogy (2008–10) centralizes power in the Capitol of Panem, which survives on contributions from its surrounding districts.

12 Butler, *Sower*, 56.

13 Margaret Atwood, *Oryx and Crake* (New York: Anchor Books, 2004); and *The Year of the Flood* (New York: Anchor Books, 2010), 25.

14 Atwood, *Oryx*, 28.

15 Atwood, *Oryx*, 82–83.

16 Atwood, *Flood*, 98.

17 Atwood, *Flood*, 189.

18 Atwood, *Flood*, 107.

The district peasants labor for resources they "owe" the Capitol, such as coal, food, and clothing. In return, district residents are offered protection, mainly from the Capitol itself.[19] Collins's neomedievalism is more subtle than Atwood's or Butler's, but it is implicit in the relationship between the Capitol and the districts: for instance, hunting outside the districts is an offense punishable by public lashing or even death.[20] And panoptical neomedieval social control is also a feature of Panem. The Capitol can hear everything, even private conversations in one's home, and they inflict brutal punishment for transgressions (the verbally disobedient have their tongues removed for treason).[21] Panem controls its subjects by publicizing these punishments, televising executions and massacres of disobedient districts, and, of course, by hosting the Hunger Games themselves, which are televised competitions to the death among district "tributes." Tributes are children under eighteen chosen by lottery as yet another "debt" to the Capitol, owed for past rebellions. Katniss, like Atwood's and Butler's heroines, also employs medieval motifs to generate the hope of resistance. With her bow and arrow, her comfort in the woods, her scrappy subversion of the Capitol's power, and her folk-hero status, Katniss evokes Robin Hood, manipulating the rich to inspire the poor. But Robin Hood is merely a surface meme in *The Hunger Games*; what lurks beneath it – just as in Butler and Atwood – is a mode of resistance far older and far more feminist.

*

Atwood, Collins, and Butler's dystopian visions incorporate an implicit feminist analysis that links corporate abuses of power to patriarchy through neomedieval tropes. The elevation of masculinity and the oppression of women are viewed as inextricable from class-based oppression, religious fundamentalism, and environmental destruction. Rape is a fact of life for girls as young as three to women as old as eighty in all three dystopian visions, and for many young boys as well. This is the logical conclusion of patriarchy, a system that victimizes and feminizes the young, the vulnerable, and the disempowered, but the heroine's connection to nature can also heal that abuse. Atwood's heroine Oryx is sold into sex slavery by her parents – other characters first encounter her on HottTotts, a website that films her

19 Suzanne Collins, *The Hunger Games* (New York: Scholastic, 2008); *Catching Fire* (New York: Scholastic, 2009); and *Mockingjay* (New York: Scholastic, 2010).
20 Collins, *Hunger Games*, 17.
21 Collins, *Hunger Games*, 5.

encounters.[22] Female debtors are "farmed out for sex" by CorpSeCorps and others sell their eggs on the black market just to survive.[23]

In the *Hunger Games*, the Capitol sells attractive champions to the highest bidder: "If a victor is considered desirable, the president gives them as a reward or allows people to buy them for an exorbitant amount of money. If you refuse, he kills someone you love."[24] Katniss's district peacekeeper also "bought desperate girls to devour and discard because he could."[25] Butler's Crusaders cut out the tongues of some disobedient women and collar others to sell into sexual slavery.[26] Since womanhood is perilous, the heroines often protect themselves by passing as men. Lauren cross-dresses whenever she is on the road because "a girl alone faced only one kind of future outside."[27] When Atwood's Toby and Ren leave the compound in which they have been hiding in *The Year of the Flood*, they cut their hair short: "It's a shorn look," Toby remarks, "it reminds her of Joan of Arc on a bad day."[28] Katniss's typical attire is masculine: leather hunting boots, trousers, her father's jacket, and her long braid tucked into a cap.[29] When the Capitol makeup artists have to prepare her for television appearances, they complain about how hairy she is and take drastic pains to feminize her.[30]

Power and patriarchy, medievalism and feudalism, the abuse of the vulnerable and the abuse of the earth are inseparable in these visions of the future. Perhaps it is unsurprising, then, that each author's heroine leads a distinctly ecofeminist resistance against neomedieval oligarchy. The rate of women to men fleeing Atwood's CorpSeCorps is three to one, and the novels imply that this is due to women's heightened empathy for the suffering of others, including animals.[31] Butler's Lauren is born with hyperempathy syndrome, which causes her to feel the pain that she or anyone else inflicts on others.[32] Collins's Katniss volunteers to take her sister's place as tribute and when she is in the televised Hunger Games, she stirs rebellion against the Capitol by protecting and healing her competitors.[33] Ren and Toby in Atwood's *Year of the Flood* are members of The Gardeners, who preach the interdependence

22 Atwood, *Oryx*, 89–91.
23 Atwood, *Flood*, 30–32.
24 Collins, *Mockingjay*, 178.
25 Collins, *Mockingjay*, 178.
26 Butler, *Talents*, 55.
27 Butler, *Sower*, 138.
28 Atwood, *Flood*, 364.
29 Collins, *Hunger Games*, 4.
30 Collins, *Hunger Games*, 51–52.
31 Atwood, *Flood*, 247.
32 Butler, *Sower*, 11.
33 Collins, *Mockingjay*, 74–75.

of every living thing, from leopards to mushrooms to snails.[34] In *The Hunger Games*, Katniss sings to young Rue, a fellow competitor, as she dies. The song invokes meadows and grass and a cloak of leaves, repeating the refrain: "Here the daisies guard you from every harm."[35] The mockingjays of Panem, even though they are mutant birds, take up Katniss's song as she decorates Rue's body with wildflowers.[36] Indeed, Katniss often seems to be in communication with mockingjays, who become her symbol. Finally, Lauren's mode of resistance is through her faith, Earthseed, which leads her to start a new sustainable colony of gardeners called Acorn in northern California.

Each heroine is not only attuned to suffering, but suffers horrible losses, torture, and degradation herself. That suffering is precisely what allows them to recruit followers against the neomedieval conglomerate. Butler's Lauren creates her own faith despite the fact that her home is burned, her followers are slaughtered, her daughter is stolen, and she herself is enslaved, beaten, and raped. Atwood's Oryx is sexually exploited and brutalized as a child, prostituted as an adult, and martyred by her lover, but she becomes the goddess of a new species after her death. Katniss undergoes public trials, loss, abuse, torture, and even multiple burnings, all televised. Cinna, Katniss's stylist, titles her "the girl who was on fire," an epithet that first refers to her flaming costume, then takes a more sinister tone when she is badly burned in the first Hunger Games and burned again during her rebellion; that fire also kills her sister.[37] Katniss seizes fire's transformative power, though, leading the revolutionaries in a battle cry: "If we burn, you burn with us!"[38] Butler's Lauren also grows through multiple fires: first, when her childhood community is burned by "paints," pyromaniac drug addicts who paint themselves blue and green and burn communities, stealing, raping, murdering in the wreckage.[39] The first fire sets Lauren on her pilgrimage north, where she collects converts and creates the first Earthseed community. The Earthseed verse at the beginning of the chapter underscores the trope:

> In order to rise
> From its own ashes
> A phoenix
> First

34 Atwood, *Flood*, 12–13.
35 Collins, *Hunger Games*, 234–35.
36 Collins, *Hunger Games*, 235–37.
37 Collins, *Hunger Games*, 57, 71–72, 119–20; Collins, *Mockingjay*, 171–79.
38 Collins, *Mockingjay*, 186.
39 Butler, *Sower*, 110.

Must
Burn.[40]

Later, repeating the phoenix verses above, Lauren and other escapees burn "Camp Christian," the Crusader reeducation camp in which they have been enslaved.[41] Martyrdom and sacrifice in these novels are amplified by symbolic connections to female divinity. When Lauren is young, she renounces her father's Baptism and creates Earthseed, which specifically rejects a "big-daddy-God" as well as the patriarchal faith of Jarret's Crusaders, instead defining God as change itself.[42] Butler gives Lauren Olamina the middle name "Oya" after the Yoruba goddess of change, and she becomes Oya's avatar on earth, unraveling religious and social structures through her movement. Oryx's apotheosis elevates her to the sacred position of the mother of all animals. And Katniss, though Robin Hood on the surface, is symbolically Dianic: killer with a bow, protector of mothers and daughters, and at home in nature and the woods.

Cross-dressing, tormented, suffering leaders of resistance movements both political and religious, followed by peasants, manipulated by the powerful, semi-divine, and publicly martyred: to medievalists, these heroines should be nothing if not familiar. In their condemnation of totalizing medieval patriarchy, Atwood, Butler, and Collins have awoken the heroines of a period in which women were supposedly dormant: Joan of Arc, Margaret of Antioch, Ursula, Godelina, Marguerite Porete, Margery Kempe, and Julian of Norwich. Katniss, Oryx, Toby, Ren, and Lauren – heroines who appear to be vessels of modernity, aligned with change and progress against a backward-looking neomedieval world – are engaged in subversions of a neomedieval future that also reproduce the past, acting as neomedieval mystics, heretics, and saints. And medieval activists and rebels communicated the same message as these contemporary ecofeminist heroines: that the potential for subversion lies in getting connected to nature, to one other, and to the divine.

Corporate neo-feudalism advances because of our isolation, as Atwood, Butler, and Collins predict. Atwood's walled CorpSeCorps territory is separated from the "pleeblands" both physically and psychologically. Butler's poor live in walled communities, yet even as the streets run red with rape and murder, people escape through "Dreamasks" that submerge them in "simpler, happier lives."[43] Collins's Panem districts are surrounded by electri-

40 Butler, *Sower*, 153.

41 Butler, *Talents*, 284.

42 Butler, *Sower*, 15, 25, 36.

43 Butler, *Sower*, 10; *Talents*, 240.

fied fences and watchtowers, so isolated from one another that the Capitol can lie about having destroyed one of them completely.[44]

We live in a world enamored of the finite – literalism, Wikipedia entries, the bubbles on a Scantron test – and even many religions prioritize the letter over the spirit. This world feeds the neo-feudal corporate oligarch, the sadist who thrives on limits, boundaries, enclosures, trademarks, and property. Today's feminist heroines urge us instead toward the infinite: they are subterranean, disruptive, but networked and wise, like their medieval ancestors Marguerite, Joan, Margery, and especially Julian of Norwich, who saw the whole world in a hazelnut. In fact, Atwood quotes Julian's famous revelation at the end of *The Year of the Flood*, which closes on Saint Julian's day:

> He showed me a little thing, the quantity of a hazel nut, lying in the palm of my hand [. . .] as round as any ball. I looked at it and thought, What may this be, and I was answered generally thus: It is all that is made. I marvelled how it might last. For I thought it might fall suddenly to nothing, for little cause; and I was answered in my understanding: It lasts and ever shall, for God loves it. And so has everything its being, through the love of God.[45]

For Atwood's protagonists, Saint Julian's day is a day of reunification, a day for feeding one's enemies and friends together and understanding oneself as a part of a universe both microscopic and impossibly huge. It may take the burning martyrdom of medieval saints and heroines to remind us that structures like church, state, corporation, and patriarchy are never as omnipotent as we think they are. The transcendent connectivity neomedieval saints inspire may lead us, in the end, to a pragmatic spirituality that an everyday medieval person might have recognized, an alchemical mixture of heaven and earth.

44 Collins, *Mockingjay*, 7–8.
45 Qtd. in Atwood, *Flood*, 424.

The Good Corporation? Google's Medievalism and Why It Matters

Richard Utz

In 1997, in one of the most widely received essays discussing questions of desire and sublimation among teachers and scholars of the Middle Ages, Louise Fradenburg includes a quick reading of director Chris Noonan's Oscar-winning 1995 movie, *Babe,* as a contemporary artifact with a "recognizably medievalist agenda." She explains that the film:

> celebrates love between master and servant (these days, animals have to stand in for the peasants), and rural life as the scene in which such love might be rediscovered. It expresses distaste for technology, focused especially on communications in the form of a Fax machine, but also recuperates the Fax, as well as discipline, training, technique. These figures recall the master tropes of anti-utilitarian medievalism in the nineteenth century. So does the film's insistent association of meaningless speech with commercialism and disbelief in the remarkable, and its association of meaningful speech with Babe's taciturn but loving farmer – a man behind the times who nonetheless is able to succeed because he recognizes the distinctive gifts of his animals, even when they want to do the work of the "other" (even, that is, when the pig Babe wants to do the work of a sheep dog).[1]

For this essay, I am less interested in Fradenburg's subsequent subjecting of *Babe* to a Lacanian reading than in her brilliant reminder that medievalism, at least in many of its modern manifestations, continues to be aligned

1 Louise Fradenburg, "'So That We May Speak of Them': Enjoying the Middle Ages," *New Literary History* 28:2 (1997): 204–5.

with romanticism and nostalgia for the premodern, the allegedly golden age which preceded machines, mechanization, science, technology, and industrialization. In his seminal essay on medievalism's genesis, "Medievalism and Romanticism," Leslie J. Workman demonstrated that, at least during the nineteenth century and in the English-speaking world, the concepts of medievalism and romanticism had become well-nigh synonymous, and I have recently been able to confirm medievalism's semantic heritage by linking its terminological "birth" to that of a number of similarly traditionalist nineteenth-century English coinages (e.g., "conservatism") clearly invented in response to progressive and democratic ones (e.g., "republicanism" and "socialism") which had invaded the British Isles from the politically tumultuous European continent.[2] The unique continuity of a more than half-hearted Anglo-American medievalist/romanticist resistance to introducing scientistic/scientific paradigms into the reception of medieval texts is noticeable, for example, in the reluctant acceptance of Lachmannian philology at British and American colleges and universities. Many Anglo-Saxon proponents of an allegedly more holistic and humanistic study of historical language and literature habitually dismissed their positivistic colleagues' work as an "unhealthy over-production," a "useless pyramid" of knowledge, and an overly "abstract," "pedantic," and "mechanical" enterprise that had lost its connection to any "artistic imperative."[3] The radical solution for this epistemological and ideological conflict between these competing paradigms came about when academic scholars adopted "Medieval Studies" as the term to describe their serious professional work and relegated all popular, creative, and journalistic receptions of medieval culture as "Medievalism." This traumatic semantic split has only recently begun to heal, most prominently under the influence of postmodernist, feminist, and postcolonialist scholarship that seeks to reunite "presentist" and "pastist" positions and discourses among medievalists.[4]

2 Leslie J. Workman, "Medievalism and Romanticism," *Poetica* 39–40 (1994): 1–34; Richard Utz, "Coming to Terms with Medievalism: Toward a Conceptual History," *European Journal of English Studies* 15:2 (2011): 101–13.

3 For these and a number of additional revealing terms and expressions by anti-modernist Anglo-Saxon scholars, see Richard Utz, "*Them* Philologists: Philological Practices and Their Discontents from Nietzsche to Cerquiglini," *The Year's Work in Medievalism* 26 (forthcoming).

4 Kathleen Biddick has expounded the potentially "traumatic" effects of this separation in *The Shock of Medievalism* (Durham, NC: Duke University Press, 1998). Excellent comprehensive definitions of "pastism" (the Middle Ages and contemporaneity are not only separated by a temporal boundary between the premodern and the modern, but a more radical form of alterity that almost defies comprehension) and "presentism" (the basic humanity of medieval people renders them similar to ourselves in their motivations and emotive responses) can be found in Juanita Feros Ruys, "Playing Alterity: Heloise, Rhetoric, and *Memoria*," in

I see the technology companies founded in the late 1980s and thereafter as caught in a similar conceptual situation: As the postmodern inheritors of modern processes of industrialization, mechanization, and corporatization, they display a keen awareness of the need to disassociate from the negative reputation these science- and capitalism-based organizations and practices still retain. Thus, many of them have sought to present themselves as organizations which drive technological and scientific innovation, albeit without the various negative consequences traditionally associated with such innovation since the eighteenth century. Some of them, most notably Google, have managed to construct themselves as organizations that can bridge the divide, brought about by the scientific revolution of the modern age, between humanistic and creative ideas and practices on the one hand and scientific and technological ideas and practices on the other. The result is a corporate image that a) coopts the creativity and benign humanism which *Babe* and dominant cultural modern narratives nostalgically locate in the past, and b) projects them as something that new and smart technologies can achieve in the present and future: The love between master and servant celebrated in *Babe* has been transformed into the "love" story of the corporation's founding, announced on the company website under the heading "When Larry [Page] Met Sergey [Brin]," and these young masters and their multicultural management team have but one goal, "to serve hundreds of thousands of users and customers around the world."[5] Like Babe's loving farmer, Googlers (i.e., Google's employees) can communicate weekly and directly with "Larry, Sergey and other execs about any number of company issues," and the value of their ideas and opinions is based on quality and "ability," not predetermined by specific prior "experience" (i.e., a pig can become a sheepdog at Google). And like the motley crew of animals on Babe's farm, Googlers "hail from all walks of life and speak dozens of languages."[6] Nature – in *Babe* that which guarantees human and animal sanity far from the madding crowd of fax machines and modernity – dominates Google offices all around the globe, with a jungle-like lobby in Sydney, the park-like atrium in London, and, most of all, the company headquarters in picturesque Mountain View, California, named for its magnificent views of the Santa Cruz Mountains, and at 111 Eighth Avenue in Manhattan. In all locations, nature and natural behavior are omnipresent, as in the fancy "Hatching" or "Meeting Eggs" in the Zurich office and "Mother's Room" in Cambridge, Massachusetts. In fact, the various recreational facilities, recy-

"Maistresse of My Wit": Medieval Women, Modern Scholars, ed. Louise D'Arcens and Juanita Feros Ruys (Turnhout: Brepols, 2004), 211–43.

5 "Company Overview," May 2012, www.google.com/about/company/.

6 "Our Culture," May 2012, www.google.com/about/company/facts/culture/.

cling initiatives, emphasis on healthy, local, organic, sustainable nutrition (available for free to the company's employees), and grass-trimming herds of goats (in Mountain View) are consciously designed to make the workplace feel like a (premodern) farming community.[7] The philanthropic Google.org, a well-funded nonprofit that focuses on issues regarding global public health, education, poverty, democracy, and climate change, further confirms goal six on the company's published corporate philosophy: "You can make money without doing evil" (often misquoted as "Don't be evil").[8] Google clearly wants to be seen as a good corporation, and more than one million job applicants per year and the first place in *Fortune Magazine*'s "Best Companies" competition in 2012 indicate that their "humanistic capitalism," a particular synthesis of (relatively) clean technology, (relatively) ethical commercialism, (relatively) democratic creativity, and vaguely neo-romantic/neomedieval resonances, has brought about what *Babe* could only achieve within the utopia of a fictional farm, with animals standing in for humans.[9]

While the multinational giant Google has been accused of censorship, copyright infraction, and violation of privacy, few would dispute that the corporation's considerable efforts at reaching a more "humanistic" form of capitalism differentiate it from more "massively exploitative" or "significantly predatory" companies. Such companies, when dealing with aspects of the medieval to promote their products, employ:

> chivalry, honor, and other values traditionally associated with the medieval to argue that what is needed is not a systematic re-evaluation of the role that corporations play and their cost to a society, but a return to a corporate model that, with a nostalgia characteristic of the neomedieval, is constructed as more noble and, therefore, more moral, ethical, and socially responsible than its present incarnations.[10]

7 The impression of visiting a farm-like environment is common to visitors of Googleplex in Mountain View, CA. See, e.g., Marion Nestle, "What Google's Famous Cafeterias Can Teach Us About Health," *The Atlantic*, August 2011, www.theatlantic.com/health/print/2011/07/what-googles-famous-cafeterias-can-teach-us-about-health/241876/).

8 "Ten Things We Know To Be True," May 2012, www.google.com/about/company/philosophy/. For the genesis and actual practice of the "Don't do evil" principle, see Richard L. Brandt, *The Google Guys: Inside the Brilliant Minds of Google Founders Larry Page and Sergey Brin* (London: Penguin, 2009).

9 By "humanistic capitalism" I understand, with the J[ust]E[nough]P[rofit] Foundation, "profit that is gained honorably, respectfully, and preserves human dignity; the purposeful distribution of a company's profits to: promote a higher standard of living for employees, create fulfilling jobs, reduce prices, encourage shareholder philanthropy, and spawn other types of pro bono contributions to society. It also promotes financial openness and transparency." (www.humanisticcapitalism.com/).

10 Kevin Moberly and Brent Moberly, "Reincorporating the Medieval: Morality, Chivalry,

In my view, Google probably inhabits a place among "mildly predatory" and "somewhat humanistic" companies.[11] As it moves away, by innovative leaps and bounds, from being "a harmless drudge," who would simply record and make available information (similar to the descriptive lexicographer), to becoming selective about information (similar to a prescriptive lexicographer), it will find, just like the makers of the *Oxford English Dictionary* or *Roget's Thesaurus*, that organizing knowledge involves incomparably more ethical, political, and cultural decision-making than the comprehensive collection and dissemination of data.[12]

Even in its most "harmless" (pre-Web 3.0) incarnation, the mildly predatory, somewhat humanistic, and vaguely neomedievalist Google revolutionized what we may know about medievalism. In December 2010, Google Labs released the Ngram Viewer, a tool that makes it possible to search for concepts and words in a database of five million digitized books, most of

and Honor in Post-Financial-Meltdown Corporate Revisionism," in *Studies in Medievalism XXI: Corporate Medievalism*, ed. Karl Fugelso (Cambridge: D. S. Brewer, 2012), 11–25. See further Harry Brown ("Knights of the Ownership Society: Economic Inequality and Medievalist Film," in *Studies in Medievalism XXI: Corporate Medievalism*, ed. Karl Fugelso [Cambridge: D. S. Brewer, 2012], 37–47 [46]), who shows that many neomedievalist works erase the abject poverty and dependence of the majority of medieval people on a very small class of elites and therefore reimagine the period "as a proto-capitalist playground, where there are no hopeless peasants, only a lot of scruffy lads waiting to become knights."

11 These are the six "maturity levels" the Just Enough Profit Foundation lists on its website (www.humanisticcapitalism.com/). Level 4 is defined as "Very humanistic. Company has a nice blend of beneficial products and services and demonstrates a propensity to share the wealth." Level 5 is defined as "Completely humanistic. Company exists only for the benefit of mankind. It is altruistic, philanthropic, promotes the general welfare, and makes just enough profit to innovate while serving its customers and employees." And level 5+, at the absolute apex of humanistic capitalism, would demonstrate "full financial transparency" in addition to level 5's virtues.

12 An illustrative example of Google's increasing move toward creating a more "semantic" web search is the recently launched Knowledge Graph, which contextualizes words and phrases to match the searcher's query as closely as possible. See Matthew Shear, "Google Knowledge Graph Attempts Next Generation of Search," *Christian Science Monitor*, 17 May 2012, www.csmonitor.com/Innovation/Horizons/2012/0517/Google-Knowledge-Graph-attempts-next-generation-of-search?utm_source=feedburner. I include the expression of the "harmless drudge" from Samuel Johnson's self-ironic entry, "lexicographer," in his 1755 *Dictionary of the English Language* to remind readers of the scientific claims lexicographers, surely the most positivistic among philologists, made in compiling their reference works during the second half of the nineteenth and the early twentieth centuries. On these investigating subjects' claims about their subjects of investigation see Charlotte Brewer, *Treasure-House of the Language: The Living OED* (New Haven, CT: Yale University Press, 2007), and Joshua C. Kendall, *The Man Who Made Lists: Love, Death, Madness, and the Creation of Roget's Thesaurus* (London: Penguin, 2008).

them published between 1800 and the present.[13] By the time I heard about and fully understood the potential of this tool for anyone interested in sound contemporary humanistic inquiry, I had just submitted the final version of an essay, "Coming to Terms with Medievalism," invited by Andrew James Johnston (FU Berlin) and Ute Berns (Hamburg) for a special edition of the *European Journal of English Studies* on "Medievalism."[14] In this essay, which was based on earlier observations made by Leslie J. Workman, the founder of the academic study of medievalism, the theories of the conceptual historian Reinhart Koselleck, and my own work on reception studies since the early 1990s, I drew a number of conclusions which, given the traditional standards of diligence in the humanities and social sciences, were perfectly plausible and legitimate:

a) "Medievalism" as a concept can be shown specifically to be the product of what Koselleck calls the process of temporalization which marks the transition from early modern mentalities to modernity and the modern university.
b) "Medievalism" (like "conservatism") is an English term, coined in Britain and in conservative response to progressive movements and corresponding coinages (republicanism; socialism) making their way to Britain in the mid-nineteenth century.
c) In the late nineteenth century, scholars dismissed "Medievalism" as the dilettante "Other" of academic medieval studies in the late nineteenth century, and the term survived only due to the unique continuity post-medieval British subjects (and, to a certain degree, all Anglo-Americans) have felt with their medieval past.
d) Since the late 1970s, "Medievalism" has transmuted into a scholarly practice ("Medievalism Studies"), spawned a subfield ("Neomedievalism"), competed with coeval movements ("New Medievalism"), and is now, for example, on the pages of Palgrave Macmillan's journal *postmedieval* (2010–), the intellectual paradigm of choice for scholars who would like to heal the rigidly "othering" attitude toward medieval culture with the assistance of presentist empathy, memory, subjectivity, resonance, affection, desire, passion, speculation, fiction, imagination, and positionality.

13 The details on the corpus construction were provided in an article by Jean-Baptiste Michele et al. ("Quantitative Analysis of Culture Using Millions of Digitized Books") for the journal *Science* 331:6014 (14 January 2011): 176–82. Perhaps the most illustrative explanation of ngrams as measurements of cultural trends is Erez Lieberman Aiden and Jean-Baptiste Michel's TED talk, "What We Learned From 5 Million Books," filmed July 2011, posted September 2011, www.ted.com/talks/what_we_learned_from_5_million_books.html.

14 Richard Utz, "Coming to Terms with Medievalism," *European Journal of English Studies* 15:2 (2011): 101–13.

Workman, Koselleck, and I based our scholarship on the traditional gold standards of lexicological reference, the *Oxford English Dictionary* and the *Deutsches Wörterbuch*. Both these great dictionaries were, of course, compiled by individuals who, while doing their best to be scientific and comprehensive, were limited in the construction of their works by their pre-computer age lexicographic corpora as well as by their own cultural, linguistic, and political notions of which kinds of text, written by which kinds of authors, could find inclusion. When I entered the terms "medievalism" and "mediaevalism" into Google's Ngram Viewer, I was overwhelmed by the wealth and wide distribution of instances in which the term was used. Even if a majority of entries on the list turned out to be incorrect due to faulty optical character recognition (OCR) in the scanning of historical printed texts,[15] there was nevertheless a solid number of new results that considerably expands the concept's semantic shadings: Thus, I was able to find that John Ruskin, whom the *OED* (and therefore Leslie Workman, I, and numerous others) had credited with one of the first (and the most consequential) British uses of "mediaevalism" in a 1853 lecture on Pre-Raphaelitism, was preceded by the British surveyor and engineer William Laxton (1802–54), who employs the term as a descriptor in the history of architecture and as a synonym for the medieval period as early as 1837, in the *Civil Engineer and Architect's Journal*.[16] An anonymous essay (by a certain "B") in the September 1849 issue of the *Southern Literary Messenger*, entitled "A Plea for Art," uses "medievalism" to denounce "all manners of retrogradism and rottenness in opinion, all manners and moods of contempt for ourselves and for each other, all variations of desire for false and ruinous conservatism."[17] And another anonymous author expresses his disdain for the remnants of medieval Catholic monasticism in an article entitled "Monachism" in the August 1844 edition of a Church of England journal, *The British Churchman*, attacking Catholic "mediaevalism" as a "monastic and antisocial poison."[18]

15 On the various potential sources for errors produced by the Ngram Viewer, see Danny Sullivan, "When OCR Goes Bad: Goggle's Ngram Viewer & the F-Word," *Search Engine Land*, 19 December 2010, http://searchengineland.com/when-ocr-goes-bad-googles-ngram-viewer-the-f-word-59181. The most common error in my own searches was due to "misreadings" of publication dates on low-quality scans, e.g., 1833 instead of the correct 1888.

16 http://books.google.com/books?id=fA5AAAAAYAAJ&q=%22mediaevalism%22&dq=%22mediaevalism%22&hl=en&sa=X&ei=LDPGT6C-BIKa9gSV-aG1Bg&ved=0CDsQ6AEwAA.

17 http://books.google.com/books?id=vlIFAAAAQAAJ&pg=PA626&dq=%22medievalism%22&hl=en&sa=X&ei=5lTGT6igK9KB0QHbsoySCw&ved=0CEAQ6AEwAQ#v=onepage&q=%22medievalism%22&f=false.

18 http://books.google.com/books?id=RC0EAAAAQAAJ&pg=PA291&dq=%22mediaevalis

These three examples of some unexpectedly early and heretofore unknown uses of "medi[a]evalism" do not challenge all the conclusions in my pre-Ngram essay. However, they complicate it by:

a) broadening the scope of our investigations from the belles-lettres and the history of ideas to additional fields (engineering, architecture, theology);
b) extending the time frame of our work to the period before John Ruskin; and
c) expanding the geographical distribution of early uses of the concept from the British intelligentsia to the pre-Civil War American South.[19]

The semantic sifting of these numerous additional texts has already begun, as David Matthews' fascinating 2011 essay on the "new semantic history" of "medieval" and "medievalism" demonstrates.[20] Although Matthews does not specifically credit Google Ngram Viewer for the impressive expansion of his project's corpus, I am convinced that his revision of the semantic histories of both terms would not have been possible without the help of Google's new technologies. Whatever we may think about the moderately neomedieval resonances in Google's corporate identity, Google's innovative information technologies are already proving transformational for the study of medievalism (and myriad other subjects). As we continually refine the obvious weaknesses of current electronic searches and include additional terms like "chivalry," "antiquities," and "obscurantism" to our comparative semantic projects, we will come to understand that Google's medievalism truly matters to the future of humanistic inquiry. I, for one, will actively test, accompany, and even request such new technologies to assist me in my future studies.

m%22&hl=en&sa=X&ei=aVbGT4vpOMOygwelodjWBg&ved=0CDsQ6AEwAA#v=onepage&q=%22mediaevalism%22&f=false.

19 This specific example might challenge the tacit assumption that the British spelling (and use) of "mediaevalism" necessarily preceded the American one (medievalism).

20 "From Mediaeval to Mediaevalism: A New Semantic History," *Review of English Studies* 62 (2011): 695–715.

"Longest, oldest and most popular": Medievalism in the Lord Mayor's Show

Clare A. Simmons

> The Lord Mayor's Show is the longest, oldest and most popular civic procession in the world. It winds through nearly 800 years of London history to arrive in the 21st century more splendid than ever. In 1213 a grateful King John awarded the City of London the right to choose its own Mayor, but he had a condition: every year, when a new Mayor took office, he had to make his way upriver to Westminster and pledge loyalty to the Crown. The Lord Mayor of London is one of the world's oldest elected officials, and the Lord Mayor's Show is the public festival that has grown up around his journey.[1]

This introduction to the Lord Mayor's Show is posted on the opening page of its website. The reference to King John places the practices that led to the show firmly in the medieval period. Moreover, the narrative as given here suggests that John willingly granted London rights in contrast to the forced concessions of Magna Carta. The official voice of the Lord Mayor's Show identifies its origins in loyalty to political structures, rather than as a form of resistance to them. By pairing the phrase "one of the world's oldest elected officials" with the idea of "public festival" the current introduction also creates the suggestion that the Lord Mayor's Show, claimed as the "longest, oldest and most popular civic procession in the world," originated in the medieval period. The Lord Mayor's procession certainly dates from the Middle Ages, but the Lord Mayor's Show came to prominence after the

1 www.lordmayorsshow.org, accessed 5 April 2012. Elsewhere on the website the charter date is given as 1215. On King John's charters, see, for example, Lindsey German and John Rees, *A People's History of London* (London: Verso, 2012), 22–23.

English Reformation and almost certainly substituted for earlier forms of public performance suppressed during the sixteenth century. The Show is thus an intriguing example of how a public event that took form after the Middle Ages claims legitimacy and official sanction through the medievalist strategies of historical claims to ancient practice and to mythmaking.

Not only has the Lord Mayor's Show utilized medieval motifs drawn from history and myth since the later sixteenth century, but, as the current financial support of the London Stock Exchange suggests, from its development by the London livery companies to the present, it has also historically united public spectacle with corporate funding and image-creation. The emergence of the Show as a major public event in the early modern period has been well studied, but my focus here is on historicizing and mythmaking since the beginning of the nineteenth century, especially the later Victorian period; and how it creates a medieval story for the postmedieval Lord Mayor's Show that justifies its continued existence as both an antiquarian curiosity and a popular festival.

From early times, the Lord Mayor of the City of London was not considered a politician but a representative of trade, being elected from one of the major trade companies; the first Mayor of London was Henry Fitz-Alwin, a mercer, who was mayor until 1211.[2] There can be no doubt that, during the medieval period, monarchs chartered trade and craft companies for, as W. Carew Hazlitt was later to describe it, "valuable consideration."[3] The reign of Henry V was a particularly active period in the granting of charters, and it was also the era of a future London folk-hero, Richard Whittington, who left his mark on London in the form of a college, prison improvements, and other charitable endowments.[4] From the monarch's point of view, such charters, renewed at least until the early 1700s, were a useful source of revenue; presumably, the London guilds of Henry V's time were helping

2 Occasionally, claims were made for even earlier origins. For example, the 1761 *Guide to the Lord Mayor's Show* maintains that the position of Lord Mayor was "so constituted from and before the time of William the Conqueror; yet going under various Denominations" (introduction). The "Dissenting Report" in the Royal Commission of the 1880s points to references that guilds existed in Anglo-Saxon times (1:58).

3 William Carew Hazlitt, *The Livery Companies of the City of London* (London: Swan Sonnenschein and Co., 1892), 63.

4 Ballads and narratives about Richard Whittington dating from the seventeenth and eighteenth centuries sometimes include a woodcut of Whittington on horseback in a parade, with what Tracey Hill has suggested are fireworks. See Tracey Hill, *Pageantry and Power: A Cultural History of the Early Modern Lord Mayor's Show, 1585–1639* (Manchester: Manchester University Press, 2010), 130–32. This is not in itself evidence that Whittington himself was part of grand Lord Mayor's Show, but indicates that later audiences liked to think that he was. In the nineteenth century, this champion of the Mercers was to become the pantomime character Dick Whittington.

finance the Hundred Years War. From the livery companies' point of view, charters granted to their trades were a historical validation. It is beyond the scope of this essay to determine whether companies really had a continued existence and membership, or whether later charters were in effect creations of new companies. In terms of mythmaking, however, post-Reformation companies made much of their medieval origins. For example, the Mercers, whose folkloric origin was in the family of Thomas Becket, point to a lawsuit in 1308 as "the first reference to the Mercers acting as a corporate body."[5] The first royal charter for the Mercers was in 1394. While the Mercers had a continuous tradition of sorts at least since the time of Richard Whittington, the Butchers' Company had no written evidence of their existence before 1592; they nevertheless pointed to references to a Butchers' Guild late in the reign of Edward III and in 1573.[6]

Yet as scholars, most recently Tracey Hill, have demonstrated, although the Lord Mayor had traveled to Westminster to show his allegiance to the monarchy since the time of King John, the Lord Mayor's Show did not take the form of a major public event until the late 1500s, although claims for antiquity were common even in the early 1600s.[7] By this time, most religious pageants organized by craft guilds had succumbed to Protestant suspicions of saints' days; fears that the representation of biblical figures onstage was idolatrous; and concerns about the social dangers of large-scale gatherings. The London tradition of the Midsummer Watch, celebrated with bonfires and religious pageants, was also suppressed after the Reformation, and some of its practices transferred to the Lord Mayor's Show, celebrated on 29 October, the Feast of St. Simon and St. Jude.[8] After Britain's move to the

5 www.mercers.co.uk/700-years-history, accessed 24 July 2012.

6 See *The Report of the Royal Commission on the City of London Livery Companies*, 5 vols. (London: Eyre and Spottiswoode, 1883–85), 3:212.

7 Hill remarks that the "mayoral Shows' roots" can be traced back to late medieval pageants but that any "exploration of the early days of civic pageantry is inhibited by a lack of certainty as to when pageantry on Lord Mayor's Day began to be established practice, although the Shows' continuities with existing traditions were, on the whole, numerous" (*Pageantry and Power*, 27). Given the amount of documentation that the livery companies were able to produce for the Royal Commissions in the nineteenth century, it is significant that none of it points to major celebrations of Lord Mayor's Day before the 1580s. For the borrowing of earlier public traditions connected with other calendar dates, see also Ronald Hutton, *The Rise and Fall of Merry England: The Ritual Year 1400–1700* (Oxford: Oxford University Press, 1994), 76.

8 For a brief period, some religious pageants may have been transferred to the Lord Mayor's Show but its performances were usually symbolic rather than drawn from Bible stories. See Hutton, *The Rise and Fall of Merry England*, 76; also David Cressy, *Bonfires and Bells: National Memory and the Protestant Calendar in Elizabethan and Stuart England* (London: Weidenfeld and Nicholson, 1989).

Gregorian Calendar in 1751, the Show moved to 9 November and effectively became a public holiday in the City of London.[9] Depending on the era, the Lord Mayor traveled by barge, horse, foot, and coach to Westminster, returning back to the Guildhall for a banquet; by the nineteenth century the travel was exclusively by the mayor's state coach.

The advantage of the Lord Mayor's Parade, or Triumph as it was often called, was that it was primarily secular in nature; it was, moreover, centered on a public act of loyalty to the crown and thus was a celebration that could be safely sanctioned both by rulers and by conscientious citizens. In an age when the period now known as the Middle Ages was frequently characterized as filled with ignorance and superstition, the Show chose to celebrate what was good about the past as seen through the eyes of the London livery companies. These companies claimed their origins in medieval guilds, the groups of craftsmen in a specific trade who banded together for mutual benefit ratified by royal charter; such a group would have apprentices learning the needed skills and trained craftsmen (journeymen). In his extensive 1892 study of the livery companies, W. Carew Hazlitt notes the "obscurity of origin" of the companies but identifies the continuity by calling them "Livery Gilds" and explaining, "The LIVERY is so called from the ancient practice of periodical delivery of clothing" to the group (Hazlitt, 19). Even then Hazlitt concedes "an inherent tendency on their part to diverge from their original gospel and *role*, and, whereas the incidence of apprenticeship was the very essence and foundation for their being, to develop a cliental and charitable principle into a sub-municipal autocracy" (21).

For as the focus on apprenticeship waned, in London many of the most powerful groups were not practicing a craft but a trade, and protecting the interests of that trade. In using the Show to create myths of origin for themselves, the livery companies and the productions that they commissioned did not only draw from the medieval period. For example, in the early modern period, rather than using the term "pageant," which was connected with the medieval religious-themed dramas performed on specific dates in the Christian calendar, companies tended to prefer the word "triumph," which has classical associations. Moreover, some of the entertainments devised to celebrate the Show in the early modern period hinted at myths of origins of the early British people, such as the story that the ancient Britons were escapees from the fall of Troy. Even a production titled *Troia-Noua Triumphans*, which was written by Thomas Dekker, pays almost as much attention

9 Tradespeople grumbled throughout the nineteenth century at the loss of a day's income; only in 1959, however, was the Show moved to the second Saturday in November. See, for example, a letter signed "An Old City Subscriber" who objected to paying a day's wages to his employees for no work (*The Times*, 12 November 1849).

to the medieval origins of the livery companies as to the ancient Britons; after a prologue emphasizing how much expense has gone into the production and scenes on land and water, "Fame" provides a list of medieval royalty and other leaders who have worn the Merchant Taylors' livery.[10]

Because the livery companies tended to choose show themes that solidified the historical importance of their trade, the medieval period was a fruitful source of inspiration. One example of the combination of specifically medieval history and myth in the early modern period is Anthony Munday's *Chrysanaleia, Or the Golden Fishing* (1616). In 1616 the new Lord Mayor was John Leman, from the "auncient and worthie Companie of Fishmongers." Munday's pageant therefore centers on the fourteenth-century Lord Mayor Sir William Walworth. In some accounts, Walworth is portrayed as an opportunist who treacherously struck down Wat Tyler while he was parleying with King Richard II and thus helped end the democratic promise of the Peasants' Revolt.[11] For the Fishmongers, in contrast, Walworth, who may have been a dealer in kippers, is a hero who proved the loyalty of their trade to the crown. *Chrysanaleia* opens with a medievalist justification of the association between the Fishmongers and the Goldsmiths, asserting that during the Crusades the two trades worked together "in a late begun league of loue and amity, by many friendly helpes and furtherances each to other, in diuers dangerous aduentures, as well on the Seas, as the land, no men being more forward in those affaires, and in those times then they."[12] The procession includes some symbols without historical specificity such as a fishing boat and a lemon tree to honor the name of the new mayor John Leeman (Lemon);[13] but it also features figures representing the time of the Crusades and of the Peasants' Revolt: among these are "the King of Moores, gallantly mounted on a golden Leopard, he hurling gold and siluer euery way

10 "[It is] a *Memoriall* of an *Exemplary Loue* and *Duty* (in those who are at the *Cost* of these *Triumphs*) to haue *added* some *Heightning* more to them then was intended at first, of purpose to do honor to their Prince and Countrey. And I make no doubt, but *many worthy Companies* in this City could gladly be content to be partners in the *Disbursements*, so they might be sharers in the *Glory*." Thomas Dekker, *Troia-Noua Triumphans; or, London Triumphing* (London, 1612).

11 For example, in Robert Southey's *Wat Tyler* (1817), Walworth remarks that if the "rabble" lose their leaders, they will be easily dispersed, and strikes down Tyler from behind. Later in his life, Southey would probably have been more sympathetic to Walworth.

12 Anthony Munday, *Chrysanaleia, Or the Golden Fishing* (London, 1616), introduction. Very possibly this medievalist preamble describing the association between the Fishmongers and the Goldsmiths was added for the printed edition.

13 The lemon tree was not simply a pun on the Lord Mayor's name. It was "richly laden with the fruite and flowers it beareth" and under it was a pelican, emblematic of self-sacrifice and hence an "excellent type of gouernment in a Magistrate, who, at his mere entrance into his yeares Office, becommeth a nursing father of the Family."

about him"; King Richard II and the Virtues; and finally a "goodly Bower" containing the tomb of Sir William Walworth.[14] Walworth rises from his tomb and explains the pageant elements, and notes that "as my Dagger slew the Rebell then," it is represented in the London coat of arms:

To honor *London* more (if more it may)
The *Red-Crosse*, in a *Siluer-field* before,
Had *Walworths* Dagger added to it more.
And now my Lord, this goodly Monument
Or Chariot of *Triumphall Victory*
Some shape of that daies honour doth present,
By *Heauens protection* of *True Maiestie*,
And beating downe *Treason* and *Mutinie*.[15]

Walworth's return from the shades like a corporate King Arthur recalls the "honor" of the events of medieval times, the triumph of loyalty over rebellion, and the importance of fishmongers to the destiny of London.

The lavish productions of the late sixteenth and early seventeenth centuries had waned by the eighteenth century. In the early 1800s, the Lord Mayor's Show did not aspire to their scale, yet the livery companies continued their emphasis on medieval origins. The Lord Mayor of London[16] was still elected from one of the twelve "great" livery companies and they appointed "bachelors in foins and budge" to form part of the procession at their personal expense. The Elizabethan terms "foins and budge" refer to grades of fur, one being fur from martens or similar animals and one from lambs; by the 1880s these terms seem to have been used exclusively by livery companies in reference to their members' obligations in the Lord Mayor's procession.[17] Over the course of the nineteenth century two strands of medievalism develop: an

14 Tracey Hill reproduces some of these in her study of the Lord Mayor's Show (*Pageantry and Power*, 140–41, 235); they are mentioned in William Herbert's 1836–37 history discussed on p. 36 below.

15 The spirit of Walworth is referring to the coat of arms of the City of London, which is the cross of St. George with a sword or dagger in one quarter; folklore claimed that this represented Walworth's weapon. According to most accounts, Walworth struck down Tyler with a sword or mace, and then later had the wounded man dragged from his bed and beheaded.

16 The Lord Mayor is the honorary title of the head of the aldermen of the City of London at the heart of London's commerce. The areas that the aldermen represent are often in combination called the Corporation. The Lord Mayor is chosen from one of the twelve livery companies. The Lord Mayor's procession pointedly makes a distinction between London and Westminster. The office is distinct from the very recent position of Mayor of London, an American-style local administrator and head of the City Council and an elected office.

17 Usually, bachelors in foins (also spelled foynes) were expected to pay more than bachelors

antiquarian justification for continuing the power of the livery companies as manifested in the Show; and the popular appreciation for medieval elements.

The main antiquarian justification for the Show was not, as might reasonably be expected, that it was a celebration of corporations, but that it was a surviving emanation of lost traditions of the medieval period. William Hone included an account of the Lord Mayor's Show in *Ancient Mysteries Described* (1823), which aimed to reclaim medieval "miracle plays" as a form of popular drama.[18] Hone identifies the Lord Mayor's Show as "the only stated exhibition in the metropolis that remains as a memorial of the great doings in the time of the pageants" and for this reason he provides "some account of its ancient appearance" (246). Immediately, Hone performs the historical elision that recurs in accounts of the Show. Having identified it as a "memorial" of medieval religious drama, he then provides an account of its "ancient" practices that date from the Elizabethan period, specifically 1575. Hone is well aware that the secular "London Pageants" emerged about this time since he cites printed sources that make this point. He is especially interested, though, in finding continuities with medieval mysteries. Ironically, scholars of the later nineteenth century found another way to claim continuity by asserting that the term "mystery play" itself derived not from religious revelation but from the trade companies that sponsored and performed them, an idea that might have appealed to Hone had he thought of it. According to Hazlitt's study of the livery companies:

> The ordinary orthography of the term *mystery* is calculated to favour an erroneous impression on the part of those who do not remember that the true word is mistery, the old French *maistre* and *maistrie* having been translated indifferently into English *master* and *mister*, *mastery* or *mistery.* Mistery, mester, maistrie, are all closely allied to *mestier* or *métier*, a trade. (Hazlitt, 24)

Even if this were true, it has little to do with the Lord Mayor's Show, which is Hazlitt's purpose for including this questionable derivation.

Because they owned so much property, ran many charitable institutions, and controlled so much of the commercial market, twice during the nine-

in budge; for example, in the 1880s the Haberdashers expected the bachelors in foynes to pay £10 and the bachelors in budge to pay £6.13.6d (*Report*, 2:xx).

18 While some scholars distinguish between "mystery plays" based on scripture and "miracle plays" based on the lives of the saints, Hone uses both terms, appropriately enough since he is especially interested in plays based on the Apocryphal New Testament. William Hone, *Ancient Mysteries Described, Especially the English Miracle Plays* (1823; repr. London: William Reeves, n.d.).

teenth century the London livery companies found that they needed to defend their structures and practices to government commissions. As early as the government "Commission for Inquiring into Municipal Corporations" in the reign of William IV, the companies claimed their origins in ancient guilds and that they were the original corporations that led to the growth of commerce. William Herbert, librarian of the Corporation of London, published two large volumes in 1836–37 tracing the London guilds back to Anglo-Saxon times, and especially focusing on the origins of "the ancient trading Corporations," the twelve great livery companies.[19] In describing their ancient halls and banquets, Herbert explains that the "city Guildhall, on the lord mayor's day, now affords the best idea of the company's ancient halls and feasts, though certainly on a scale of greater magnitude and splendour" (1:87). Herbert mentions many medieval instances of the Mayor of London and the livery companies riding in their regalia to meet the monarch or to celebrate other significant occasions (1:89–101). He hints that the Lord Mayor's Show of the late 1500s and 1600s was the successor to such "ridings" and the Midsummer Watch:

> *The Lord Mayor's Show*, as exhibited with all the increased splendour we have alluded to, was the king of City sights. – To the simple procession of minstrels, whom we have seen with the Companies' beadle on horseback, first succeeded spectacles on the water, chiefly in the nature of sham fights, with a few allegorical characters on land, who sang or recited complimentary verses. (1:199)

Herbert's account of the evolution of the Show follows Hone's in assuming a continuity with, although a development from, medieval practices. A generation later, in 1864, Toulmin Smith similarly claimed that corporations had their origins in the medieval guilds. He also insisted that: "Charters of Incorporation do not and cannot *create* Corporations. They have always depended, and still depend, for even their validity upon the pre-existence of the 'Communitas.'"[20] Corporations, then, were founded for the welfare of their members and interests that they supported.

By the Victorian period some of the livery companies had major power in London, having assumed the role of quality-control officers for their

19 William Herbert, *The History of the Twelve Great Livery Companies of London*, 2 vols. (London: printed for author, 1836–37), 1:iii. Herbert is well aware that Anglo-Saxon guilds "were, at first, political" (1:3); the early pages of his study intermingle trade guilds with other kinds of companies.

20 Toulmin Smith and Lucy Toulmin Smith, *English Gilds: The Original Ordinances* (London: Published for the Early English Text Society by N. Trübner and Co., 1870), xii.

trades.[21] All, at least in theory, offered aid to the sick and elderly among their numbers; and many sponsored charitable institutions such as schools and housing; certainly, today, the livery companies, whose members are frequently not associated with the trade that gave the company its name, claim that their main function is to support and administer their charitable foundations.[22] The companies were thus seeking to maintain status in the community. While it could certainly be argued that the ultimate intent of achieving such status was to increase profits, community standing was a more immediate goal, and the public spectacle of the Lord Mayor's Show was a means of celebrating a collective history.

The 1870s and 1880s were a crucial point in the history of the Lord Mayor's Show, since opinions were so strongly divided as to what it meant. In 1870 Lucy Toulmin Smith claimed the Show as a true medieval survival. In her Preface to her late father's edition of the records of medieval guild activity, she remarks that "In the present day, when the race of life is to the swift, and there is scarcely any time left for anything else, these popular pageants are despised, and a barren imagination can see in the last relic of them, the Lord Mayor's Show, nothing but 'a bore.'" She goes on to quote Canon Rock's *Church of our Fathers*: "such an age will not understand the good which, in a moral and social point of view, was bestowed upon this country by the religious pageants, and pious plays and interludes of a by-gone epoch. Through such means, however, not only were the working-classes furnished with a needful relaxation, but their very merry-making instructed while they diverted them" (xxxiv–xxxv). For the Toulmin Smiths, the Lord Mayor's Show is indicative of the popular nature of civic pageants. *English Gilds* also contains a lengthy treatise by Lujo Brentano arguing that medieval guilds were the forerunners of present-day trade unions.

In 1880 a new Royal Commission was appointed to inquire into the state of the London livery companies. The government was interested in how charitable trusts were administered; whether the companies were functionally monopolies; whether their administrative structures should be revised;

21 For example, the Royal Commission reported that "The Fishmongers' Company, relying on its charters but without authority by any Fish-statute, appoints and pays 'fish meters' who attend at Billingsgate Market, examine the fish offered for sale there, and condemn any which may be proved to be unsound. The company defrays the expense of deodorizing and removing the fish thus condemned" (1:19).

22 For example, the Merchant Taylors' official history states that "by the end of the 17th century its connection with the tailoring trade had virtually ceased and it became what it is today – an association of philanthropic and social character, devoting its energies to educational and charitable activities" (http://merchant-taylors.co.uk, accessed 16 August 2012). The Merchant Taylors are nevertheless now encouraging tailors to join the organization and sponsor tailoring training and contests.

and whether they were paying appropriate taxes (Hazlitt, 2–3). Hazlitt explains that:

> the hostile critics of the Corporation and the Companies made a good deal of the serious loss to the Imperial revenue from the enormous amount of property held in mortmain and exempt from succession-duty in perpetuity [. . .]. There was also a contention that the Companies were independent of the Corporation, and were, at least no longer, what they nominally or ostensibly professed to be – representatives, guardians, and promoters of various trades and callings. (2)

It also seems possible that in an era of growing fears about the spread of anarchy and communism, the government may have believed the Toulmin Smiths' claims that the livery companies were popular working-class organizations, even though they also claimed them as the original corporations and founders of "commerce," and by this time most of them were run by prosperous businessmen.[23] In 1884 the Commission produced a five-volume report which began with a historical overview of the medieval origins of the livery companies. Drawing on some of the Toulmin Smiths' archival work, the Commission repeated the evidence for medieval survivals claimed by the companies. Quoting other authorities, the introduction to the Commission's report conceded that "it is doubtful whether any primitive merchant guild ever existed in London, and the process by which a popular form of the livery local government became established at the period just mentioned is obscure." Yet it emphasizes the importance of the companies to London's development: "There is no doubt, however, that some of the corporations which are the subject of this inquiry (some had existed before the Norman conquest), were, to a great extent, the instruments through which the municipal independence of London was achieved."[24]

While the Royal Commission's final report did not present a threat to the continued existence of the livery companies, William Carew Hazlitt's *Livery Companies of the City of London* seems to have been composed in anticipation of a need to defend them. Hazlitt stresses the respectable nature of the companies in a quiet refutation of the idea that they were a crucible for socialist rebellion, and even justifies their expenditure on banquets as "almost the only survivals of ancient English hospitality" (5). In fact they

23 The original guilds appear not to have been gender exclusive but by the Victorian period members were all male. Women livery company members made a resurgence in the twentieth century, but the current picture of the Merchant Taylors' leadership shows them as mainly male.

24 *The Report of the Royal Commission*, 1:9.

hardly needed it; they became liable to the Corporation Tax of 1884, but the government did not interfere with their administrative structures. In keeping with his emphasis on the respectability of the livery companies, Hazlitt treads lightly over the issue of the Lord Mayor's Show, but in his summary of the history of each company he provides an extensive list of the pageants of early modern times. Hazlitt's reluctance to address the Lord Mayor's Show directly, even though it would seem the most obvious emanation of the continued relevance of the livery companies, is probably because the "popular" elements of the Show lack antiquarian dignity. An element that contemporary commentary reveals to have been particularly welcome to the large crowds who attended the parade was the inclusion of "men in armour."

For much of the nineteenth century, the "men in armour" represented for the crowds the imagined medieval past of Lord Mayor's Day. A 1761 guide to the show mentions a man in armor with attendants as representative of the "Armourers and Brasiers" company.[25] Spectators, though, seem to have interpreted the men in armor as a tradition in its own right. In 1790, *The Times* stated that the "man in armour, the last of the city pageants, who, with his attendants, formed a spectacle that gratified the curiosity of many, has ceased to grace the show" (10 November 1790). In 1808, however, the "man in armour was restored to this ancient ceremony, after a lapse of some years, to the great satisfaction of the spectators" (*The Times*, 10 November 1808). An account of the parade in 1826 mentions a "Man in brass chain armour, mounted on a black charger"; the parade also included two men in copper armor and another in "brass scale" armor (*The Times*, 10 November 1808).[26] The "men in armour" seem to have become an expected sight for the large crowds who attended the procession. In 1865, the parade was scaled down and the "men in armour" abandoned: in 1868 *The Times* noted with satisfaction:

> The men in armour will be "conspicuous in their absence." Two or three years ago that grotesque part of the spectacle was abolished, and will probably henceforward exist only in the popular recollection as a subject of ridicule. (9 November 1868)

25 *A Guide to the Lord Mayor's Show, or the gentleman and lady's companion to that magnificent procession* (London, 1761), 8. In 1761 the newly crowned George III and family attended, and the banquet cost £4,889.4.0, roughly equivalent to $750,000 today.

26 The different-colored suits of armor, apparently chain-mail rather than plate armor, may possibly be a response to the immense popularity of Walter Scott's *Ivanhoe* (1819), which was to become a leading inspiration for arms, armor, and tournaments.

This prognostication proved, however, to be incorrect. In the 1870s the parade took on an imperial flavor and the 1876 parade included "Indian elephants, in Oriental trappings with howdahs, guided by Mahouts; attendant equestrians in State costumes; [and] six Knights in armour, with each a lance and pennon" (10 November 1876). The word "pageant" began to be used more frequently, as, returning to the early modern practices, parades once again started to include carts drawing displays. In 1877, *The Times* noted that "in spite of the wishes of some who look with no friendly eyes upon the Corporation and its surroundings, the Lord Mayor's Show is still as it has been from the earliest recollection of all" (10 November 1877). Even in rain, the procession was more ambitious and more topical than ever, and included:

> Two immense dromedaries from Sangers Circus, ridden by "Egyptians," and after them came an ornamental car, drawn by six horses, carrying an insignificant model of Cleopatra's Needle, surrounded by a group of persons representing Egypt. It had been originally intended to carry the model perpendicularly, but Temple-bar again proved a thorn in the side of the Civic authorities, and so this "Egyptian loan," as it was called, had to recline on its car, amid representations of the Sphinx and the Pyramids. A pair of elephants followed the Needle, and then came what was described as an elaborate ornamental tableau car, drawn by ten horses, and representing "Peace and Plenty," – questionably appropriate at this juncture; – the Muses, the Four Seasons, and other trophies and emblems, more or less absurd.

The parade therefore looked back to the early modern period, where representations of camels (possibly horses in pasteboard trappings[27]) were sometimes included as part of the emblem of the Mercer's Company. At the same time, it anticipated the arrival of the obelisk known as Cleopatra's Needle by a year, and also shows the interest in Egypt that was to lead to British occupation in 1882. Yet the subject matter was not merely topical; to keep everyone happy, it also included six men in armor. The 1884 Show included "floats" with episodes in London history:

> There was, for instance, a car drawn by 12 ponies, with the immortal Dick Whittington beside the Highgate mile-post in the act of listening to Bow Bells, and in close proximity to a representative of his famous cat. [. . .] William the Conqueror was represented, and so was Richard

27 See Hill, *Pageantry and Power*, 150.

> Coeur de Lion, Henricus Fitz-Alwyne, the first Mayor of London, Richard II, and Queen Elizabeth, all beautifully mounted and carefully costumed after the manner of the habits in which they lived. Lord Mayor Walworth standing over the slain Wat Tyler was not a popular figure. It evoked groans and hisses. (*The Times*, 11 November 1884)

The reaction to William Walworth, once a hero of the Fishmongers, suggests class divisions in the reception of the Lord Mayor's Show. While the livery companies took the opportunity to assert their status in the City, the Show itself gave the people of London an opportunity to voice their opinions of the new and retiring mayors. As early as 1787, *The Times* remarked that the new mayor's parade through the City "gives the vast multitude of citizens and inhabitants an opportunity of knowing his person, and paying him every proper degree of reverence and respect. Here too, the former Lord Mayor goes through the popular ordeal; and his conduct is generally marked with approbation, or reproach" (8 November 1787). The "men in armour" had clearly been a favorite with ordinary Londoners, the classes who, unless they had a life story like Dick Whittington's, would never have the opportunity to share in the lavish banquets that followed the day's events.

As the parade expanded to become more like a carnival, the editors of *The Times* felt entitled to point out the absurdity of some of the representations, even though these scenes endorsed the crown, the empire, and trade. Still, while *The Times* conceded that "some iconoclasts maintain that the Lord Mayor's Show is only meant for bumpkins and children," it also defended it as "by no means an empty fiction. It symbolizes in a manner the power and repute of the Corporation of London, which are no shadows, but substantial realities" (Editorial, 9 November 1882).

Yet the public celebration of the ancient Corporation's continued existence, the Lord Mayor's Show, was moving more in the direction of folk-tradition and carnival – or perhaps even freak-show. A popular song of the early twentieth century, "The Ogo-Pogo," for example, describes a creature whose "mother was an earwig, his father was a whale," and concludes that "the Lord Mayor of London wants / To put him in the Lord Mayor's Show."[28] Far from an occasion of civic pomp, then, the Lord Mayor's Show is a chance to escape the everyday world of London commerce. The Square Mile of the City has few residential properties, and on a typical Saturday the area is very quiet. On the day of the Lord Mayor's Show, however, an estimated quarter of a million people come out to watch the parade, which

28 "The Ogo-Pogo, A Funny Foxtrot," words by Cumberland Clark. See http://karlshuker.blogspot.com/2010/12/when-ogopogo-was-going-for-song.html, accessed 27 July 2012.

now claims to have participants in the "thousands."[29] In the later twentieth and early twenty-first centuries, as the Lord Mayor's show of allegiance to the crown has become irrelevant and London's economy has grown increasingly dependent on heritage culture, traditions themselves become the justification. The most visible example of this transformation is the Guildhall giants.

The Guildhall giants are large carved wooden figures kept in the building at least since the earlier 1600s. Often described as the "traditional guardians of London" (www.lordmayorsshow.org), they are not representations of medieval characters but rather mythological figures. William Hone calls them Corinaeus and Gogmagog, although they are more frequently known as Gog and Magog.[30] In some sources they were Trojans who migrated with Brutus the great-grandson of Aeneas to ancient Britain, and in others they were already resident and defeated by the Trojans.[31] Further myth also suggests that after being defeated (by the Trojans or by the Cornish giant Corinaeus) the giants were chained to a palace on the site of the Guildhall. The very confusion over who the giants are and what they represent indicates that their story has largely been handed down by oral tradition. Although they are associated with ancient Celtic times, for Hone they are a remnant of the medieval pageants ended at the Reformation, marking the continuity between the Middle Ages and the present. Hone includes in his 1823 study an engraving of the giants of his time, themselves replacements of earlier figures. The giants are a significant aspect of the guild tradition that has survived to the present day, although the figures have changed over the years. Early wooden statues were destroyed in the Great Fire of London in 1666; a replacement pair was destroyed in the Second World War; and a new pair was sponsored by a former Lord Mayor in 1953.

An interesting recent innovation, however, is the introduction of Gog and Magog into the Lord Mayor's Show itself. The current parade features new wickerwork giants labeled Gog and Magog who wear Romano-British kilts. The official Lord Mayor's Show website explains:

> Queen Elizabeth I will have seen Gog and Magog standing at Temple Bar when she visited the City, and perhaps even Henry V on his return from Agincourt. The old giants were carnival figures standing 14 feet

29 See the website of the City of London Corporation, www.cityoflondon.gov.uk/things-to-do/special-events/Pages/city-events, accessed 17 August 2012. Strangely, the website states that the Lord Mayor's Show is on the first Saturday in November, when it is normally on the second Saturday.

30 Gog and Magog are mentioned in the Bible; according to some sources Corinaeus killed Gogmagog.

31 Hone, *Ancient Mysteries*, 272.

> high and made from "wickerwork and pasteboard". They must have towered over the sixteenth century crowds, and between outings they stood guard at the Guildhall. They suffered many repairs and reconstructions due to time, rodents and finally the Great Fire, until eventually in the early 18th century they were replaced with wooden statues: more durable, but sadly no longer light or mobile enough to lead the Lord Mayor's procession. The statues remained at the Guildhall until they were destroyed in the blitz and replaced yet again.
>
> Olivia Elton Barratt is a Basketmaker who is given to having ideas. They tend to be the sort of idea that leaves a person floating down the Thames in a coracle of her own construction, and this was one of the bigger ones: wouldn't it be great to recreate the ancient giants and see them walking the city streets again? She had nursed the plan for years, and when she learned that she would become Prime Warden of the Basketmakers' Company in 2006 she decided it was time to put it into practice.[32]

The ambiguity of the word "ancient" (does it refer to the giants' mythical origin or to the possibility that they may have been in use in the medieval period?) enhances the sense of history. Again, in describing the history of the giants, the website makes use of references to known practices in the Lord Mayor's Show in Elizabethan times, yet simultaneously suggests that the giants may have been part of the ceremony in the medieval period (the time of Henry V and Dick Whittington). The phrase "carnival figures" implies that, as in some European festivals, the giants were part of the parade.[33] Eighteenth- and nineteenth-century antiquarians, possibly drawing on European analogues, made the assumption that the pasteboard and wood figures of before the Great Fire were paraded in the "triumphs" (Hone, 266–67), and the story of Barratt's giants does the same. Hone goes so far as to assert: "That wicker was used in constructing figures for the London pageants is certain" (267), implying that the early Guildhall giants were such parade figures even though the evidence is scanty. The Guildhall giants were certainly part of London folk-culture, but not necessarily ever a part of the parade for the Lord Mayor's Show until their recent recreation.

Yet the final significant element of this account is its emphasis on Barratt's

32 www.lordmayorshow.org/visitors/procession/gogmagog, accessed 24 May 2012.

33 On the role of giants in festival culture, see Dorothy Noyes, *Fire in the Plaça: Catalan Festival Politics after Franco* (Philadelphia: University of Pennsylvania Press, 2003), particularly pp. 42–46. The Catalonian Corpus Christi celebrations coincide with the traditional time of English mystery plays in the Christian calendar. Intriguingly, Noyes identifies the 1890s as the point when the festival moved to become a more directly orchestrated tourist event (45).

continuation of earlier practice in providing a beautiful and ingenious tribute to her livery company. The description is vague as to who actually paid for the giants, but the implication is that the funding came from the same source as in the early modern period, that is, that members of the company made contributions. The new Guildhall giants, although not medieval in costume and most likely not medieval in how they are used, confirm that in the Lord Mayor's Show, medievalism and corporations go hand in hand.

Gendering Percy's *Reliques: Ancient Ballads* and the Making of Women's Arthurian Writing

Katie Garner

In December 1807, almost fifty years after the publication of Thomas Percy's foundational three-volume collection of ballads, sonnets, and songs, *Reliques of Ancient English Poetry* (1765), a rather less impressive-looking duodecimo volume appeared on the literary market announcing itself as *Ancient Ballads; Selected from Percy's Collection; with Explanatory Notes, taken from Different Authors, for the Use and Entertainment of Young Persons*. Containing only a slim seventeen of Percy's 180 pieces, *Ancient Ballads* is a fraction of the size of the *Reliques*' weighty three tomes. This single-volume redaction was the work of an anonymous "lady" who felt compelled to compile a "selected" version of the influential anthology after hearing her female benefactor repeatedly complain that she was "under the necessity of refusing [her] daughters the pleasure of reading Percy's Collection of Ancient Ballads, on account of the great number amongst them which were unfit to meet the eye of youth."[1] Indeed, modern readers might be inclined to agree with the lady's decorous patron. As Nick Groom has strikingly put it, "[t]he *Reliques* [. . .] welters in gore: the bloodiness of death and dismemberment incarnadines the entire three volumes, and if occasionally watered by humour or levity, it is more often deepened by a colossal amorality."[2] For the lady editing Percy's ballads in 1807, so pervasive was the amorality and violence that even those poems

1 "Dedication – To Mrs. ****.," in ["A Lady"], *Ancient Ballads; Selected from Percy's Collection; with Explanatory Notes, taken from Different Authors, for the Use and Entertainment of Young Persons. By a Lady* (London: Vernor, Hood, and Sharpe, 1807), iii–iv (iii).

2 Nick Groom, *The Making of Percy's Reliques* (Oxford: Clarendon Press, 1999), 45. The title of my own essay reflects my debt to Groom's work.

which passed her strict selection process were subject to further bowdlerization in her edition. "I believe you will not meet with any thing to disapprove of in this little volume," the lady reassured her patron in the introduction to her collection, "for I have selected my ballads with the greatest care, and have omitted all objectionable passages" (iv).

Long overlooked by scholars, *Ancient Ballads* has much to tell us about the relationship between gender and medievalism in the nineteenth century, and, more specifically, about how Arthurian material was presented to women readers. An exploration of the anonymous lady's editorial treatment of Percy's texts reveals both the epistemological limits of her censored redaction, as well as its significance as one of the earliest examples of the treatment of Arthurian material under a female editorial hand. In contrast to many contemporaneous ballad collections, *Ancient Ballads* pays particular attention to the role of female voices in the texts it contains, and, in doing so, seeks to (re)connect its young female readers with the poetry of Britain's medieval past. The final section of this essay considers the impact of the *Ancient Ballads* on the development of women's popular Arthurian writing through an examination of "A Dream" (1815), a juvenile Arthurian work by the poet and translator Louisa Stuart Costello (1799–1870). Written in response to her encounter with Arthurian material in the lady's edition, the style and narrative of Costello's "A Dream" can be partly understood as a reaction to the bowdlerized nature of the lady's Arthurian texts.

Addressed to a reading audience of "young persons," *Ancient Ballads* would appear to be, as Steve Newman notes, "the earliest redaction of Percy [. . .] for children."[3] As well as being the first of its type, *Ancient Ballads* is also distinctly unusual in comparison to its better-known successors, such as John Gilbert's *The Boy's Book of Ballads* (1861) and Sidney Lanier's *The Boy's Percy* (1882), both of which firmly connected Percy's texts with the growth of a boy's "manful" character.[4] In contrast, by virtue of its being edited by a "lady" and produced in response to the needs of a mother and her daughters, contemporary reviewers largely assumed that the *Ancient Ballads* was directed toward young women. The *Monthly Review* considered it to be a "very pretty as well as very innocent" book which would "appear to great advantage in any young lady's library."[5] Likewise, the *Anti-Jacobin* admired the lady's

3 Steve Newman, *Ballad Collection, Lyric, and the Canon: The Call of the Popular from the Restoration to the New Criticism* (Philadelphia: University of Pennsylvania Press, 2007), 259.

4 *The Boy's Book of Ballads*, ed. John Gilbert (London: Bell and Daldy, 1861); *The Boy's Percy: Being Old Ballads of War, Adventure and Love from Bishop Thomas Percy's Reliques of Ancient English Poetry*, ed. Sidney Lanier (New York: Charles Scribner's Sons, 1882), vii–xxxi (xxx).

5 "Ancient Ballads; selected from Percy's Collection," *Monthly Review* 58 (February 1809): 212.

"very judicious selection from Percy's Ancient Ballads" and thought it altogether a "very elegant volume," as well as one with clear educational benefits:

> These Ballads will be found very proper for young ladies, to convey to them some knowledge of the style and manner of life of their forefathers, as they will probably interest their feelings enough to prevent their modern artificial blandishments from mocking the simplicity and innocence of ancient language and sentiment.[6]

Under the umbrella of the separation between past and present, the reviewer arranges a number of further oppositions: between "ancient" and "modern," simplicity and artifice, "forefathers" and "young ladies." Masculinity is associated with simplicity and the innocence of a natural past, whereas femininity is linked to modernity, artifice, and flattery. For the reviewer, women readers are naturally inclined to ridicule ancient texts on account of their gender; the ballads themselves, as the work of patriarchal "forefathers," are inadvertently positioned as part of a masculine literary tradition which modern women will struggle to understand. This is why the lady's carefully managed collection of medieval ballads – selected particularly to appeal to ladies' "feelings" – is deemed to be "very proper."

The comments in the *Anti-Jacobin* emerge from a broader background of anxieties about women's reading and misreading of literary texts which were gathering pace from the 1750s onwards. As Jacqueline Pearson has demonstrated, Romantic-period discourses are saturated with concerns about "girls [. . .] who read the wrong books, in the wrong ways and in the wrong places."[7] The revival of interest in medieval texts which began in Britain in the second half of the eighteenth century, much fostered by the appearance of Percy's *Reliques*, was almost exclusively the province of male antiquarians, but their various publications – scholarly essays as well as reprints of medieval fragments, ballads, and romances – entered a market populated with higher numbers of active women readers than ever before.[8] The concurrent rise in the production of antiquarian texts alongside what Pearson terms the "feminization of the reading public" was bound to raise new questions about the suitability of medieval texts for female study.[9]

6 "Ancient Ballads, selected from Percy's Collection," *Anti-Jacobin Review and Magazine* 31:123 (September 1808): 57–58 (58).

7 Jacqueline Pearson, *Women's Reading in Britain: A Dangerous Recreation, 1750–1835* (Cambridge: Cambridge University Press, 1999), 15.

8 Pearson, *Women's Reading in Britain*, 14–15.

9 Pearson, *Women's Reading in Britain*, 15.

When Joseph Haslewood edited Malory's *Le Morte Darthur* for R. Wilks in 1816, he too emphasized the ways in which he had taken care "to render the text fit for the eye of youth; and that it might be no longer secreted from the fair sex." Like the anonymous lady, Haslewood was keen to reassure his readers that "every indecent allusion has been carefully expunged; and the work may now, with confidence, be placed in the hands of the most scrupulous."[10] The editions by Haslewood and the anonymous lady not only point toward the ways in which women and children were offered a different, sanitized version of medieval poems and romances in contrast to the wider (masculine) reading public, but they also involuntarily offer an indication of the levels of interest women readers had in Britain's medieval literary past. The lady's report of her patron's recurring refusal to let her daughters read the *Reliques* is a powerful demonstration of their desire to encounter older texts. In similar fashion, Haslewood's claim that Malory's epic was "secreted" from women readers suggests that they were otherwise keen to read his Arthuriad. After all, there is little need to secrete books from a social group which has no interest in reading them.

"A very foolish and paltry book": The Limits of the Ancient Ballads

Advertised as containing texts "selected from Percy's Collection," the full title of the *Ancient Ballads* placed the roots of its origin firmly in the Bishop of Dromore's earlier work. The lady's choices for the *Ancient Ballads* show that she, like Percy, held an immediate preference for the martial, northern ballads. Like the *Reliques*, *Ancient Ballads* opens with "The Ballad of Chevy-Chase," and retains a further two poems describing the exploits of the Northumberland Percys ("The Rising in the North" and "Northumberland Betrayed by Douglas"). Ballads connected to the romance tradition also dominate the lady's slimmed-down collection which contains "King Estmere," "Valentine and Ursine," "Robin Hood and Guy of Gisborne," and four of Percy's original six Arthurian poems. The lady also seems to have been keen to preserve the hidden national diversity in Percy's ostensibly "English" collection, and includes two popular Scottish examples: "Hardyknute" and "Sir Patrick Spence."

When arranging the *Reliques*, Percy had carefully positioned "more modern attempts in the same kind of writing" at the end of each volume

10 [Joseph Haslewood], "Advertisement," to [Sir Thomas Malory], *La Mort d'Arthur: The Most Ancient History of the Renowned Prince Arthur and the Knights of the Round Table*, [ed. Joseph Haslewood], 3 vols. (London: R. Wilks, 1816), 1:iv.

in order to "atone for the rudeness of the more obsolete poems."[11] In her much shorter collection, the lady abandons Percy's chronological structure in favor of a more thematic arrangement. As a single-volume work, it is inevitable that items which appeared previously in separate books in Percy's three-volume anthology achieve new and greater proximity in the *Ancient Ballads*, but it would appear that the editor carefully rearranged Percy's items to highlight similarities she perceived between individual texts. For example, "The Heir of Linne" (from Percy's first volume), a cautionary tale which describes how the "unthrifty" laird of Linne loses and eventually regains his estate, appears immediately before the avaricious tale of "Gernutus, the Jew of Venice" (from volume two), an analogue to the pound-of-flesh plot told in Shakespeare's *The Merchant of Venice*. When Percy compiled the *Reliques*, he placed "Sir Lancelot du Lake" in his first volume under the category of "Ballads that illustrate Shakespeare," separated from the other "Ballads on King Arthur, &c." which otherwise appeared all together in volume three. In her edition, the lady simply collates her Arthurian specimens, uniting "Sir Lancelot" with "The Marriage of Sir Gawaine," "King Ryence's Challenge," and "King Arthur's Death" to form one group at the center of her volume (88–130). In the *Reliques*, the reader does not encounter Percy's main group of five Arthurian ballads until almost the end of the anthology, but in the lady's abridgement the Arthurian specimens are given pride of place and account for almost a fifth of her content.[12] Their centrality in her redaction for "young persons" in part reflects a general association between the Arthurian story and childhood reading that was already in evidence; as Roger Simpson points out, Robert Southey read Malory when at Westminster School between 1788 and 1792.[13] Southey, however, held a firm concep-

11 Thomas Percy, "Preface," to *The Reliques of Ancient English Poetry: Consisting of Old Heroic Ballads, Songs and Other Pieces of our Earlier Poets; Together with some few of later date*, 4th edn., 3 vols. (London: John Nichols for J. and C. Rivington, 1794), 1:viii–xx (xiv). As Groom notes, this edition was published in 1795, though 1794 appears on the title page (see Groom, "The Formation of Percy's *Reliques* [Introduction]," in Percy, *Reliques of Ancient English Poetry*, with an introduction by Nick Groom, 3 vols. [London: J. Dodsley, 1765; facsimile repr. London: Routledge, 1996], 1:1–68 [2]). I have used the 1794 fourth edition of the *Reliques* throughout this essay, as it was the most recent at the time when the lady was compiling her version (a fifth edition appeared in 1812). The presence of editorial material from this edition in the *Ancient Ballads* strongly suggests that the 1794 edition was the lady's working text. All further references to the *Reliques*, unless otherwise stated, are to the 1794 edition.

12 Arthurian material covers 42 of the 211 pages of *Ancient Ballads* (88–130), equating to 20 percent, compared with 4 percent, or 48 pages out of 1324, in Percy's three-volume *Reliques* (1:214–19, 3:1–41). (Figures based on the 1794 edition.)

13 Roger Simpson, "'Revisiting Cramalot': An Arthurian Theme in the Correspondence of William Taylor and Robert Southey," in *Studies in Medievalism IV: Medievalism in England*, ed. Leslie J. Workman (Cambridge: D. S. Brewer, 1992), 143–60 (143).

tion of *Le Morte Darthur* as a "book for boys," whereas the lady's strong preference for Arthurian material in her collection for her patron's daughters suggests that she deemed the legend to be equally suitable reading matter for young ladies.[14]

Alongside the ballads themselves, the *Ancient Ballads* also includes what the lady describes as "a few explanatory notes for the information of [. . .] young readers" (vi). In her detailed analysis of Lanier's editorial approach to *The Boy's Percy*, Marya DeVoto points out that the substantial scholarly apparatus of essays, footnotes, and often lengthy headnotes to individual ballads in the *Reliques* clearly advertised Percy's volumes as an "antiquarian recovery project," but that such a myriad of paratextual additions was considerably "less appropriate for the modern child."[15] Quite logically, then, the *Ancient Ballads* contains far less critical material and apparatus than the *Reliques*: gone are Percy's introductory essays to each volume, as well as a substantial proportion of his footnotes and introductory headnotes. Percy systematically prefaced each item in the consciously erudite *Reliques* with some form of commentary (sometimes a single paragraph, but often stretching to several pages) elucidating details of the poem's origin, content, location, and editorial treatment. In the lady's text, only ten of her seventeen ballads merit their own scholarly introductions, which are compiled by extracting select passages from Percy's equivalents. The *Monthly Review* noticed another missing paratextual feature: *Ancient Ballads* appeared without a contents page.[16] Hence Percy's scholarship was not only substantially reduced, but the lady's entire text was far less searchable and readable. Occasional glosses of archaic words and phrases were added to help younger readers with some of the more challenging Middle English, but this, like the lady's approach to headnotes, was an uneven practice. While up to six words might be glossed on a page for "The Ballad of Chevy-Chase," only three words are given similar treatment throughout the entirety of "King Arthur's Death." Admittedly, the northern dialect of "Chevy-Chase" makes it a more challenging text for any reader than "King Arthur's Death" and thus the poem may be deserving of more glosses, but reviewers still felt that the *Ancient Ballads* needed to do far more to make Percy's texts fully accessible for younger readers, pointing out that

14 Robert Southey, "Preface," to [Sir Thomas Malory], *The Byrth, Lyf, and Actes of Kyng Arthur; of his noble knyghtes of the rounde table* [etc.], 2 vols. (London: Longman, Hurst, Rees, Orme, and Brown, 1817), 1:i–xxxix (xxviii).

15 Marya DeVoto, "The Hero as Editor: Sidney Lanier's Medievalism and the Science of Manhood," in *Studies in Medievalism IX: Medievalism and the Academy I*, ed. Leslie J. Workman, Kathleen Verduin, and David D. Metzger (Cambridge: D. S. Brewer, 1999), 148–70 (152).

16 "Ancient Ballads; selected from Percy's Collection," *Monthly Review* 58 (February 1809): 212.

"for children, indeed, [the *Reliques*] was never designed; but neither is this selection, in which the old orthography is preserved, by any means level to their comprehensions."[17]

While the reduction of some of Percy's more copious notes and annotations was undoubtedly necessary to fit the material for a younger audience, the lady's contractions in the pursuit of simplicity often produce rather confusing results. When Percy edited "The Marriage of Sir Gawaine," he added a note to the ballad's description of the loathly lady "clad in red scarlette," observing that this was "a common phrase in our old writers" and citing as proof the similarly "scarlet red" clothing of the Wife of Bath in Chaucer's prologue to the *Canterbury Tales* (*Reliques* 3:15).[18] In the *Ancient Ballads*, a footnote appears at the same point in the poem, but its meaning and function are less than clear: the female editor's equivalent merely reads "so the original" (102). It is possible, perhaps, that rejecting Percy's (incorrect) hypothesis that the ballad was Chaucer's source, the female editor wished to assert the *Wife of Bath's Tale* as the "original" upon which the ballad was based, but ultimately the brevity and obscurity of the note render it comparatively useless to a child reader.

In addition to the truncated and often unclear notes, indications of any "supplements" or additions that Percy had made to the ballads he found in his mutilated folio were also rendered invisible in the lady's edition. Without Percy's headnote to "The Heir of Linne," young readers of the poem in the *Ancient Ballads* encountered the text unaware that several "breaches and defects" in the manuscript had "rendered the insertion of supplemental stanzas necessary" (*Reliques* 2:128). Also printed without a headnote, "Hardyknute" appeared simply subtitled (as it is in Percy) "a Scottish fragment," without the attribution of the poem to Lady Wardlaw which accompanied the poem in the *Reliques* from 1767 onwards (*Reliques* 2:96). The treatment of "The Marriage of Sir Gawaine" provides another good example of the lady's lack of interest in either the origin or the authenticity of Percy's texts. Following repeated complaints from an outraged Joseph Ritson, Percy had finally added a transcript of the fragmentary Arthurian poem to the fourth edition of the *Reliques* published in 1794.[19] Yet despite having access to the now-published fragment, when the female editor published her version of the text in 1807,

17 "Ancient Ballads; selected from Percy's Collection," *Annual Review and History of Literature* 7 (January 1808): 474.

18 See Geoffrey Chaucer, "The General Prologue," to *The Canterbury Tales*, in *The Riverside Chaucer*, ed. Larry D. Benson, 3rd edn. (Oxford: Oxford University Press, 1988), Part I, line 456.

19 See Groom, *The Making of Percy's Reliques*, 227; also Bertrand H. Bronson, *Joseph Ritson: Scholar-at-Arms*, 2 vols. (Berkeley: University of California Press, 1938), 2:567.

she simply presented Percy's former version (presumably less objectionable because more complete). Like "The Heir of Linne," "The Marriage of Sir Gawaine" appears without an introductory headnote in the *Ancient Ballads* and so again none of the ballad's complex textual history was explained.

In her volume's dedication, the editor had openly advertised that some of her selections had warranted close editing to ensure the removal of "all objectionable passages" (iv). Made mostly for the sake of propriety, often these changes were minor and of little consequence to the overall narrative of the ballad: for example, in "King Ryence's Challenge," the poem's original description of "Guenever the gay" (*Reliques* 3:26–27, line 3) becomes, in the lady's edition, "Guenever the royall" (116). Other modifications, however, were both more manipulative and more subtle. In "Sir Lancelot du Lake," which describes Lancelot's fight against the villainous knight Sir Tarquin, Lancelot eventually gains the victory when he strikes his opponent's "necke in two" (*Reliques* 1:214–19, line 121). In the lady's version of the poem, Tarquin's gruesome beheading is cleverly reconfigured: the problematic "in two" is replaced with the homonymous "into" (96). Subsequently no heads are cleaved from bodies in the dénouement to the lady's version of "Sir Lancelot du Lake," as Lancelot achieves his victory by delivering his foe a slightly more restrained stab in the neck.

Indeed, the violence endemic to "Sir Lancelot du Lake" makes it somewhat surprising that the lady chose to retain such a high proportion of the Arthurian ballads from the *Reliques* in her sanitized collection. Recent commentators have tended to emphasize the "coarseness" of Percy's Arthurian ballads; Groom summarizes their content as a lively mix of "sexual politics and adultery, sexual misdeeds (lewdly described), and cat fights."[20] The lady chose not to include the lewdest ballad of the set, "The Boy and the Mantle," in which a courtly chastity test ends with Arthur pronounced a "cuckold" and Guinevere "a bitch and a witch / And a whore bold" (*Reliques* 3:1–11, lines 150, 147–48). "The Legend of King Arthur" was also left out, though probably more for reasons of space than on account of any particularly objectionable content.[21]

Just as bawdy as "The Boy and the Mantle," however, was "The Marriage of Sir Gawaine," which rather more surprisingly was retained in the lady's "instructive and entertaining" edition (iv). Beginning with a typical interruption at court by a damsel abused by a villainous baron, the first part of the poem describes Arthur's quest to appease his aggressor by uncovering what "women most desire" (101; *Reliques* 3:11–24, line 70). The baron's

20 Groom, *The Making of Percy's Reliques*, 55.

21 "The Legend of King Arthur" provides a first-person summary of Arthur's life; thus, the poem's latter stanzas overlap to a certain extent with the narrative of "King Arthur's Death."

dialogue is pitted with crude language which the editor felt it imperative to censor. Single words are regularly substituted for more agreeable alternatives; the baron calls Arthur a "cuckold kinge" in Percy's version (*Reliques* 3:13, line 39), which is changed to "boasting kinge" by the lady (99), and similarly "swore" (*Reliques* 3:17, line 150) becomes the more polite "sayd" (106), and "whore" (*Reliques* 3:17, line 152) the more acceptable "jade" (106). As the spelling of the inserted "sayd" suggests, the lady both antiquated and modernized the spelling of Percy's texts as she thought appropriate.

The second part of the ballad required the most pervasive changes due to its increasingly sexualized content. After the marriage takes place between Gawain and the loathly lady who provides Arthur with the answer to the riddle, the narrative culminates in a climactic scene set in their "wed-bed" (*Reliques* 3:22, line 93). Determined to avoid such a backdrop of sexual intimacy, in the lady's text, Gawain and the lady simply converse at "home" (111), where, rather than "lying" next to her newly wedded knight (*Reliques* 3:22, line 110), the lady is more properly "sitting there by his side" (112). Omitted altogether from the lady's copy is the stanza describing the couple's enjoyment of one another between the sheets:

> Sir Gawaine kiss'd that lady faire,
> Lying upon the sheete:
> And swore, as he was a true knighte,
> The spice was never soe sweete. (*Reliques* 3:22, lines 105–8)

Presumably, this stanza was so riddled with sexual references that the lady came to the conclusion that its problematic four lines were best left out altogether.

These changes to the narrative of "The Marriage of Sir Gawaine," made in pursuit of the amelioration of its sexual content, result in a very different poem. The lady's appeal to Gawain to choose whether to see her beautiful either "by night, or else by day" (*Reliques* 3:23, line 119) becomes, in *Ancient Ballads*, a choice between her appearance "at home or else abroad" (112). Couched in these terms, Gawain's deliberation between having her appear "foule still in my house" or "foule in companie" (112) (in Percy "foule still in the night" and "foule by daye" [*Reliques* 3:23, lines 121, 124]) is recast in terms which do more to reflect eighteenth-century ideas about the privacy of the home against more public spaces, than the original ballad's more coarse association of the night with sexual freedom, and the day with public propriety.

The various scholarly weaknesses of the lady's edition did not pass unnoticed by contemporary reviewers. The *Eclectic Review* remained skeptical about the educational benefits of the collection: "We do not think [. . .]

that this particular species of reading is peculiarly adapted to improve the minds of youth, either by exalting their sentiments, expanding their conceptions, or refining their taste; and better ways unquestionably will be found of providing for their amusement."[22] Unsure whether children, of any gender, should be exposed to Britain's early poetry, the comments of the *Eclectic Review* are unusually devoid of any of the preconceived ideas about "proper" feminine reading which characterize much of the critical commentary on the volume. A particularly savage account in Arthur Aiken's *Annual Review* began by classifying the *Ancient Ballads* as a "very foolish and paltry book" compiled "for the benefit of some *very* delicate lady."[23] The remainder of the review pointed up various further shortcomings: "[n]either taste nor judgement is displayed in the choice of pieces inserted," proclaimed the reviewer, while "the notes are very trifling, and the printing very inaccurate."[24] Finally, the very appearance of the *Ancient Ballads* was declared "injurious to the memory of the late respectable Bishop of Dromore."[25] Holding the lady's text up to the standard of Percy's *Reliques*, the *Annual Review* found it distinctly wanting.

Feminizing Percy's Reliques

Yet to dismiss the lady's *Ancient Ballads* on account of its faulty scholarship would in many ways repeat the anti-feminist criticisms of the writer for the *Annual Review*. While the above discussion illuminates some of the limits of the lady's scholarship and her "selections," it distracts attention away from the numerous similarities between Percy's and the lady's editorial approaches. Percy's late acquisition of the Countess of Northumberland as patron for the *Reliques* in 1764 prompted him immediately to consider his "ancient" content in a new light. As he explained in a letter to Sir David Dalrymple, Lord Hailes: "After a lady had accepted of the Book I was obliged to cancel all the more indelicate pieces and substitute others more inoffensive."[26] In a bid to temper some of the collection's more lewd content, Percy made the last-minute decision to cut fifteen already-printed poems from the anthol-

22 "Ancient Ballads; selected from Percy's Collection," *Eclectic Review* 5:1 (May 1809): 489.

23 "Ancient Ballads; selected from Percy's Collection," *Annual Review* 7 (January 1808): 474. (Emphasis in original.)

24 "Ancient Ballads," *Annual Review*: 474.

25 "Ancient Ballads," *Annual Review*: 474.

26 Percy to Dalrymple, 16 December 1764, in *The Correspondence of Thomas Percy and David Dalrymple, Lord Hailes*, ed. A. F. Falconer (Baton Rouge: Louisiana State University Press, 1954), vol. 4 of *The Percy Letters*, general ed. Cleanth Brooks and David Nichol Smith, 16 vols., 4:91–92. Also quoted in Groom, *The Making of Percy's Reliques*, 223.

ogy.[27] He also embarked on some significant restructuring. The group of five Arthurian ballads which were originally due to appear at the front of the first volume were now moved to the beginning of the third, with the dual benefit of privileging the ballads concerning the countess's ancestors, the Northumbrian Percys, and lessening the prominence of the bawdy Arthurian poems.[28] With the cancellations and this new structure in place, Percy could confidently assure his readers that "great care has been taken to admit nothing immoral or indecent" (*Reliques* 1:xx). Nearly fifty years later, the editor of the *Ancient Ballads* made the same claims for her "selected" edition.

There are yet further parallels. In her dedication, the lady was careful to mention that she had compiled her "little volume" in her "leisure hours" (iii), but before judging this as evidence of the lady's lack of scholarly ambition, it is worth remembering that Percy had made much the same apology for the *Reliques*. Toward the end of his own preface the bishop confessed: "[t]o prepare [the *Reliques*] for press has been the amusement of now and then a vacant hour amidst the leisure and retirement of rural life, and hath only served as a relaxation from graver studies" (*Reliques* 1:xx). The lady's substantial "omissions" and alterations to her texts also pale in comparison to Percy's more numerous and sustained "improvements" from his mutilated folio. As Groom summarizes:

> Percy [. . .] compiled single texts of ballads from a variety of unacknowledged versions, and liberally rewrote these collages to suit the taste of a late eighteenth-century readership. Although noteworthy interpolations were often pinned with quotation marks (thus ''), many minor revisions, and some major rewritings, were rendered completely invisible.[29]

In fact, one of the changes Percy made to the end of "Robin Hood and Guy of Gisborne" altered the climax of the narrative in much the same way as the lady's later adjustments revised the ending of "Sir Lancelot du Lake." In the folio copy of the ballad, Little John shoots an arrow at the Sheriff that "did cleave his head in twinn," yet in the printed *Reliques* the same line declares

27 Groom, *The Making of Percy's Reliques*, 223–25.

28 Groom, *The Making of Percy's Reliques*, 223. Similarly, David Matthews surmises that "the change may have been made because Percy felt that it was important to spare the countess finding, in what was originally to have been the anthology's opening poem, a stanza on Queen Guenevere describing her as 'a bitch and a witch, / And a whore bold.'" David Matthews, *The Making of Middle English, 1765–1910* (Minneapolis and London: University of Minnesota Press, 1999), 11.

29 Groom, *The Making of Percy's Reliques*, 8–9.

that Robin's right-hand man "shott him into the 'backe'-syde" (*Reliques* 1:81–95, line 236).[30] (The more prudent lady opts simply for "he shott him into the side" [60].) Multiple scholars have observed how Percy's position as a "man of taste" dictated the shape of the *Reliques*.[31] His own alterations were very much in accordance with the type of changes that the female editor of his text, fifty years later, deemed necessary in order to make the same ballads fit for her patron's daughters. Both Percy and the lady handled and selected their texts based on similarly discerning principles.

Percy was subject to more than his fair share of critical attacks from the antiquarian community on account of his uninhibited "improvements" to his folio copies, but the criticisms (and, indeed, the praise) levied at the lady's redaction suggest that her gender had an important role to play in the reception of her text. Romantic antiquarianism was a ubiquitously masculine field of enquiry, and one which, it would appear, viewed female entrants into the field with considerable suspicion. From the second half of the eighteenth century onwards, emerging theories about the origin of romances, rediscoveries of medieval texts, transcripts of rare material, and plans for new editions or collections were passed between an exclusively male network of scholars including Percy, Thomas Warton, Joseph Ritson, Walter Scott, and George Ellis. As Philippa Levine observes, late eighteenth- and early nineteenth-century antiquarians were "[o]verwhelmingly male and middle class," and most (like Percy and Warton) had university educations.[32] Women, on the other hand, were excluded not only from the benefits of university study, but also from many of the venues for antiquarian research; Rosemary Sweet has outlined how "public records in the depositories in London or in the libraries of Oxford and Cambridge were closed to them, except as visitors."[33] In a climate hostile to women working directly with primary materials, women's

30 This alteration is examined in detail by Bronson in *Ritson: Scholar-at-Arms*, 2:572. For a transcript of the poem in the original folio, see *Bishop Percy's Folio Manuscript*, ed. John W. Hales and Frederick J. Furnivall, 3 vols. (London: N. Trübner and Co., 1867–68), 2:227–37 (237).

31 As well as Groom's work, see Leah Dennis, "Thomas Percy: Antiquarian *vs.* Men of Taste," *PMLA* 57:1 (1942): 140–52; Gwendolyn A. Morgan, "Percy, the Antiquarians, the Ballad, and the Middle Ages," *Studies in Medievalism VII: Medievelism in England II*, ed. Leslie J. Workman and Kathleen Verduin (Cambridge: D.S. Brewer, 1996), 22–32; and Matthews, *The Making of Middle English*, 3–24.

32 Philippa Levine, *The Amateur and the Professional: Antiquarians, Historians and Archaeologists in Victorian England 1838–1886* (Cambridge: Cambridge University Press, 2003), 8. See also Susan Manning, "Antiquarianism, Balladry and the Rehabilitation of Romance," in *The Cambridge History of English Romantic Literature*, ed. James Chandler (Cambridge: Cambridge University Press, 2009), 45–79 (56).

33 Rosemary Sweet, *Antiquaries: The Discovery of the Past in Eighteenth-Century Britain* (Cambridge: Cambridge University Press, 2004), 71–72.

first forays in medieval studies were limited to redactions of works resulting from archival research by male scholars, such as the lady's *Ancient Ballads*, or Susannah Dobson's translated abridgements of the works of the French medievalist Jean-Baptiste de La Curne de Sainte-Palaye.[34]

Ballad-collecting, as a sub-branch of antiquarianism, was ostensibly little different. With the exception of Charlotte Brooke, the editor of *Reliques of Irish Poetry* (1789), eighteenth-century ballad collectors were almost exclusively male. Yet when the antiquarian went out into the field to source his ballads, he consistently found himself in the company of women; as Deborah Symonds points out, "most of the recorded singers, by the time the collectors came in the eighteenth and nineteenth centuries, were women."[35] Similarly, Susan Stewart observes: "[o]nce we look beyond the invention of the minstrel tradition, we find a genre predominantly continued by women in both its 'authentic' and imitated forms."[36] A dramatization of this innate connection between balladry and women's oral culture occurs in Sir Walter Scott's *The Antiquary* (1816), when his idiosyncratic protagonist, Jonathan Oldbuck, overhears a song sung by Elspeth Meiklebackit. Immediately diagnosing her song as an "historical ballad," Oldbuck can scarcely believe his good fortune at discovering "a genuine and undoubted fragment of minstrelsy! – Percy would admire its simplicity – Ritson could not impugn its authenticity."[37] As Oldbuck diligently scribbles down Elspeth's "legendary scraps of ancient poetry," Scott illuminates the contrast between the lower-class, illiterate female singer and the moneyed, male antiquarian who commits her song to writing.[38]

The old woman who acts as a repository of ancient poetry is recognized for her value and contribution in Scott's novel, but more recent commentators on the ballad revival have argued that the same process of transmission – from female singer to male-authored text – was seldom foregrounded in eighteenth-century ballad anthologies. Maureen McLane has shown how antiquarians like Percy, though keen to name their distinguished correspondents who had contributed scholarship or ballad transcripts, were more reluctant to provide the names of women who had "preserved" the newly

34 Susannah Dobson (d. 1795) translated and abridged two popular works by the French medievalist Jean-Baptiste de la Curne de Sainte-Palaye: *The Literary History of the Troubadours* (London: Wilson, 1779) and *Memoirs of Ancient Chivalry* (London: Dodsley, 1784).

35 Deborah A. Symonds, *Weep Not for Me: Women, Ballads and Infanticide in Early Modern Scotland* (University Park: Pennsylvania State University Press, 1997), 1.

36 Susan Stewart, *Crimes of Writing: Problems in the Containment of Representation* (Durham, NC: Duke University Press), 119.

37 Sir Walter Scott, *The Antiquary*, ed. Nicola J. Watson (Oxford: Oxford University Press, 2002), 375–76.

38 Scott, *The Antiquary*, 375.

prized songs "in memory."[39] As Nigel Leask puts it, "Romantic ballad theory [. . .] showed a stubborn resistance to a feminized oral tradition."[40] Citing Percy's fabled "rescue" of his folio manuscript from the hands of Humphrey Pitt's fire-lighting maids, Susan Stewart concludes that from the eighteenth century onwards, "the ballad [. . .] is thus constantly being rescued not so much from 'history,' as from the general oblivion of the feminine."[41] McLane suggests, somewhat more sinisterly, that "balladeering could be seen as a particular traffic in women – e.g. Mrs Brown of Falkland, Mrs Arrot of Aberbrothick – conducted in the course of homosocial exchange."[42] Ballad collectors like Percy had cleaved the ballads from their feminine roots, and wrapped them in a protective and exclusive web of scholarship. Far from being the preserve of eighteenth-century ballad collectors alone, the textual marginalization of the ballad's domestic materiality was still in full swing at the beginning of the nineteenth century; Adriana Craciun has examined how Scott's *Minstrelsy of the Scottish Border* (1802–3) was similarly marked by a repressed debt to texts collected from the strains of Scottish female "spinstrelsy."[43]

In contrast, the *Ancient Ballads* is openly addressed to the "daughters" of the lady's patron, as well as, by implication, to a wider generation of young women, and is organized in a number of ways which draw attention to the feminine heritage of the ballads it contains. The female editor's obvious debt to Percy for her texts does not prevent her from asserting her ownership over what she calls "my ballads," and her professed "care" in preparing them for publication couches her editorial practice in domestic, maternal terms (iv). Perhaps most indicative of the editor's proto-feminist politics is her decision to extract a particular paragraph from Percy's "Essay on the Ancient Minstrels" pertaining to the existence of female minstrels and place it among her notes to "King Estmere." Percy had emphasized how this particular ballad helpfully illustrated "the character of old Minstrels" in accordance with the aspects of the figure's dress, class, and manners put forward in his own essay (*Reliques* 1:63). In the *Ancient Ballads*, the female editor uses the same poem to promote her interest in female contributors to the minstrel tradition. The

39 Maureen N. McLane, *Balladeering, Minstrelsy, and the Making of British Romantic Poetry* (Cambridge: Cambridge University Press, 2008), 52–54.

40 Nigel Leask, "'A degrading species of Alchymy': Ballad Poetics and the Meanings of Popular Culture," in *Romanticism and Popular Culture in Britain and Ireland*, ed. Phillip Connell and Nigel Leask (Cambridge: Cambridge University Press, 2009), 51–71 (69).

41 Stewart, *Crimes of Writing*, 118–19.

42 McLane, *Balladeering, Minstrelsy, and the Making of British Romantic Poetry*, 63.

43 Adriana Craciun, "Romantic Spinstrelsy: Anne Bannerman and the Sexual Politics of the Ballad," in *Scotland and the Borders of Romanticism*, ed. Leith Davis, Ian Duncan, and Janet Sorensen (Cambridge: Cambridge University Press, 2004), 204–24.

remainder of Percy's essay is deemed unnecessary for the lady's edition, but the bishop's observation that "there should seem to have been women of this profession, as well as those of the other sex" is considered by the lady editor to be too important to leave out (38–39; *Reliques* 1:xlii).[44]

It is not only on a textual level that the *Ancient Ballads* promotes the presence of women in the ballad tradition. Like the majority of later Victorian ballad collections for children, the *Ancient Ballads* appeared accompanied by several illustrations. A scene from "Northumberland Betrayed by Douglas" is chosen for the volume's frontispiece and depicts the ubiquitous earl's departure from his lady before his journey to England by sea. The figure of Northumberland occupies the center of the plate, but his gaze is directed firmly left toward his lady, and to his right lies the ship which will carry him away. Below the engraving is an excerpted stanza from the ballad containing the lady's parting words to her lover:

> And wilt thou goe, noble lord?
> Then farewell truth and honestie:
> And farewell heart and farewell hand.
> For never more will I see thee. (Frontispiece; also 182)

What the frontispiece illustrates, then, is not Northumberland's departure *per se* but the woman's "farewell" speech. The combination of text and image not only gives prominence to the role of Northumberland's lady in a ballad otherwise bearing the names of two men, but, placed at the opening of the volume, it immediately articulates a connection between the lady's "selected" ballads and acts of female orality.

The volume's second and only other engraving, this time accompanying "The Heir of Linne," also visualizes the role of a woman in its narrative. It depicts the scene in which the ballad's eponymous protagonist appeals to the "wife of John o' the Scales" for alms (facing 70). As in the frontispiece, the female figure again stands off-center to the left of the picture, but with her arm extended upwards and outwards toward the shadowy side-profile of the impoverished heir. With her arms outstretched and uplifted eyes, her pose is reminiscent of the stance of an oral performer. Positioned in a vaguely gothicized hall where her husband and another man sit feasting, she doubles as a visual representation of the female minstrel offered to readers in the note

44 Percy's thoughts on this particular aspect of minstrelsy had completely turned around by 1794. In the original 1765 version of the "Essay on the Ancient English Minstrels," he had firmly concluded: "I do not find that any of the real Minstrels were of the female sex." See Percy, *The Reliques of Ancient English Poetry* (facsimile repr. of 1765 edition; 1996), 1: xv–xxiii (xviii).

to "King Estmere." The two engravings, then, emphasize the presence of women in the "ancient" texts they illustrate, and, in doing so, go some way towards articulating and rehabilitating the ballad's otherwise repressed feminine oral history of transmission. Mistakes in scholarship aside, the lady's *Ancient Ballads* responds to a particular need to reconnect young female readers with the ballad's feminine roots.

Rather than interpreting the lady's limited scholarship as imposing a limit on the usefulness of her text, it is perhaps more productive to read her departure from the familiar structures of the eighteenth-century ballad collection, with its dense textual apparatus of "introductions, headnotes, footnotes, appendices, dissertations, [and] commentaries," as a move toward a new or alternative kind of (feminine) antiquarianism.[45] Ann Wierda Rowland has suggested that such paratextual elements perform an important consolatory as well as elucidatory function: "[t]he impressive scholarly apparatus that the ballad revival bequeaths to British literature is, in fact, a way of *not* reading or responding to the contents of popular literature."[46] *Ancient Ballads*, on the other hand, inherits a portion of this scholarly apparatus, but also substantially reduces it. Thus, the lady's collection illustrates the other side of Rowland's statement: without a reinforcing structure of scholarly appendages, *Ancient Ballads*, as the less "impressive" ballad collection, forces its young readers to read and respond to the often sensational material of Percy's most popular ballads.[47]

In particular, the *Ancient Ballads* is responsible for bringing young women readers into greater proximity with the Arthurian ballads in the *Reliques*. Marion Wynne-Davies credits Lady Charlotte Guest with "the first female rewording of the Arthurian narrative in English"; however, though not translations *per se*, the substantial editorial changes that the anonymous lady makes to both "Sir Lancelot du Lake" and "The Marriage of Sir Gawaine" demonstrate that women were "rewording" and taking an interest in the presentation of Arthurian texts several decades before the first of Guest's *Mabinogion* installments appeared in 1838.[48] The new centrality of Percy's Arthurian ballads in the *Ancient Ballads* impressed the importance of these poems upon the volume's young female readers, and encouraged at least one

45 McLane, *Balladeering, Minstrelsy, and the Making of British Romantic Poetry*, 45.

46 Ann Wierda Rowland, "'The fause nourice sang': Childhood, Child Murder, and the Formalism of the Scottish Ballad Revival," in *Scotland and the Borders of Romanticism*, 225–44 (227). Emphasis in original.

47 McLane, *Balladeering, Minstrelsy, and the Making of British Romantic Poetry*, 45; Rowland, "'The fause nourice sang,'" 227.

48 Marion Wynne-Davies, *Women and Arthurian Literature: Seizing the Sword* (Basingstoke: Macmillan, 1996), 111.

young woman writer to pen her own poetical reflection on the legend in response.

The Legacy of the Ancient Ballads*: Louisa Stuart Costello's "A Dream"*

Did young women read the *Ancient Ballads*? Certainly, not all parents and guardians hid Percy's *Reliques* from their young daughters in quite the same manner as the lady's prudish patron.[49] With her father's permission, Mary Russell Mitford (b. 1787) began reading Percy's "charming volumes" at the very young age of "four or five."[50] "King Estmere," "The Children of the Wood," and those ballads describing "the Loves of King Arthur's Court" subsequently became her favorite childhood reading.[51] Indeed, in the course of reviewing the *Ancient Ballads*, the commentator for the *Annual Review* defended Percy's volumes by affirming that "it does not appear to us that his collection is likely to be at all injurious to young women of correct and really virtuous minds."[52] Percy himself also encouraged a female readership of his work. When the Scottish poet Anne Bannerman drew on the *Reliques* for her collection of Gothic ballads, *Tales of Superstition and Chivalry* (1802), which includes her Arthurian poem, "The Prophecy of Merlin," Percy sent her a "superbly bound" copy of the *Reliques* as a token of his appreciation.[53]

49 This is not to say that the policing behavior of the lady's benefactor was completely isolated. In 1881, the American editor Sidney Lanier told a very similar anecdote to his publisher, Charles Scribner, pertaining to his decision to compile *The Boy's Percy* (1882): "I recently discovered my three boys reading this book [Percy's *Reliques*] with the uttermost avidity, – even in the old form – and had much grief in finding myself obliged to hide it from them, because it contained so much matter that no-one, boy or man, should read" (Sidney Lanier to Charles Scribner, 19 April 1881, in *The Centennial Edition of the Works of Sidney Lanier*, ed. C. R. Anderson and A. H. Starke, 10 vols. [Baltimore, MD: Johns Hopkins University Press, 1963], 10:302; also quoted in DeVoto, "The Hero as Editor," 162). Contrary to the earlier practices of the female editor of the *Ancient Ballads*, Lanier actually increased the scholarly apparatus accompanying the ballads in his redaction. For a detailed discussion of Lanier's editorial treatment of Percy's text, see DeVoto, "The Hero as Editor," 148–70.

50 Mary Russell Mitford, "My Earliest Recollections: Percy's *Reliques*," in *Recollections of a Literary Life; or, Books, Places and People*, new edn., 2 vols. (London: Richard Bentley, 1857), 1:1–17 (3).

51 Mitford, "My Earliest Recollections," 1:13.

52 "Ancient Ballads," *Annual Review*: 474.

53 [Anne Bannerman], *Tales of Superstition and Chivalry* (London: Vernor and Hood, 1802), 142. Percy's "present" of the *Reliques* to Bannerman is recorded in the correspondence between Percy and the editor Robert Anderson. See Anderson to Percy, 26 July 1804, in *The Correspondence of Thomas Percy and Robert Anderson*, ed. W. E. K. Anderson (New Haven, CT: Yale University Press, 1988), vol. 9 of *The Percy Letters*, general ed. Cleanth Brooks and A. F. Falconer, 16 vols., 9:153.

As well as the ballads themselves, Percy's scholarship had an equally influential effect on women's literary criticism, including their knowledge of Arthurian literature. In her essay entitled "Cursory Remarks on the Spirit of the Old Ballads" (1825), the writer and poet Maria Jane Jewsbury referred to Percy's two versions of "The Marriage of Sir Gawaine" to illustrate that many of the "old ballads" were "considered abridgements of the longer metrical romances."[54] The *Reliques* could even function as a touring lady's guidebook to British sites; when the American poet Lydia Sigourney visited the English border town of Carlisle on 31 August 1840, she immediately connected the place with the "sacred festivities of olden time" she had read of in Percy's "The Boy and the Mantle," the revised version of which begins: "In Carlisle dwelt King Arthur [. . .] and there he kept his Christmas."[55] This range of responses would seem to confirm that Percy's *Reliques* was a largely accessible text for women writers from the 1780s onwards, as well as a popular source of information about the Arthurian legend.

However, for other women (who were not as lucky as Bannerman was to receive a copy of the *Reliques* direct from the author), Percy's volumes were harder to come by. The writer and translator Mary Howitt had to wait until her marriage in 1821 to gain access to "Percy's Relics of Ancient English Poetry" which she had tantalizingly "heard of but till then never seen."[56] Substantially smaller than the *Reliques*, and relatively affordable at four shillings and sixpence, the *Ancient Ballads* was a well-placed cheaper alternative to Percy's full anthology (in comparison, as Groom notes, the 1765 edition of the *Reliques* sold for half a guinea).[57] Both born in the same year, Howitt and her contemporary Louisa Stuart Costello were part of a second generation of Romantic women writers who were ideally placed to encounter the lady's abridged version of the *Reliques* in their formative years. In particular, we know that Costello read the *Ancient Ballads* closely because she included an extract from the lady's text in her debut volume of poetry, *The Maid of the Cyprus Isle and Other Poems* (1815), published when she was just sixteen

54 Maria Jane Jewsbury, "Cursory Remarks on the Spirit of the Old Ballads," in *Phantasmagoria: or, Sketches of Life and Literature*, 2 vols. (London: Hurst, Robinson and Co., 1825), 1:279–309 (289).

55 Lydia Sigourney, "Carlisle," in *Pleasant Memories of Pleasant Lands* (Boston: James Monroe and Co., 1842), 56–64 (62). "The Boy and the Mantle, as revised and altered by a modern hand," *Reliques* 3:340–49 (lines 1–6).

56 Mary Howitt, "Preface," to *Ballads, and Other Poems* (London: Longman, Browne, Green, and Longmans, 1847), v–viii (v–vi). The *Reliques* was the first book Howitt borrowed from her husband's library.

57 See "Ancient Ballads; selected from Percy's Collection," *Monthly Review* 58 (February 1809): 212, and Groom, "The Formation of Percy's *Reliques* [Introduction]," in Percy, *Reliques of Ancient English Poetry* (facsimile repr. of 1765 edition; 1996), 1:1–68 (2).

years old. Material from the *Ancient Ballads* provided the young poet with the inspiration for "A Dream," a fifty-seven-line narrative poem in which a somnolent narrator is magically transported to an aerial world and given a rare glimpse of King Arthur.

"A Dream" is prefaced by an introductory note alerting readers to the "popular tradition in Wales, that King Arthur did not die, but was carried away by fairies to some place, where he will remain some time, and then return to earth again, and reign in as great authority and power as ever."[58] Bar a few slight variations and additions, these words are lifted straight from the explanatory headnote to "King Arthur's Death" in *Ancient Ballads*. They also appear in the same position in Percy's volume, as it was from there that the female editor extracted them for her edition. In both the lady's and Percy's texts, the lines are attributed to Raphael Holinshed, but, where Percy's fellow antiquarians would have been able to decode the citation of "Holingshed, B.5. C.14" (56; *Reliques* 3:28), the lady's younger readers would have had little idea what text was being referred to.[59] By the time Holinshed's words are attached to Costello's poem, the extract has been thoroughly divorced from its original authorship and attributed solely to the *Ancient Ballads*. The unattributed quotation which prefaces Costello's poem demonstrates how intermediary texts like the *Ancient Ballads* – marketed specifically toward "young ladies" – placed women readers and writers at an increased distance from Arthurian sources. Given this context, it is hardly surprising that Costello's poem also situates itself at a distance from the medieval or Arthurian world.

"A Dream" makes no attempt to portray its medieval subject in an archaized style; rather, it is a composition firmly in the tradition of the Romantic visionary poem. Written in heroic couplets, the poem begins with a lyrical description of its first-person speaker lying languidly on the bank of "a wandering stream" amidst a meadow of "buds of scarlet poppy" (lines 1, 4). In the idealized surroundings of this opium-heavy Eden, the speaker is coaxed into sleep by the lulls of "Sweet Morpheus" (line 3). The parallels with the narrative, if not the form, of Coleridge's later "Kubla Khan" (1816) continue as Costello's somnambulant dreamer experiences a fantastic vision: a mysterious "fairy form" rises from the nearby stream and escorts the dreamer to "distant worlds unseen by mortal eye" (lines 8–10). Their destination is a Romantic fairyland populated by nymphs and sylphs where "soft airs of music play" (line 14). There is little of the medieval in Costello's poem,

58 Louisa Stuart Costello, "A Dream," in *The Maid of the Cyprus Isle and Other Poems* (London: Sherwood, Neely and Jones, 1815), 56–58 (56).

59 For the original text, see Raphael Holinshed, *Chronicles of England, Scotland and Ireland*, 2nd edn., 6 vols. (London: [Henry Denham], 1587), 2:92.

but this is perhaps partly understandable considering that the Arthurian texts in the *Ancient Ballads* had been shorn of much of their medieval language and mood in the process of the lady's modernization.

Now magically "suspended in the skies" by an "airy chain," the dreamer spies a warrior asleep on an idyllic "flowry plain" below (lines 11–12). When asked about the identity of the sleeping man, the guide answers:

> The knight thou see'st is well to mortals known,
> And once in triumph sat on Britain's throne;
> By friends admir'd, and dreaded by his foes –
> What infant but the name of Arthur knows? (lines 21–24)

The guide's observation that King Arthur is well known to young children again seems to reflect the fact that Costello herself encountered Percy's Arthurian ballads in a text produced for the "amusement" of "children" (iii). Her version of Arthur, then, was already strongly associated with childhood reading. Indeed, much is infantilized in the first half of the poem, including the sleeping Arthur. As the dreamer watches, the king's disturbed "slumbers" are "sooth'd" by an "attending train" of nurse-like sylphs who mind him until he "clos'd his eyes and sunk to rest again" (lines 17–18). In the same way that *Ancient Ballads* placed Arthurian material in a new juvenile context, Costello places Arthur in a nursery-like environment in her poem.

As well as an infantilized figure, Costello's Arthur is also intangible, located in "distant worlds" (line 10) and only observed by the dreamer from a distance set and maintained by the "beauteous fairy guide" (line 19). The guide continues to speak on the subject of Arthur's death, but offers the dreamer little in the way of definitive answers, proclaiming: "none below know how the hero died; / Conjecture only has the tale supplied" (lines 25–26). Yet instead of recounting, from "King Arthur's Death," Arthur's mysterious departure "from the lande" in a "barge [. . .] of ladyes" (130; *Reliques* 3:36, lines 180–81), Costello's guide offers a number of more fantastical possibilities:

> By some 'tis said he yet on earth remains,
> And in the figure of a raven reigns;
> And some believe, by mermaids borne away,
> In Neptune's court he lives beneath the sea (lines 27–30)

While Costello is drawing on Cornish beliefs (well known to contemporaneous antiquarians) that Arthur may have taken up a posthumous existence in the form of a raven, the prospect of an underwater Round Table seems to be entirely her own invention. As Alan and Barbara Lupack have cogently pointed out, "while the taking of liberties with the Arthurian stories is not exclusive to women [. . .] it seems clear that women, by virtue of being outside the mainstream of Arthurian tradition, have been more inclined to radical interpretations and innovative reworkings of it."[60] As an offshoot of Percy's *Reliques*, the *Ancient Ballads* demonstrates how the source of Costello's Arthurian inspiration placed her in a position already "outside the mainstream" circulation of antiquarian Arthurian texts. In particular, the unmooring of "King Arthur's Death" from its scholarly context in the *Reliques* seems to have made space for a more imaginative interpretation of Arthurian material in "A Dream."

Soon, however, the guide's lively indulgence in imaginative "conjecture" is swiftly curtailed (line 26), and the dreamer strongly reminded that "unto mortals 'tis not given to know / How he [Arthur] forsook their transient realms below" (lines 31–32). With this authoritative voicing, the fairy guide's educational role becomes most readily apparent: throughout the poem, the guide is employed in didactically releasing and setting the limits of the dreamer's knowledge of the Arthurian legend. In this way, the relationship between the guide and the dreamer reflects the wider didacticism of the *Ancient Ballads*, whose "young readers" receive the poems as they have been selected and censored according to the lady's "judgement" (iii). After failing to resolve the "mystery" of Arthur's death by quizzing the equivocal guide (line 49), the dreamer is violently "seized by hands unseen" and "hurl'd" to earth (line 53). Simpson calls the poem a "playful enquiry," but this downplays the unsettling "fear" that the dreamer experiences when they find themselves so swiftly dispatched (line 51).[61] The poem ends with the brief return of the voice of the dreamer, who, reflecting on their somnambulistic journey, concludes: "I woke [. . .] lamenting that my dream was vain, / Resolv'd to drive King Arthur from my brain / And live, content in darkness to remain" (lines 54–57). Though it tentatively attempts to create an imagined dialogue with Arthur, "A Dream" ends with a frank withdrawal from the legend. Banished to a metaphorical darkness, the dreamer ends the poem less enlightened than they were at its beginning. The narrative of the poem encapsulates Costello's compromised encounter with "King Arthur's Death" in *Ancient Ballads*, a text which, lacking any clear sources for its notes on Arthur's death, similarly left the young female reader with no scholarly leads

60 Alan Lupack and Barbara Tepa Lupack, "Arthurian Literature by Women: The Forgotten Tradition," in *Arthurian Literature by Women*, ed. Alan Lupack and Barbara Tepa Lupack (New York: Garland, 1999), 3–34 (4).

61 Roger Simpson, *Camelot Regained: The Arthurian Revival and Tennyson, 1800–1849* (Cambridge: D. S. Brewer, 1990), 158.

to follow. *Ancient Ballads* thus provides an important context for the poem's final inability to contemplate almost anything Arthurian.

The early abandonment of a juvenile curiosity toward the Arthurian legend which characterizes "A Dream" sits somewhat uneasily in the context of Costello's later literary career. Clare Broome Saunders has drawn attention to Costello's life-long "fascination" with medieval texts; in 1823, she published eight lines entitled "Part of Pierce Plowman's Vision (1350), Modernised" anonymously in William Jerdan's *Literary Gazette* which serve as an example of both the breadth of her medieval interests and her desire to represent medieval texts to the public in popular and accessible forms.[62] Nor did she abandon her imaginative interest in the Arthurian legend, for she continued to publish several Arthurian poems in literary annuals. In 1829 she published "The Funeral Boat" in the *Forget Me Not*, and in 1837 her ballad entitled "The Deaths of Tristan and Yseult" appeared in the gift book *The Tribute*.[63] When Costello turned to writing travel books in the 1840s, she continued to draw on her wealth of antiquarian knowledge, assuring her readers of her familiarity with the romances of "Little Arthur of Brittany, Lancelot du Lac, Tristan the Adventurer [. . .] and others in ancient verse which I have seen in multiple libraries."[64] By the 1840s, Costello's accumulated knowledge of Arthuriana is evident from a glance at the subtitles for various chapters in her European travelogues: passages are dedicated to "Tristan and Yseult," the "Phantom of King Arthur," "Merlin," and "Viviana."[65] The frustrations and withdrawals which characterize her juvenile Arthurian poem are long gone, replaced by a new confidence brought about by either visiting landmarks associated with the legends, or, better, by holding an Arthurian manuscript in her hands. The limited scholarship of the lady's *Ancient Ballads* may have left the sixteen-year-old poet scrabbling in an unenlightened "darkness,"

62 Clare Broome Saunders, *Women Writers and Nineteenth-Century Medievalism* (Basingstoke: Palgrave Macmillan, 2009), 9; "M.E." [Costello], "Part of Pierce Plowman's Vision (1350), Modernised," *Literary Gazette* 348 (1823): 603.

63 Costello, "The Funeral Boat," in *Forget Me Not: A Christmas and New Year's Present for MDCCCXXIX*, ed. Frederic Shoberl (London: R. Ackermann, 1829), 185–92. Costello, "The Deaths of Tristan and Yseult," in *The Tribute: A Collection of Miscellaneous Unpublished Poems, by Various Authors*, ed. Lord Northampton (London: John Murray, 1837), 289–92. The latter poem was republished under the alternative title of "The Legend" in the first of Costello's French tours, *A Summer amongst the Bocages and the Vines*, 2 vols. (London: Bentley, 1840), 1:299–301.

64 Costello, *Béarn and the Pyrenees: A Legendary Tour to the Country of the Henri Quatre*, 2 vols. (London: Bentley, 1844), 1:147.

65 Costello, *Summer*, 1:297–300; Costello, *Béarn and the Pyrenees*, 1:285, 302–3; Costello, *The Falls, Lakes, and Mountains, of North Wales* (London: Longman, Brown, Green, and Longmans, 1845), 112, 122–23.

unable to make sense of the Arthurian legend, but without the lady's redaction Costello's lifelong interest in Arthur might never have been piqued at all. Providing one of the earliest examples of the treatment of Arthurian texts under a female editorial hand, *Ancient Ballads* deserves wider recognition for its role as a foundational text in the making of women's Arthurian writing.

Romancing the Pre-Reformation: Charles Reade's *The Cloister and the Hearth*

Mark B. Spencer

Although largely forgotten today, Charles Reade's *The Cloister and the Hearth* when it first appeared in 1861 "struck the reading public as well as the American and English press like a tidal wave." It was particularly popular in the United States, where it went through eight editions in the first few weeks and was universally hailed by the leading newspapers as "a masterpiece of historic fiction."[1] Indeed, many critics regarded it as the perfect historical novel, superior even to Sir Walter Scott, well into the twentieth century. Reade drew his original inspiration from the opening pages of a brief autobiography by Desiderius Erasmus (1466–1536) known as the *Compendium vitae*, where the famous humanist describes the circumstances of his birth and the ill-fated relationship of his parents. The story was then richly embroidered by Reade with the wildest inventions of romance and a wealth of vivid historical detail gleaned from scrupulous research in a host of primary sources from the fifteenth and sixteenth centuries. Given the recent sesquicentennial of the novel's original publication, it seems worthwhile to revisit *The Cloister and the Hearth* and assess how well the novel stands up today, both as a historical representation of life in the later Middle Ages and as a monument of Victorian medievalism.

Reade would not have been entirely pleased to know that of all his works only *The Cloister and the Hearth* would live beyond his lifetime (1814–

1 C. H. Muller, "Charles Reade and *The Cloister and the Hearth*: A Survey of the Novel's Literary Reception and Its Historic Fidelity," *University of South Africa English Studies* 9 (1971): 18–26 (19).

84).[2] In the 1850s the American novelist William Dean Howells and his friends were all avidly reading Reade's "jaunty, nervy, knowing books," and wondering "whether we ought not to set him above Thackeray and Dickens and George Eliot [. . .] so great was the effect that Charles Reade had with our generation."[3] The young Henry James called him "to our mind the most readable of living English novelists [. . .] a distant cousin of Shakespeare,"[4] while Charles Algernon Swinburne declared shortly after Reade's death that "he has left not a few pages which if they do not live as long as the English language will fail to do so through no fault of their own, but solely through the malice of time."[5] By the turn of the century, however, only *The Cloister and the Hearth* had achieved classic status, while Reade's other works were generally dismissed as mere "dross" compared with *The Cloister*'s "gold."[6] As late as 1921 *The Cloister* was still a bestseller in England, when one scholar observed, "Three generations of sober and accredited critics have praised this book in terms of just extravagance."[7]

According to Howells, Reade was "a man who stood at the parting of the ways between realism and romanticism," but rather than firmly choosing the former as Howells himself had done, Reade "remained content to use the materials of realism and produce the effect of romanticism."[8] This may well explain the longevity of *The Cloister and the Hearth* over Reade's other novels and plays, for romance remained viable in the historical novel long after it had faded in serious contemporary fiction. Reade's prodigious labors in the service of realism were notorious, especially the immense notebooks in which he gathered together innumerable cards, clippings, copies, and notes from every imaginable source. Reade himself referred to it as his "Baconian" method, because it sought the truth purely through investigation of the empirical evidence, rather than *a priori* reasoning as demonstrated by the Greek sophists, the medieval schoolmen, and Thomas Carlyle.[9] One

2 Diana Vitanza, "Naturalism in Charles Reade's Experimental Novel Griffith Gaunt," in *Victorian Sensations: Essays on a Scandalous Genre*, ed. Kimberly Harrison and Richard Fantina (Columbus: The Ohio State University Press, 2006), 64–73 (64, 73 n. 2).

3 William Dean Howells, *My Literary Passions* (New York: Harper, 1895), 144.

4 Henry James, "Felix Holt the Radical," in *Notes and Reviews* (Cambridge, MA: Dunsten, 1921), 207.

5 Charles Algernon Swinburne, *Miscellanies* (London: Chatto & Windus, 1886), 271–72.

6 Lewis Melville, *Victorian Novelists* (London: Constable, 1906), 167. Swinburne claimed that *Griffith Gaunt* was actually Reade's best novel (285), a judgment with which several of Reade's more recent critics have generally agreed. See Elton Smith, *Charles Reade* (Boston: Twayne, 1976), 148–49.

7 E. W. Hornung, "Charles Reade," *London Mercury* 4 (June 1921): 153.

8 Howells, *Literary*, 144.

9 Wayne Burns, *Charles Reade: A Study in Victorian Authorship* (New York: Bookman, 1961), 57–63. Burns fully elaborates on Reade's marked antipathy to Carlyle.

early work, *It Is Never Too Late to Mend* (1856), focused on the terrifying conditions in English prisons, and Reade assiduously visited several of these, interviewing warders and inmates, and even having himself locked up in a cell.[10] Such proclivities were obviously well suited for historical fiction, and although the notebooks for *The Cloister and the Hearth* have been lost, an extant letter to a friend contains a quick list of seventy-four sources in English, French, and Latin that he consulted in its composition, ranging from Froissart's *Chronicles*, Erasmus's *Colloquies*, and Luther's *Table Talk* to Henry Shaw's *Dresses and Decorations of the Middle Ages* (1843), Francisque Michel's *Le livre d'or des métiers: Histoire des hôtelleries, cabarets, hôtels garnis, restaurants et cafés* (1851), and Nathaniel Wanley's *The Wonders of the Little World* (1678).[11]

If Reade was something of a methodological forerunner to the naturalism of Zola and the Goncourt brothers,[12] the romance element in his work, as noted by Howells, remained strong as well, especially in *The Cloister and the Hearth*. As mentioned above, Reade was originally attracted to the story of Erasmus's parents by the opening passage in the *Compendium vitae*, which Erasmus composed when he thought he was mortally ill in 1524. The humanist says that his father Gerard had a secret affair with his mother Margaret, "hoping for marriage," and "there are those who say they were betrothed." Gerard's parents and ten brothers, however, were determined that he should enter the church and refused to countenance his matrimony. In frustration Gerard fled to Rome, where "he lived as youths do," taking up the profession of copying, which still flourished there, since the printing press had not yet arrived. After a while his parents sent him a letter claiming that Margaret was dead, and in his despair Gerard became a priest, turning "his whole mind to religion." Returning home a few years later, Gerard discovered that he had been tricked, for Margaret was most certainly alive and living with their young son at her mother's house. She steadfastly refused to marry anyone else, nor did Gerard "ever lay a hand on her." The young Erasmus was put to his letters at the age of four, and sent to the grammar school at Deventer in his ninth year, where his mother moved to watch over him. Several years later she perished during a pestilence, and Gerard

10 Smith, *Charles Reade*, 106–7; William J. Dawson, "Charles Reade," in *The Makers of English Fiction* (New York: Revell, 1905), 164–78 (172–73).

11 The full title of the last is *The Wonders of the Little World: Or, a General History of Man in Six Books, wherein by many thousands of examples is shewed what Man hath been from the First Ages of the World to these Times, in respect of his Body, Senses, Passions, Affections: his Virtues and Perfections, his Vices and Defects, his Quality, Vocation, and Profession*. For the complete list see Alfred Turner, *The Making of the Cloister and the Hearth* (Chicago: University of Chicago Press, 1938), 4–12.

12 Vitanza, "Naturalism," 64–66.

hearing the sad news likewise "began to languish" and soon died himself, both parents being just past their fortieth year.[13] The *Compendium* does not say whether Gerard knew that Margaret was pregnant before he left.

The story appealed to Reade for at least two reasons. First, like Gerard he himself had lived a life of enforced celibacy as a Magdalen fellow at Oxford well into middle age, since the proceeds from his writings did not provide sufficient income to support him. Two memoirs by Reade's friends and relatives mention a Scottish girl whom Reade may have fallen in love with and desired to marry about 1840, but the celibacy rule for his fellowship, and the possible opposition of his family, prevented it. Although he went on to have other relationships later in life, the Scottish girl remained "the one lady whom in the best days of his manhood he idealized, and never forgot, even in his dying moments."[14] Secondly, in the late 1850s Reade was working on a book entitled "Heroes and Martyrs," which would "glorify obscure men and women who performed noble deeds, but were soon forgotten," in direct opposition to Thomas Carlyle's great-man theory and his idealization of the Middle Ages.[15] The projected book was never written, but in its place appeared *The Cloister and the Hearth*. Much later Reade did publish another novel, *A Hero and Martyr* (1875), based on the true-life achievements of a Glasgow workman, who had heroically saved several people from drowning in the river Clyde over a number of years.[16]

Reade announces this theme of the unknown hero in the opening paragraphs of *The Cloister and the Hearth*, which deserve full quotation, for, as will be seen below, his words reveal not only the strengths and weaknesses of Reade's novel, but of nineteenth-century historical fiction in general:

> Not a day passes over the earth, but men and women of no note do great deeds, speak great words, and suffer noble sorrows. Of these obscure heroes, philosophers, and martyrs, the greater part will never be known till that hour, when many that are great shall be small and the small great; but of others the world's knowledge may be said to sleep: their lives and characters lie hidden from nations in the annals that record them. The general reader cannot feel them, they are presented so curtly and coldly: they are not like breathing stories appealing to

13 English translation in Turner, *The Making*, 16–17.

14 Smith, *Charles Reade*, 140–41. The memoirs are Charles L. Reade and Compton Reade, *Charles Reade, D. C. L., Dramatist, Novelist, Journalist: A Memoir, Compiled Chiefly from His Literary Remains* (London: Chapman and Hall, 1887); John Coleman, *Charles Reade as I Knew Him* (London: Treherne, 1903).

15 Turner, *The Making*, 2–3; Smith, *Charles Reade*, 136–38.

16 Burns, *Charles Reade: A Study*, 303; Smith, *Charles Reade*, 136–38.

his heart, but little historic hailstones striking him but to glance off his bosom: nor can he understand them; for epitomes are not narratives, as skeletons are not human figures.

According to Reade, such records of prime truths remain a dead letter to plain folk; the annalists have left too much to the imagination, and imagination is so rare a gift. Here, then, the modern writer of fiction may be of use to the public – as an interpreter:

> There is a musty chronicle, written in tolerable Latin, and in it a chapter where every sentence holds a fact. Here is told, with harsh brevity, the strange history of a pair, who lived untrumpeted, and died unsung, four hundred years ago; and lie now, as unpitied, in that stern page, as fossils in a rock. Thus, living or dead, fate is still unjust to them. For if I can but show you what lies below that dry chronicler's words, methinks you will correct the indifference of centuries, and give those two sore tried souls a place in your heart – for a day.[17]

This chapter from the "musty chronicle, written in tolerable Latin" has been identified as the *Compendium* from other sources among Reade's letters and notes.[18] Thus, from a mere two paragraphs of "harsh brevity" in the Latin of Erasmus, Reade proposes to spin over a thousand pages of "breathing stories" in the four volumes of his original 1861 edition.

As an imagined life of the parents of Erasmus, Reade's plot is just about as fantastically romantic as a seventeenth-century *roman* or *nouvelle historique.* Indeed, the separation of two lovers and their eventual reunification after many misadventures and tribulations is one of the oldest romance plots and forms the basis of almost all Reade's novels.[19] In *The Cloister and the Hearth* Gerard meets Margaret Brandt and her father Peter on his way to Rotterdam to compete in a contest sponsored by Philip the Good, Duke of Burgundy, in the arts of painting, illuminating, and writing on vellum, at which Gerard is highly adept, having studied under the occasional patronage of Margaret Van Eyck, sister of the painters Jan and Hubert. Along the way they encounter Ghysbrecht van Swieten, the burgomaster of Tergou, who had cheated Peter Brandt out of his rightful inheritance twenty years before. Gerard falls deeply in love with Margaret, and after a few complications they are about to be wed, when the hostile intervention of Ghysbrecht and two

17 Charles Reade, *The Cloister and the Hearth: A Tale of the Middle Ages* (New York: Random House, 1937), 5–6.

18 Turner, *The Making*, 15–16; Smith, *Charles Reade*, 138–39.

19 Burns, *Charles Reade: A Study*, 315.

of Gerard's brothers forces him to flee Holland, but not before he consummates his irregular union with Margaret and stumbles upon a document that exposes Ghysbrecht's fraud.

Acting upon Margaret Van Eyck's advice, Gerard determines to make for Rome, but experiences a long series of picaresque adventures on the way, including attack by a bear, a robbery and murder attempt at an inn, a battle between bandits and the followers of a local count, a siege, a meeting with gypsies, and a spell of beggary through the towns of the German Empire, until finally reaching Italy via the trading route from Augsburg to Venice. Once in Rome Gerard's adventures continue as he joins the circle of the humanist Fra Colonna, meets the Pope in person, and inspires the love of Clælia, a beautiful young princess of the Cesarini family. Disaster strikes again, however, when he receives a forged letter from Margaret Van Eyck, actually written by Ghysbrecht and the two brothers, informing him that Margaret Brandt has died. After a period of riotous living as "one of the wildest, loosest, wickedest young men in Rome," Gerard prepares to drown his unendurable despair by throwing himself in the Tiber, when he spies an assassin sent by Clælia, whose carnal advances he had spurned. Gerard approaches and begs the man to kill him, forcing a purse into his hands, but the assassin refuses because he recognizes Gerard as the one who had saved his wife and child during a shipwreck en route from Venice to Rome. Gerard casts himself into the water anyway, but the assassin pulls him out and bears him to a Dominican monastery, where Gerard ultimately joins the order and takes the vows of the priesthood.

As a Dominican friar Gerard undergoes a great spiritual conversion and travels throughout Europe as an impassioned preacher. While speaking to a crowd in Rotterdam he sees a vision of Margaret in the audience. Upon inquiry he discovers the truth about her from some old friends, hunts down his brothers in a rage and curses them to everlasting perdition, visits the dying Ghysbrecht and forces him to acknowledge his crime against the Brandts and make proper restitution, and then disappears into a nearby hermitage. As Gerard battles with his spiritual and sensual demons seeking release in hyper-asceticism, Margaret tracks him down and draws him back into the world by revealing his child to him. Reluctantly the hermit becomes the vicar of Gouda, taking up a position promised by the young princess Mary of Burgundy many years before. Although Margaret and Gerard dare not live as man and wife, they take care of young Erasmus together, and Margaret helps out with Gerard's parochial duties until their early deaths as related in the *Compendium.*

The plot has many more twists and turns, but hopefully enough has been provided to reveal how thoroughly preposterous the story is as a history of Erasmus's parents. Contrary to Reade's claims in the opening paragraphs, the short passage in the *Compendium* speaks far more eloquently of their domestic tragedy than this concatenation of implausible and melodramatic events. The historical link with Erasmus hurts the novel more than it helps, at least to a twenty-first-century sensibility, and either a strong dose of distancing irony as found in Scott, or a further retreat into a more profound vision of pure romance like Victor Hugo's *Notre-Dame de Paris* might make the tale more palatable. On the other hand, if one ignores the Erasmus connection and views the novel primarily as a historical picaresque, then its realistic pretensions can be viewed in a different light.

All the critics have agreed on Reade's great narrative power, and his marvelous inventiveness keeps the story moving at a smart and exciting clip.[20] Reade's minute antiquarian investigations also bring a wealth of fascinating detail on the quotidian texture of late medieval life both high and low, whether describing elaborate banquets at the Burgundian and papal courts, the national character of the resident merchants in Venice, or the life of wandering soldiers and beggars on the open roads. Many of Reade's cameo portraits are highly amusing, such as Fra Colonna's learned humanism and his disquisition on the decayed greatness of Rome, or Reade's wonderfully satiric depiction of medieval physicians. The Cesarini Princess Clælia is great fun as well, a sort of Lucrezia Borgia figure. From Margaret Van Eyck we receive a detailed lecture on the art of oil painting, and Gerard's spiritual struggle with his sexual desires as the hermit of Gouda, if rather unlikely for the fifteenth-century father of Erasmus, still bears a certain degree of psychological insight, presumably in part from Reade's own personal experience, for the monastic asceticism of the earlier Middle Ages or the Catholic Reformation. As one critic has remarked, "*The Cloister and the Hearth* may be considered a picture gallery bringing the visitor a personal experience of the dangers, discomforts, and glories of the Middle Ages [. . .] the activities of the vermin at one German inn make one itch along with Gerard and Denys."[21]

Much of this material is lifted directly from primary sources such as the *Colloquies* of Erasmus and the *Voyages* of Michel de Montaigne, although it must be admitted that despite the enthusiasm of Alfred Turner, who tracked these sources down, the original versions, much like the passage in Erasmus's

20 Emerson Grant Sutcliffe, "Plotting in Reade's Novels," *PMLA* 47 (1932): 834–63; Wayne Burns, "'The Cloister and the Hearth': A Classic Reconsidered," *Nineteenth Century Fiction* 2 (1947): 71–81 (72); Arthur Thomas Quiller-Couch, "Charles Reade," in *Studies in Literature* (New York: Putnam, 1918), 274–88 (275); J. B. Price, "Charles Reade and Charles Kingsley," *Contemporary Review* 183 (1953): 161–66 (165); Muller, "Charles Reade and *The Cloister*," 25; Swinburne, *Miscellanies*, 283.

21 Smith, *Charles Reade*, 144.

Compendium, are sometimes more compelling than Reade's dramatization of them.[22] This is particularly true when Reade attempts to pump up an episode with his rather "commonplace" and "burlesque" humor.[23] As George Orwell remarked, Reade was much better at describing things than people, because he had "no sense whatsoever of character or probability," but a vast range of "penny-encyclopedic learning," which his powerful narrative gift allowed him "to cram into books which would at any rate pass as novels." His stories were perfect for the reader with "the sort of mind that takes a pleasure in dates, lists, catalogues, concrete details, descriptions of processes, junk-shop windows" or "likes knowing exactly how a medieval catapult worked or just what objects a prison-cell of the eighteen-forties contained."[24] Apparently, Reade's contemporary novels were even more stuffed with factual information and tortuously complex plot developments, and the documentary record on Erasmus actually exerted some beneficial restraint.[25]

Two examples will serve as an illustration of Reade's method on this score in *The Cloister and the Hearth*. The first is a medieval siege that Gerard's traveling companion Denys, a French soldier he befriended on the way to Italy, is temporarily forced to join by troops operating under the command of "Anthony, Bastard of Burgundy, the son of Duke Philip the Good" (82) against an unnamed rebellious city. All the typical ingredients of medieval siege warfare are incorporated into the eight-page account, including the walls, moats, wooden towers or "mantelets" of the besiegers, the "hoards" or "penthouses" constructed on the curtain walls by the defenders in response, the "cats" used to fill in the moat with rubble, the catapults, mangonels, and trébuchets to batter the walls and penthouses, the mines and countermines, as well as the constant covering fire supplied by archers, crossbowmen, and arbalastriers. The chronicles of Jean Froissart and Enguerrand de Monstrelet provided the historical warrant for these various elements, even if the overall account does not conform to any specific siege. Medieval audiences were likely to be well informed on such matters and required no further elaboration beyond a mere mention, so Reade resorted to secondary sources, such as the eighteenth-century antiquarian researches of Joseph Strutt and the

22 The examples are innumerable as Turner whenever possible provides full quotations from both the original and Reade's version side by side. As Elton Smith observes, Turner's "exhaustive analysis of the sources now sounds more impressive than the novel itself" (*Charles Reade*, 173). See also Turner's "Charles Reade and Montaigne," *Modern Philology* 30 (1932–33): 297–308 and "Another Source for *The Cloister and the Hearth*," *PMLA* 40 (1925): 898–909.

23 Ellen Cumpston, "Why Is Charles Dickens a More Famous Novelist than Charles Reade?," in *Four Years of Novel Reading: An Account of an Experiment in Popularizing the Study of Fiction*, ed. Richard G. Moulton (Boston: Heath, 1895), 52.

24 George Orwell, "Books in General," *New Statesman* 20 (17 August 1940): 162.

25 Burns, "'The Cloister,'" 76; Sutcliffe, "Plotting," 863.

relevant articles and illustrations in the more recent French medieval and Renaissance encyclopedia edited by Paul Lacroix and Ferdinand Seré,[26] for the necessary details that would enable him to explain to his contemporary readers precisely how everything worked, especially in this case the catapult.[27] Most people today probably derive their image of a medieval siege from Hollywood films; Reade's vivid set piece offered the same service in print, and in an equally easy-to-digest form.

The fabled city of Venice receives even more extended attention when Gerard makes a visit there, as reported in a letter to Margaret. First, he treats her to a hilarious comparison of the best and worst aspects of the various European nations he has encountered as a way of passing the time while he waits for an injured leg to heal. The respective customs and conditions of the Germans, English, French, and Italians in regard to their drinking habits, wives, inns, beds, furniture, windows, and honesty or dishonesty pass in review. Moving on to Venice itself, we learn that the "bread is lovely white," but "their meats they spoil with sprinkling cheese over them," while "their salt is black; without a lie." The women are "encouraged to venal frailty, and pay a tax to the State," which not content with the great profits derived from every manner of exotic luxury product, "must also trade in sin." Some twenty thousand of these "Jezebels" are "pampered and honoured for bringing strangers to the city, and many live in princely palaces of their own" (541). Once Gerard has sufficiently recovered to get about in a litter, he visits the cathedral of St. Mark and sees the four famous brass horses of the upper gallery, wondrously fashioned as if "at the very next step must needs leap down on the beholder." He marvels at the pillars wrought of the most exquisite stone, and the inestimable treasures of gold and precious gems on display. "The brazen chest that holds the body of St. Mark," "two pieces of marble stained with John the Baptist's blood," "a piece of the true cross and of the pillar to which Christ was tied," and "the rock struck by Moses, and wet to this hour" are among the sacred relics viewed. Last but not least, "three ghastly heads rotting and tainting the air" were fixed upon "a great porphyry slab in the piazza," which Gerard deems a fitting end for three "traitors to the state" (542–43). In characteristic fashion, the principal sources for this welter of

26 Joseph Strutt, *A Compleat View of the Manners, Customs, Arms, Habits &c. of the Inhabitants of England, from the Arrival of the Saxons to the Reign of Henry the Eighth,* 3 vols. (London: Benjamin White, 1775–76); *Le moyen âge et la renaissance: histoire et description des mœurs et usages du commerce et de l'industrie, des sciences, des arts, des littératures, et des beaux-arts en Europe*, ed. Paul Lacroix and Ferdinand Seré, 5 vols. (Paris: 5, rue du Pont de Lodi, 1848–51).

27 Turner, *The Making*, 85–92. Turner believes the especially detailed description of the catapult was drawn from an English translation of Villard de Honnecourt's book of drawings, *The Sketch-Book of Wilars de Honecort*, trans. and ed. Robert Willis (London: J. Henry and J. Parker, 1859), which supplied additional editorial explanation.

observation and factual detail actually belong not to the fifteenth century, but rather to the European travelogues of two Englishmen, Thomas Coryat (c. 1577–1617) and Fynes Moryson (1566–1629), which were first published in 1611 and 1617 respectively.[28] Presumably, Reade felt that the slower pace of change in those days would offer some protection from anachronism.

Indeed, for a novel that was long regarded as the supreme "Tale of the Middle Ages," *The Cloister and the Hearth* often seems surprisingly unsympathetic to things medieval, especially medieval religion. The fifteenth-century setting does not help in this regard, for the corruption and laxity in both secular and ecclesiastical society during this period was by no means typical of the Middle Ages as a whole. The fact that Gerard and Margaret were the parents of Erasmus is telling as well, for although Martin Luther and John Calvin were more instrumental in the foundation of modern Protestantism, Erasmus perhaps more than any other single figure opened the way to a general reformation and renewal of the Christian faith in the two decades before 1517, "laying the egg that Luther hatched." The distaste of Erasmus for monasticism was notorious, and in the traditional interpretation of Reade's novel the "cloister" is held to represent the misery caused by clerical celibacy, while the "hearth" stands for a normal and healthy family life. The original title of the novel's first, shorter version was "The Good Fight," which Wayne Burns claims must refer to Gerard's "fight against his sexual love for Margaret – a fight so all-consuming that even after her death, when he thinks he has won, his actions belie his professions." In the end he dies of a broken heart shortly after her death, and when his body is prepared for burial, a lock of Margaret's hair is found underneath his monastic hair shirt. As a fellow Dominican, Father Jerome, told him, he was "dying for a woman" already dead, and it would have been better if he had succumbed to this earthly passion and repented before she had died rather than succumbing in body and soul afterwards.[29] Reade's final words in the penultimate chapter entreat the reader's sympathy for the two young lovers in their "rare constancy, and pure affection, and then cruel separation by a vile heresy in the bosom of the church." In case the reader misses the point, an asterisk by the word "heresy" adds "Celibacy of the clergy, an invention truly fiendish" (911).

As Dianna Vitanza has convincingly argued, the good fight was not just against clerical celibacy, but against the benighted condition of medieval

28 Turner, *The Making*, 10–11, 125–37. The titles are *Coryats Crudities; Hastily Gobled Up in Five Moneths Travells of France, Savoy, Rhaetia commonly called the Grisons Country, Helvetia alias Switzerland, Some Parts of High Germany and the Netherlands*, and for Moryson, *An Itinerary Containing His Ten Yeeres Travell Through the Twelve Dominions of Germany, Bohmerland, Sweitzerland, Netherland, Denmarke, Poland, Italy, Turkey, France, England, Scotland & Ireland*.

29 Burns, *Charles Reade: A Study*, 319.

Catholicism as a whole, and its threatened resurrection in the Oxford or Tractarian Movement in the nineteenth-century Anglican church.[30] Nor was Reade entirely alone on this score, for amid the powerful tide of nostalgia, idealism, romanticism, and genuine historical scholarship that fed the medieval revival throughout the nineteenth century,[31] there arose a significant current of "counter-medievalism," in which evangelical Protestants in particular sought to preserve their "authentic" Christian beliefs against utopian readings of the Catholic Middle Ages.[32] The medieval religious practices that Reade casts in a ridiculous light are legion. Amidst the storm on board ship to Rome, the other passengers pray to a large wooden statue of the Virgin Mary for aid, while Gerard snatches the statue away and sets it afloat bearing a mother and child, thereby saving their lives. Viewing the supposed heads of St. Peter and St. Paul at the Lateran church in Rome, Gerard is deeply dismayed to hear Fra Colonna dismiss them as mere waxen images. Transubstantiation is mocked when Gerard notices someone taste-testing the bread and wine before the Pope performs the Mass. If the bread and wine are truly transformed into the flesh and blood of Christ, how can there be any fear of poison? Papal infallibility receives the same treatment, as the Pope indulges in some idle and rambling remarks on Boccaccio, Plutarch, Herodotus, and the evidence from scripture for blessing dumb beasts, but then advises Gerard not to receive his words as "delivered by the Pope ex cathedra, but uttered in a free hour, by an aged clergyman" (605). Also in Rome, a priest is accused of sacrilege and subjected to the water ordeal, in which he proves his innocence when he sinks and nearly drowns before being dragged back out "gurgling, and gasping, and screaming for mercy" (669). The monk Polifilo delivers a merciless lecture expounding the pagan origins of Christian rituals and practices, including the polytheistic nature of the veneration of the Virgin Mary and other saints, the reincarnation of the god Pan in the Devil, the Roman holidays lurking beneath several of the most prominent Christian feasts, the Pythagorean origin of monasticism, and the use of the tonsure by Egyptian and Brahmin holy men (673–84).

Gerard, moreover, is given to some surprising pronouncements. On several occasions he disparages the idea of praying to the saints, telling the

30 Dianna Vitanza, "*The Cloister and the Hearth*: A Popular Response to the Oxford Movement," *Religion and Literature* 18 (1986): 71–88.

31 A rich critical literature on this topic stretches from Alice Chandler's *A Dream of Order: The Medieval Ideal in Nineteenth-Century English Literature* (Lincoln: University of Nebraska Press, 1971) to Michael Alexander, *Medievalism: The Middle Ages in Modern England* (New Haven, CT: Yale University Press, 2007).

32 Miriam Elizabeth Burstein, "Counter-Medievalism: Or, Protestants Rewrite the Middle Ages," in *Beyond Arthurian Romances: The Reach of Victorian Medievalism* (New York: Palgrave Macmillan, 2005), 148–68.

panicked passengers on the boat to Rome that they might as well go straight to the source in Christ himself, as there is little that Dominic or Francis could do for them now. Later he informs the Princess Clælia when they meet again and he wins her to repentance that she should "Pray much to Christ and little to his saints" (705). He opposes the Immaculate Conception of the Virgin Mary when the issue is bruited in 1476, and with his dying words he exhorts his followers not to hold by "these new-fangled doctrines of man's merit," for as the Apostles and the Church Fathers maintained, "we are justified, not by our own wisdom, or piety, or the works we have done in holiness of heart, but by faith." Reade supplies a note citing Clement of Rome in Greek to this latter remark, but every educated reader knows who is most closely identified with the theological declaration of "justification by faith alone" (908). Margaret has something to say on all of this as well, for she is the one who draws Gerard back into the world from his hermitage, declaring that it is spiritual selfishness and egotism for a priest to take care only for his own soul, since so many other worse sinners need his attention. She reminds him of his gift as a preacher, and his membership in the preaching order of Dominic, which he denies by withdrawing from the world. When her arguments at length have prevailed, Gerard cries out, "IT IS THE VOICE OF AN ANGEL!" and Reade adds "The battle was won," referring most assuredly to more than just the immediate contest between the two lovers (863).

Rather than a genuine effort to serve as a sympathetic "interpreter" of the Middle Ages by "breathing stories" into a "musty chronicle," Reade's novel in many instances simply imposes nineteenth-century romance and Protestant triumphalism upon them every bit as much as Charles Kingsley's *Hypatia* (1851). A more accurate subtitle would be "A Tale of the Early Reformation," doubly so since many of Reade's primary sources derive actually from the sixteenth century rather than the fifteenth as noted above. The "cloister" stands for all the superstitions and abuses of the old religion, not just celibacy, and the "hearth" is representative of all loving human communities ordered by the apostolic principles of Christ. Vitanza perhaps overemphasizes the secular aspect, insisting that the "hearth" represents "humanitarianism in all of its forms" and that it is primarily "acts of benevolence and human fellowship that give meaning to life."[33]

Reade was both a social reformer and a committed Evangelical in the vein of Kingsley's "muscular Christianity," and Margaret and Gerard as the vicar of Gouda and his wife seem close to his ideal. Clearly, though, since the child is also a powerful factor in luring Gerard back to the world from the hermitage, the sanctification of sexual love in marriage is intended as

33 Vitanza, "Naturalism," 83.

well. Before her death Margaret is informed by a lawyer that if her irregular marriage is performed before two witnesses it is legally binding, with or without the presence of a priest, especially if sealed by the birth of a child, and she should sue the vicar of Gouda to force him to take her into his household, which of course she declines to do. Reade certainly presents them as married:

> United by present affection, past familiarity, and a marriage irregular, but legal; separated by holy Church and by their own consciences which sided unreservedly with holy Church: separated by Church, but united by a living pledge of affection, lawful in every sense at its date. (874)

It has long been something of a mystery why Scott's popularity declined so drastically and abruptly in the 1920s and 1930s after an admirably long run of over a century, and the question is even more apt in regard to Reade, for the former still generates an ever-growing mountain of academic criticism, while both popular and critical interest in the latter has almost died off completely. In Scott's case a variety of explanations has been offered, such as the presence of *Ivanhoe* and *Quentin Durward* on required reading lists at English schools, an outmoded romanticism, weak heroes and stiff dialogue, a longwinded and tiresomely slow narrative pace, a decline in nationalistic pride, and a lack of interest in or knowledge of Scottish history.[34] Ironically, academic scholars generally limit Scott's greatness to the early novels written from 1814 to 1820 and set closer to home in time and place, while among the general public perhaps only *Ivanhoe* really still lives. Those twentieth-century critics who have addressed Reade's work have generally concurred that his undoubted gift for narrative fluency is overwhelmed by his sensationalism, melodrama, stock characters, and the general "overstuffedness" of his novels, which faithfully mirror the peculiarities of Victorian popular taste no longer palatable today.[35] More recently, several scholars have suggested that Reade's

34 See Hugh Walpole, "Sir Walter Scott Today," *Times Literary Supplement* (30 April 1938): vi–vii; Hugh Trevor-Roper, "Great Scott," *Spectator* 224 (1970): 78–79; Coleman O. Parsons, "Sir Walter Scott – Yesterday and Today," *Proceedings of the American Philosophical Society* 116 (1972): 450–57; Irving Howe, "Falling Out of the Canon: The Strange Fate of Walter Scott," *The New Republic* 207 (17–24 August 1992): 35–37.

35 For a judicious assessment see Burns, "'The Cloister,'" 71–81 and Smith, *Charles Reade*, 152–57. Mary Poovey addresses the issue again under a rather different light in "Forgotten Writers, Neglected Historians: Charles Reade and the Nineteenth-Century Transformation of the British Literary Field," *ELH* 71 (2004): 433–53.

contemporary novels may be due for a revival, even among casual readers,[36] but one wonders if *The Cloister and the Hearth* will be included. The reputation and readership of historical novels by other established canonical authors of the period such as George Eliot's *Romola* (1863) and William Makepeace Thackeray's *The History of Henry Esmond* (1852) have not measured up to that of their more contemporary efforts. Even Leo Tolstoy is not such an exception when one remembers that *War and Peace* (1863–69) is set a mere two generations at most before his own day. Despite the claims of Georg Lukács in his seminal study *The Historical Novel* (1937), few if any historical novels of the deeper past from the Romantic and Victorian eras are entirely believable today as an authentic representation of their purported historical time and place.

The reasons for this sudden eclipse, like most changes in taste and fashion, are probably complex and elusive, but a few speculative ruminations might be hazarded. Speaking of the difference between the modern and the postmodern novel, Robert Anchor declares that:

> historians cannot do without the assumption, however unprovable, that changes in literary forms follow changes in the world outside literature; that what we take a literary form to be and how we evaluate its merits depend heavily on what we make of the world outside literature. Whether it is a question of old-fashioned representational realism or the postmodern novel, our views are going to be shaped by whatever sense we are able to make of the history and culture to which they belong; for our concept of history and culture, our concept of what the extraliterary world is and is not, will determine our expectations of what a writer can and should do.[37]

This distinction holds just as well between the Romantic and Victorian historical novel and the modern realist historical novel. Both Scott and Reade evoke the premodern world in a form that is fundamentally alien to the serious understanding of the historical past today, and that form is romance. Just why the nineteenth-century historical novel should have clung to romance when the novel of contemporary life moved toward an ever deeper and richer verisimilar realism remains something of a mystery. The divide can be seen most starkly in Gustave Flaubert, whose *Madame*

36 Vitanza, "Naturalism," 64, 73 n. 6; Richard Fantina, "'Chafing at the Social Cobwebs': Gender and Transgender in the work of Charles Reade," in Harrison and Fantina, *Victorian Sensations*, 135–36.

37 Robert Anchor, "Narrativity and the Transformation of Historical Consciousness," *Clio* 16 (1987): 121–37 (129).

Bovary (1857) is still regarded by many critics as the towering masterpiece of modern realism, while *Salammbô* (1862) set in ancient Carthage is awash in romance conventions, above all in its fevered exoticism and fantastic plot elements. The example of Scott may have played a decisive role, but in many ways it seems that he was merely preserving a tendency that had already emerged in the *roman* and *nouvelle historique* of the seventeenth and eighteenth centuries. As Peter Green was perhaps the first to note, authors such as Sigrid Undset in *Kristin Lavransdatter* (1920–22) and Robert Graves in *I, Claudius* and *Claudius the God* (1934) established a new set of realist conventions for historical fiction, in which a much greater effort was expended to make the characters and plots of their novels as psychologically plausible and historically authentic and appropriate as the masses of material detail that Reade so adroitly deployed, thereby rendering most previous historical novels obsolete.[38] The genre has evolved even further since then, with recent decades witnessing the emergence of postmodern historical fiction, as noted by Anchor, in which the conventions of the realist historical novel are in turn playfully upended and challenged. For medievalists, Umberto Eco's *The Name of the Rose* (1981) probably comes most readily to mind in this regard.

It is easy to forget how recent a development the modern historical sense really is. Both the Romantic historical novel and the beginnings of modern historical scholarship arose at roughly the same time, each partly inspiring and influencing the other,[39] but history as a professional academic discipline hardly existed outside of Germany before the second half of the nineteenth century, and it did not reach full maturity until the twentieth. Thus, only in the last 150 years or so has a deep historical consciousness and a strong sense of historical period become common coin, and not just among scholars, but in the popular imagination as well. This new historical consciousness may even be "the most characteristic acquisition of our age," as Green claimed,[40] or at least it was before the advent of postmodernism. It should hardly be surprising then, that the nineteenth-century historical novel fails to satisfy the modern or postmodern historical sensibility, for our concept of the "extraliterary world" in the deep past is too different. According to Green,

38 Peter Green, "Aspects of the Historical Novel," *Transactions of the Royal Society of Literature*, 3rd series, 31 (1962): 35–60. The paper was originally read to the society in 1958.

39 Numerous critics have detailed the mutual influence of history and the historical novel in the nineteenth century. See especially Stephen Bann, *Romanticism and the Rise of History* (New York: Twayne, 1995) and *The Clothing of Clio* (Cambridge: Cambridge University Press, 1984). The practicing historian's point of view can be found in G. M. Trevelyan, "Influence of Sir Walter Scott on History," in *An Autobiography and Other Essays* (London: Longman, 1949), 200–5, and Hugh Trevor-Roper, "Sir Walter Scott and History," *The Listener* 86 (19 August 1971): 225–32.

40 Green, "Aspects," 41.

the Victorian era was too blinded by its smug complacency and absolute confidence in the patent superiority of its own ethics and institutions to ever sympathetically imagine a society other than itself,[41] a failing amply evident in *The Cloister and the Hearth*'s depiction of medieval religion. But the Middle Ages were no less anachronistic in their conception of the antique past, while the Renaissance created another romantic dream of its own from classical antiquity. Even the eighteenth century tended to view the ancient world as a more or less faithful mirror image of itself. Perhaps we should pause before thinking we have had the last word.

As Reade suggested in the opening paragraphs of *The Cloister and the Hearth*, the task of the historical novelist is essentially that of an interpreter, seeking out the "prime truths" which "remain a dead letter to plain folk," unless revivified by the power of imagination, which "reveals what lies below" the bare and dry bones of the chronicle record. In other words, the historical novelist "makes history live again," just as legions of nineteenth-century critics said about Scott. But the interpretation must be made into our own idiom. There can be no third party between ourselves and the past. A nineteenth-century historical novel is an interpretation of the past into the idiom of the nineteenth century, in terms of both style and content. As a manifestation of Romantic and Victorian culture, such novels can retain enormous interest, or as an example of how the nineteenth-century literary imagination conceived the past, but as a direct interpretation of the past *for us*, they are seriously handicapped, unless essentially grounded in nearly their own time and place like Tolstoy's Russian epic. This is especially true for the popular reading audience, which is after all the primary audience for the historical novel. Scholars can resort to the original sources. One need only read a few pages anywhere in either *The Cloister and the Hearth* or most of Scott's novels to see why their appeal would be limited today, and why it seems unlikely they can ever really speak to the present again, except as a voice from the age in which they were written. The conventions and manner of representing the past in prose fiction will surely continue to evolve in various ways, and eventually our own modern and postmodern historical novels may seem as quaint and unreal to future readers as those of the nineteenth century do to us.

41 Green, "Aspects," 41–42.

Renovation and Resurrection in M. R. James's "An Episode of Cathedral History"

Patrick J. Murphy and Fred Porcheddu

"An Episode of Cathedral History": the very title promises us a study in the synchronic and the diachronic, as a few select persons inherit and respond to a structure designed to bear witness to all of human history. And a tale of the uneasy fortunes of communal history and memory is exactly what M. R. James (1862–1936) supplies, though (as we might expect from a distinguished medievalist who became one of the masters of the ghost-story genre) whatever social and aesthetic lessons we may learn are to be gained only after serious consideration of the scholarly backdrop of a kind of writing the author once characterized as "ghost stories of an antiquary."[1] Our

1 A current upswing of interest in James's fiction is perhaps reflected in the *New Yorker* recently running a piece on the subject: Anthony Lane, "Fright Nights: The Horror of M. R. James" (13 and 20 February 2012): 105–8. Although no monograph has yet appeared on James's fiction, some of the better essays on his stories have been collected in S. T. Joshi and Rosemary Pardoe, *Warnings to the Curious: A Sheaf of Criticism on M. R. James* (New York: Hippocampus Press, 2007). Several of these originally appeared in the occasional journal *Ghosts & Scholars* (edited by Rosemary Pardoe), which from 1979 to 2001 published numerous notes, essays, and original fiction inspired by James, and presently continues online as *The Ghosts & Scholars M. R. James Newsletter*. Several annotated editions of James's collected tales have appeared recently, along with numerous adaptations of his fiction, including BBC television and radio dramatizations. The video game *The Lost Crown* (Got Game, 2008) is based on "A Warning to the Curious," and *A Podcast to the Curious*, dedicated to all things Jamesian, is currently available from iTunes. James's academic work, on the other hand, is the subject of Lynda Dennison, *The Legacy of M. R. James: Papers from the 1995 Cambridge Symposium* (Donington, Lincolnshire: Shaun Tyas, 2001), while accounts of James's life and professional career include S. G. Lubbock, *A Memoir of Montague Rhodes James* (Cambridge: Cambridge University Press, 1939); Richard William Pfaff, *Montague Rhodes James* (London:

purpose in this essay, then, is to investigate the complexity of these inspirations and, further, to offer an interpretation of how they may be understood to connect in the larger architecture of James's fiction. In particular, we argue that two very different kinds of "mysteries" shape this ghost story. The first of these is Dickens's *The Mystery of Edwin Drood* and its connections to the very specific architectural history of Rochester Cathedral. The second is the genre of the "mystery play," a form that in James's day was understood to have evolved out of church rituals built into the very fabric of the cathedral. These mysteries may be understood as most concretely linked by James's curious creation of a plain, empty altar tomb to house his horror – an object that stands at the center of medieval drama, of Rochester cathedral history, and, of course, of this ghost story itself. A long history of reform, restoration, and revival, eternally disrupting the symbiotic balance struck between a cathedral's past and its present needs, is the most obvious villain at the intersection of these mysteries, but it is equally important for us to understand how James blends these separate scholarly interests into a single meditation on who owns history and how it is properly to be used. To see these patterns we must recognize that James's background as a medievalist and a bibliographer led him to tell stories in which very precise architectural, literary, and liturgical references appear in plain sight as a kind of creative analogue to scholarly footnotes – that he entombs his horrors in layers of allusion that we may well miss if we are too quick, as have been most previous readers of the tale, to put monster over all other matters.

We will presently examine this critical tendency before moving on to our larger discussion. First, however, a brief summary of the story's plot may be useful. "An Episode of Cathedral History" is, at least on the surface, of the jack-in-the-box variety of ghost stories not uncommon to James's fiction in which a supernatural being is discovered in a sealed-off location (a chamber at the bottom of a well, a disused room in a country inn, and so on) until it is unintentionally liberated through accident or curiosity; the creature must therefore be dealt with – appeased, rendered impotent, or just driven off – before the narrator is removed from our gaze. We might winkingly call this particular version of the form a "jack-in-the-pulpit" story, for here the malignant supernatural agent is released when a Gothic Revival restoration party, against the admonitions of local citizens, removes the wooden choir pulpit of "Southminster Cathedral" and discovers an unknown tomb encased beneath it. Following weeks of unease during which a number of persons in the cathedral environs fall ill and even die, a representative assembly meets in

Scolar Press, 1980); and Michael Cox, *M. R. James: An Informal Portrait* (Oxford: Oxford University Press, 1983).

the choir to open the tomb – only to have the cause of the unhealthy effects flee and leave them, or some of them, in the dark. Our guide to these events is the cathedral's principal verger, Mr. Worby, who witnessed them as a boy (watching the memorable climax from a perch high up in the triforium) and who relates them some fifty years later to a visiting scholar, Mr. Lake.

Perhaps more than any other of the stories of M. R. James, this tale has attracted attempts to classify the species of its supernatural antagonist.[2] To be sure, James's unusual status as both a writer of fiction and an outstanding medieval scholar invites such efforts of taxonomy: his academic work on pseudepigraphica and biblical apocrypha included substantial engagement with Latin, Greek, and other texts of the supernatural, bodies of lore so remote and rhizomatic that they fascinate us into speculating how they might be transfigured in fiction by an academic expert.[3] In the particular case of "An Episode," the question of classification is at once both raised and confounded by the biblical associations made by members of James's fictional cathedral community itself, as when one canon remarks to another

2 Commentators have often linked lamia mythology with the events of the story, often emphasizing its traditional threat to children (although the creature of the tale is "downright fatal" only to older residents). In M. R. James, *The Haunted Doll's House and Other Ghost Stories*, ed. S. T. Joshi (New York: Penguin, 2006), 276 n. 14, Joshi remarks that "A *lamia* is a monster out of Roman popular mythology, often thought to devour children." Similarly, Michael Cox, *Casting the Runes and Other Stories* (Oxford: Oxford University Press, 1987), 330 n. 219, explains, "A lamia was a witch or demon supposed to suck the blood of children." In M. R. James, *Collected Ghost Stories*, ed. Darryl Jones (Oxford: Oxford University Press, 2011), 452, Jones goes a bit further, explaining that, "The lamia was a Greek succubus or night demon who devoured children, and gained particular cultural currency in the nineteenth century as a vampiric femme fatale. Thus, importantly, 'Cathedral History's' demon is *female* (as opposed to its male counterpart in 'Canon Alberic')" (452). Jacqueline Simpson, "'The Rules of Folklore' in the Ghost Stories of M. R. James," *Folklore* 108 (1997): 9–18, takes a different approach, relating features of the haunting to various motifs of Danish folklore, including, for example, "the red-eyed church-dwelling ghost" that "appears in a widespread migratory legend." Perhaps the most prolonged look into lamia lore is Peter Bell, "The Lamia and the Screech-Owl: Some Thoughts on 'An Episode of Cathedral History,'" *Ghosts & Scholars M. R. James Newsletter* 16 (2009): 27–30, where "a fascinating synthesis of interlocking traditions" of the lamia is discussed.

3 After his dissertation on the *Apocalypse of Peter* (King's College, 1887), James edited and/or translated *The Psalms of Solomon* (1891), *The Testament of Abraham* (1892), and two series of *Apocrypha Anecdota* (1893/97). For a time thereafter he shifted his energies to the manuscript catalogues for which he is best known in the academic world, but he returned to large-scale textual productions with translations of *Old Testament Legends* in 1913, followed by the pseudepigraphic *Biblical Antiquities of Philo* (1917), *The Lost Apocrypha of the Old Testament* (1920), and his magnificent *Apocryphal New Testament* (1924) and *Latin Infancy Gospels* (1927). More than sixty additional items on apocryphal topics – among them reviews, brief notes and queries, introductory essays, and critical studies – further enrich the columns of his scholarly output on the subject.

that the previous night's uneasy sleeping held "rather too much of Isaiah 34.14 for me."[4] A reader who follows Canon Lyall's suggestion to look up the passage will read in the Vulgate of Jerome:

> et occurrent dæmonia onocentauris et pilosus clamabit alter ad alterum ibi cubavit lamia et invenit sibi re quiem
>
> (The wild beasts of the desert shall also meet with the wild beasts of the island, and the satyr shall cry to his fellow; the screech owl also shall rest there, and find for herself a place of rest.)[5]

Translation quickly fails us, for even between the Latin and the English we can see the competition of natural and supernatural agencies – wild beasts and screech owls jostle for the reader's attention with *dæmoniae*, *onocentauri*, satyrs, and *pilosi* (literally, "hairy ones"). Then there is the enigmatic lamia, which is also featured in the last words of the story as a curious kind of reverse epigraph and ambiguous epitaph: Lyall affixes the inscription *ibi cubavit lamia*, "There the lamia has dwelled," to the empty tomb's northern face. The lamia of Isaiah has been variously Englished as "screech-owl," "Lilith," "she-demon," and "night-creature," as well as "night-bird," -monster, -spirit, -raven, and -hag.[6] As James supplies no translation of that particular word, readers and critics have selected freely among these choices as well as others of their own invention, while varying a good deal even in ignoring the perfect tense of *cubavit* as they have glossed the inscription in the past ("There lay a sorceress"), present ("Here lies a vampire") and future ("There shall be the lair of the night monster" [or witch, or vampire]).[7] As

4 M. R. James, *A Thin Ghost and Others* (London: Edward Arnold, 1919), 92. All citations to the story are from this edition.

5 The English here is that of the Cambridge King James translation used in the story (but see below, n. 7).

6 The renowned Hebrew scholar Joseph Addison Alexander, in *The Earlier Prophecies of Isaiah* (New York: Putnam, 1846), 568–72, provides a detailed inventory of translations up to his own time. Isaiah 34:14 also appears in James's "Canon Alberic's Scrap-book" in the context of the hairy, skeletal creature being interrogated by King Solomon. Sir Matthew Fell happens upon Isaiah 13:20 ("it shall never be inhabited") during his sortilege in "The Ash-Tree."

7 To take these citations in reverse: the third is from Rosemary Pardoe, "The Demon in the Cathedral (A Jamesian Hoax)," *All Hallows* 1 (1989): 25–26; the second from M. R. James, *A Pleasing Terror: The Complete Supernatural Writings*, ed. Christopher Roden and Barbara Roden (Ashcroft, British Columbia: Ash-Tree Press, 2001), 264 n. 15; the first is to be found as a reader's marginal gloss in the digitized copy of *A Thin Ghost and Others* (1919) currently available on Google books. We include this last example to emphasize that James has indeed left a challenge of translation that many of his readers have taken up. Numerous variations on all three of these might be cited. Many of those who have located the lamia's residence in the future have relied on the King James translation ("the screech owl also shall rest there"), which

these examples also suggest, quite some ink has been spilled in emphasizing the assumed feminine nature of the creature in question (despite the fact that it is described as "a thing like a man" by our only eyewitness) and its possible status as some kind of vampire, albeit a rather unconventional one.[8] As Peter Haining explained in 1968, "This particular story [. . .] introduces a somewhat different kind of vampire – not one of flesh and blood, but an ephemeral being nonetheless capable of creating fear and terror."[9] Indeed, the tale has enjoyed a dubious afterlife as a staple of vampire-fiction anthologies, a generic affiliation apparently grounded largely, if not solely, in the ambiguity of this single word.[10]

What is invariably lost in all this speculation is the simple observation that "lamia" comes merely as a scriptural allusion produced by one of the story's characters – Canon Lyall – in the aftermath of the haunting, and therefore is not necessarily to be taken as any authoritative or defining label for what has emerged from the tomb. In fact, it would be just as legitimate to posit an association with the other creatures mentioned in Isaiah 34:14 (those demons, satyrs, and hairy ones who cry out to one another), as indeed some critics have done. To all this published speculation we respond that the nature of the haunting in "An Episode of Cathedral History" is not so much a matter of teratological lore as it is a function of the larger narrative context from which the monstrous thing emerges. Such an argument is in line with the response of the first recorded audience of the tale, James's friend and fellow ghost-story writer Arthur Benson, who in his diary entry for 18

version is cited elsewhere in the tale for a different line ("the satyr shall cry to his fellow") but which is neither based on the Vulgate nor known for its faithfulness to verb tenses in the original. Notice, too, that translations glossing the line often flip between "there" (the literal sense of *ibi*) and "here" (a translation apparently influenced by the common epitaph formula, "Here lies . . ."). As James leaves *ibi cubavit lamia* untranslated, however, it seems best to take him as much as possible at his (or at least that of Lyall's Vulgate's) literal word: "There a lamia has lain."

8 Engagements with the tale often resolve into dubious taxonomic judgments, even in academic criticism. For example, Jack Sullivan, *Elegant Nightmares: The English Ghost Story from LeFanu to Blackwood* (Athens: Ohio University Press, 1978), 78, summarizes the story as involving "a vampire posing as a saintly relic in a fifteenth-century cathedral altar-tomb."

9 Peter Haining, *The Midnight People* (New York: Popular Library, 1968), 51; Haining includes "An Episode" alongside stories by Polidori, Benson, Derleth, Bloch, Bradbury, and others.

10 The genre affiliation has subsequently been reinforced by, among others, Alan Ryan (*Vampires*, 1987, reprinted as *The Penguin Book of Vampire Stories*, 1988), Richard Dalby (*Dracula's Brood*, 1987, and *Vampire Stories*, 1992), Stephen Jones (*The Mammoth Book of Vampires*, 1992, *The Giant Book of Vampires*, 1994, and the modest *Book of Vampires*, 1997), and Otto Penzler (*The Vampire Archives: The Most Complete Volume of Vampire Tales Ever Published*, 2009). "An Episode of Cathedral History" is James's sole representation in some of these; in others it is accompanied by "Wailing Well."

May 1913 recorded that "Monty read us a very good ghost story, with an admirable verger very humorously portrayed – the ghost part weak."[11] Arguably, what Benson senses about this excellent ghost story with a "weak" ghost is that its primary concern lies not so much with the undead but with the living community that breathes life into the ancient structure of the cathedral. We will argue, in fact, that the most useful strategy for understanding this haunting is to investigate the background materials not of the monster, but rather of its lair.

Reviving a Mystery

"An Episode of Cathedral History" is noticeably preoccupied with architecture, its narrative arc largely shaped by church layout and ornamented with the technical vocabulary of cathedral description. We would expect nothing less from a scholar who produced numerous reviews, articles, and guidebooks on the subject, and we might well assume that the cathedral of this tale simply merges in its fictional fabric various cathedral features culled from James's wide experiences in the field – as indeed James himself asserts in noting that his Southminster, like his Barchester, was a "blend of Canterbury, Salisbury, and Hereford."[12] To a certain extent this is surely the case, though we will here foreground the importance of quite a different cathedral, Rochester, as much as for its physical structure as for its very particular history. It is the literary history of Rochester with which we must begin – specifically with *The Mystery of Edwin Drood*, the legendary tale of obsession and murder set in the Rochester-based cathedral town of Cloisterham. As readers of the novel will recall, John Jasper, the chief villain of the work and

11 Cox, *Casting*, 143 n. 19. This is the earliest trustworthy reference to the story, though Pfaff quotes Lady Maisie Fletcher remembering James reading the story aloud "c. 1912" (*Montague*, 410 n. 58). "An Episode" was first printed in the *Cambridge Review* of 10 June 1914, and then reprinted in *A Thin Ghost and Others*, James's third collection, in 1919.

12 M. R. James, Preface to *Collected Ghost Stories* (London: Edward Arnold, 1931). James's descriptions of the architecture and fabric of English and French cathedrals, chapels, abbeys, and parish churches number some thirty-four books and articles; among the more notable are *The Sculptures in the Lady Chapel at Ely* (London: Nutt, 1895), *The Verses Formerly Inscribed on Twelve Windows in the Choir of Canterbury Cathedral* (Cambridge: Cambridge Antiquarian Society, 1901), *Notes on Glass in Ashridge Chapel* (Grantham: Leatton and Eden, 1906), *The Sculptured Bosses in the Cloisters of Norwich Cathedral* (Norwich: Goose, 1911), the chapter "Sculpture, Glass, Painting," in *Medieval France: A Companion to French Studies*, ed. Arthur Tilley (Cambridge: Cambridge University Press, 1922), 388–434; *St. George's Chapel, Windsor: The Woodwork of the Choir* (Windsor: St. George's Chapel, 1933); and of course *Abbeys* (London: Great Western Railway, 1925) and *Suffolk and Norfolk: A Perambulation of the Two Counties* (London: Dent, 1930), the latter of which is suffused with architectural anecdotes of every kind.

the cathedral's choirmaster, decides to murder his nephew Edwin Drood because he (Jasper) has become infatuated with Edwin's fiancée Rosa Bud. And as is known even to those who have not read it, Dickens had reached the point in his serialization where clues to Drood's disappearance were beginning to accumulate and interlace when the author suffered a sudden stroke and died the following day, 9 June 1870. Only half the novel was written; Dickens left behind no plot sketch, no indication of the functions of several recently introduced characters, and not even any proof that young Drood actually had been successfully murdered by the opium-clouded Jasper. The work thus passed into literary history as the great unfinished Victorian novel, and like *Hero and Leander*, *The Romance of the Rose*, and so many others, its lack of closure begat acrobatic feats of self-appointed authorship. Dozens of solutions and sequels were published in the following decades, though a century and a half later that profusion has been effectively replaced in popular memory by the 1985 Rupert Holmes musical whodunnit.[13]

M. R. James became a devoted reader of Dickens's works; his enthusiasm led him to recommend Dickens alongside the Bible, Homer, and Shakespeare to students at Eton as a source of the "best things" for lasting inspiration in life.[14] In 1905 he wrote a lighthearted report on an imaginary "Edwin Drood Syndicate" for the *Cambridge Review* in which he engaged some of the central questions left by the unfinished novel;[15] but after that squib James's manner toward the problem took on a more diligent aspect, perhaps because he realized how thoroughly his academic colleagues shared his interest in treating the unfinished text as a collection of clues to a soluble puzzle. In his memoir *Eton and King's* he recounts in particular how his friend Henry Jackson, the Regius Professor of Greek at Cambridge, having read James's facetious *Cambridge Review* piece, "plunged into" the subject himself, ultimately producing the monograph *About Edwin Drood* in 1911.[16]

13 By the close of the nineteenth century the solutions had accumulated to the point that even the generously spirited William Hughes had to admit that "it is a hard matter to the reader to struggle through any one of them" (*A Week's Tramp in Dickens-Land* [London: Chapman and Hall, 1891], 138). Interest in finishing the story spiked again in 1905, and in 1912 – the centennial of Dickens's birth – John Cuming Walters published *The Complete Mystery of Edwin Drood by Charles Dickens: The History, Continuations, and Solutions* (London: Chapman and Hall), with no fewer than thirty-two proposed completions.

14 Pfaff, *Montague*, 352. The presence of Dickens throughout James's fiction would reward focused study. In addition to the pervasive quoted presence in James's stories, several powerful attitudes and commitments – to the spirit of Christmas, to the glimpse of the uncanny in the corner of the retina, to universal camaraderie – link the two authors.

15 *Cambridge Review*, 30 November and 7 December 1905; repr. in *Hunted Down: The Detective Stories of Charles Dickens*, ed. Peter Haining (London: Peter Owen, 1996), 210–23.

16 Henry Jackson, *About Edwin Drood* (Cambridge: Cambridge University Press, 1911); discussed in Pfaff, *Montague*, 215.

In July of 1909, as Jackson was assembling this study, he, James, and four others formed themselves into a real Drood Syndicate and visited Rochester in order "to examine the possibilities of various theories on the spot – *e.g.* What access was there to the crypt? Was there anything answering to the Sapsea monument? What were the relative positions of the Vineyard, Durdles's yard, Minor Canon Corner? etc. – and a very memorable week-end we spent there."[17] Alas, James admits that the party "did not hit on any illuminating facts"; he seems particularly disappointed to have found no exemplar of the tomb of Mrs. Sapsea, where, in his own solution to the plot, he was convinced that Drood's still-living body had been secreted by John Jasper.[18] In his review of Jackson's book he provides an interpretation of the frontispiece of the *Edwin Drood* serial which he reads like an historiated miniature – using the same kind of attention to grouped imagery we find in his manuscript descriptions – and concludes that Dickens intended Drood to have survived Jasper's attempt at strangulation, to have returned to Cloisterham disguised as Dick Datchery, and ultimately to have confronted his uncle in the very tomb where he had been left for dead: "Central picture, end, the pale person cannot be a phantom as the figure casts a shadow on the wall behind him."[19]

Importantly for our purposes, all of this Droodish activity coincided with James's composition of "An Episode of Cathedral History," just before the Dickens centennial and not long after the publication of Henry Jackson's study and James's thorough review of it. His preoccupation with *Edwin Drood* announces itself as early as the story's opening scene, when Lake and Worby cross the Southminster Cathedral close at night with a lantern:

> "Anyone might think we were Jasper and Durdles, over again, mightn't they?" said Lake, as they crossed the close, for he had ascertained that the Verger had read *Edwin Drood.*
>
> "Well, so they might", said Mr. Worby, with a short laugh, "though I don't know whether we ought to take it as a compliment. Odd ways, I often think, they had at that Cathedral, don't it seem to you, sir? Full choral matins at seven o'clock in the morning all the year round. Wouldn't suit our boys' voices nowadays, and I think there's one or two

17 M. R. James, *Eton and King's: Recollections, Mostly Trivial, 1875–1925* (Cambridge: Cambridge University Press, 1926), 215–16.

18 James, "Edwin Drood Syndicate," 212–16.

19 M. R. James, "About Edwin Drood" [Review], *Cambridge Review*, 9 March 1911; repr. in *About Edwin Drood* (Edinburgh: Tragara Press, 1983), 16–24 (see esp. 20–22); see also James, *Eton and King's*, 215, and Walters, *Complete Mystery*, 248.

of the men would be applying for a rise if the Chapter was to bring it in – particular the alltoes".[20]

If only we listen for them, we can hear the bells of Cloisterham tolling quietly all throughout James's Southminster. Both stories are set in quiet English cathedral towns south of London in the middle of the nineteenth century; both contain important characters who are head vergers; both contain arrogant, aloof chapter deans whose comeuppance readers eagerly anticipate. James imports Dickens's lovely coinage of "cathedraly" for "cathedral-adjacent," and in both works watchful visitors stay in the cathedraly home of the verger. Mr. Worby, James's verger, inherits both the native insights and the wall-tapping mannerism of "Stony" Durdles (as James wrote in his Syndicate essay, "This person, it will be remembered, possessed an extraordinary faculty of detecting, by means of tapping, the presence and even, to some extent, the nature of foreign [or other] bodies lying behind masonry"[21]); in *Drood* there is an exchange between Jasper and Durdles about hearing portentous cries, shrieks, and the howl of a dog in the night, which is paralleled by the night-time phenomenon of "the crying" which Worby recalls from his boyhood, hiding in bed with his little scared dog (cries which, we infer, are made by the freed creature during its nocturnal perambulations). In both works the cathedral choir is the site both of the performance of worship and of the sudden, dramatic stirrings of a deadly malice; and finally, of course (and insofar as James's convictions led him to believe was the case with *Drood*),

20 James, *A Thin Ghost*, 77. The thorough saturation of this story with Dickensiana is further illustrated by noting James's sly allusion in Worby's phrase "all the year round" to Dickens's famous periodical, which variety of publication James once called "the real happy hunting ground, the proper habitat" of the ghost story: M. R. James, *Some Remarks on Ghost Stories* (Edinburgh: Tragara Press, 1985), 5. Very subtly, the thread is picked back up on the next page:

> Not many minutes had passed before Worby reappeared at the door of the choir and by waving his lantern signalled to Lake to rejoin him.
>
> "I suppose it is Worby, and not a substitute," thought Lake to himself, as he walked up the nave. There was, in fact, nothing untoward. (James, *A Thin Ghost*, 78)

The suspicion that the figure in the distance may be a "substitute," coupled with Worby's act of signaling Lake with a lantern, strongly evokes one of Dickens's most famous ghost stories, "The Signal-Man," which opens with the narrator and the tale's protagonist mistaking each other for ghosts: "The monstrous thought came into my mind [. . .] that this was a spirit, not a man" (21). Indeed, the story ends with the signal-man perishing when he mistakes the warning of an engineer for the voice of a ghostly "substitute." Dickens's story, not incidentally, first appeared in that "happy hunting ground" (*All the Year Round* 16 [16 December 1866]: 20–25), while James especially appreciated "The Signal-Man," referring to it as "a ghost story proper" (*Some Remarks on Ghost Stories*, 7).

21 James, " Edwin Drood Syndicate," 219.

both works contain a climactic confrontation with the inmate of a tomb who is . . . well, not quite dead enough.

These and scores of other more incidental verbal echoes connect the two works. But the unfinished nature of *Edwin Drood* directs us to the general concept of renovation, the alterations made to a structure as it moves forward in time. Apart from the puzzle of Dickens's last plot, we must ask ourselves, and apart from the grave that was actually dug for Dickens in its south transept before the Dean of Westminster pulled rank to enrich the soil of Poet's Corner, is there more in Rochester Cathedral for an antiquarian with sepulchral matters on his mind? The answer, it turns out, is "Yes" – for in Rochester there are two more tombs which have relevance for "An Episode of Cathedral History," two real tombs, both housing the mortal remains of medieval bishops ("them old 'uns with a crook," as Durdles would say) whose remarkable architectural histories a seasoned architectural student like James would have encountered during his investigation of the Drood plot.

The nineteenth-century renovation of Rochester Cathedral was less encompassing than those of other diocesan seats, but in one respect it stands alone: the striking alterations to the Rochester choir and to the eastern end of the cathedral generally. Between them, Lewis Cottingham (who brought the Gothic Revival with him during twenty years of projects beginning in 1825) and Gilbert Scott (who in the 1870s deliberately reworked or negated much of what his predecessor had done) dilated the choir from a restricted and claustrophobic space to the open, airy, accessible minor transept it is today.[22] Their overall vision was to refashion the "monastic" eastern end of the small cathedral for a new generation's use.[23] While much of what they accomplished was surely necessary and valuable for the stabilization of the structure, James, like his colleague Sir William Hope, could not but have despaired at a number of attempts at removing old materials and medi-

22 Other projects included those of Lewis Vulliamy (1845), J. D. Sedding and J. C. Pearson (1880s and 1890s), and C. H. Fowler (1904–5). Predictably, some of these projects – those by Cottingham and Scott in particular – were exceptionally controversial, and architectural historians still disagree on their merits (compare Janet Myles, *L. N. Cottingham, 1787–1847: Architect of the Gothic Revival* [London: Lund Humphries, 1996], 82, and David Cole, *The Work of Gilbert Scott* [London: Architectural Press, 1980], 172).

23 Unique among English cathedrals, the walled choir of Rochester formed "in effect an eastern church"; "the long walled choir, the old choir of the monks [. . .] could only be assigned to the clergy, and could not be opened to the nave" (Richard John King, *Handbook to the Cathedrals of England (Southern Division)*, 3rd edn. [London: John Murray, 1903 (1862)], 585–86). Comparisons of the floor plans of the various eighteenth-, nineteenth-, and early twentieth-century handbooks and guides to Rochester Cathedral will help the reader envision the details here and in the following pages. On the matter of the choir reduction the reader is especially encouraged to consult James Storer, *History and Antiquities of the Cathedral Churches of Great Britain*, vol. 4 (London: Rivingtons, 1819), Plate 7.

evalizing new ones into existence.[24] For his part, Cottingham "swept away" much of the older woodwork in the choir (including paneling, cornice-work, and the choir pulpit itself) and replaced it with newly made "medieval" fittings.[25] But his work resulted in two quite astonishing discoveries: a remarkable fourteenth-century painting of the Wheel of Fortune on the wall behind the destroyed pulpit, and the largely intact tomb of Bishop John de Sheppey, complete with painted figural effigy, walled up behind a thick layer of chalk and plaster between two arches leading from the choir to the presbytery where it had been secreted, invisible and unsuspected in the midst of constant traffic, for at least 200 years. In his exultation over the latter discovery Cottingham took the extraordinary step of privately printing a sort of promotional "press kit" – a multi-page pamphlet with custom engravings depicting his discovery of the tomb, the foremost of which shows the architect himself describing de Sheppey's monument to a group of visitors.[26] So similar is the triumphant response which James provides for his vindicated restorers that one feels he could almost have written it from Cottingham's engraving: "The removal of the base [of the pulpit] – not effected without considerable trouble – disclosed to view, greatly to the exultation of the restoring party, an altar-tomb – the tomb, of course, to which Worby had attracted Lake's attention that same evening."[27]

Fifty years after Cottingham, Gilbert Scott removed the eastern extension of the choir stalls which had cut up the minor transept since the Middle Ages; in so doing he reduced the size of the choir but opened up the entire

24 W. H. St. John Hope (1854–1919) spent four years in Rochester compiling his *Architectural History of the Cathedral Church and Monastery of St. Andrew at Rochester* (London: Mitchell and Hughes, 1900); his capacious knowledge and keen ability to extrapolate based on observation make him something of an architectural counterpart to James, and they are of one voice on matters of nineteenth-century "restoration" (as Hope's frequent ironic use of the term in inverted commas indicates). Michael Cox asserts that James, "appealing to the authority of Ruskin, insisted that ancient buildings belonged to the men who built them: 'it was only our duty to preserve them for posterity if we could do so without altering them. Restoration was unjustifiable, reparation was beneficial'" (*Casting*, 43), and this Ruskinian attitude is explored in detail by Martin Hughes, "Murder of the Cathedral: A Story by M. R. James," *Durham University Journal* 87 (January 1995): 73–98; and Françoise Dupeyron-Lafay, "Les cathédrales de Montague Rhodes James" (in *La Cathédrale*, ed. Joëlle Prungnaud [Villeneuve d'Ascq: Université Charles-de-Gaulle, 2001], 203–14).

25 Hope uses this metaphor at least four times when discussing the Gothic Revival restorations at Rochester (*Architectural History*, 88, 96, 109, 115); Mr. Worby despairingly remembers how Southminster's dean orders a "clean sweep" of its choir (James, *A Thin Ghost*, 84).

26 *Some Account of an Ancient Tomb, etc. etc. etc., Discovered at Rochester Cathedral, 1825, by L. N. Cottingham, Arch.* (London: Taylor, 1825). Both it and the Wheel of Fortune are visible on the cathedral's panoramic tour, online at www.rochestercathedral.org/pano/.

27 James, *A Thin Ghost*, 87.

eastern transept. In an act of passive aggression or aesthetic integrity (take your pick), he moved the new choir pulpit which Cottingham had designed out into the nave and built his own new one for the choir; this he chose to place in its current position against the pillar across the northeast transept from its traditional location across from the bishop's throne, and next to the de Sheppey tomb which Cottingham had discovered.[28] The single disruption to the complete openness of the minor transept was now the monument of Bishop John Lowe: a plain rectangular fifteenth-century altar tomb which had been built lengthwise against the outside of the altar screen behind the former pulpit, but which now sprouted like a mushroom from the floor of the wide open north–south transept. Because of the chain reaction of other restoration decisions – the removal of the choir pulpit, the removal of the eastern choir stalls – Gilbert Scott may have felt that he had no other option than to dismantle and move the tomb of Bishop Lowe some thirty feet away, adding it to a sort of ghetto of seventeenth-century monuments in the onetime Chapel of St. William. But Lowe, a former confessor to Henry VI (whose "two great foundations" were James's own Eton and King's), had specifically directed in his will that his tomb be placed *ex opposito sedis episcopalis*, "across from the bishop's seat," and its position had been used by several generations of architectural historians to localize monuments and altars that had been subsequently destroyed. Unmoved by Scott's defense that the reorganization was made necessary by the other alterations and the close quarters of the small cathedral, Sir William Hope did not disguise his contempt: he maintained that Lowe's tomb was "an ancient landmark in the topography of the church, and its removal is therefore the more unjustifiable."[29]

The reason we have reviewed this architectural work in such detail is to emphasize that by the time M. R. James and his Edwin Drood Syndicate visited Rochester in July of 1909, a trail of restoration, tomb discovery (de Sheppey), and tomb movement (Lowe) was not just available in print resources like Hope's *Architectural History* but was still within the living memory of many persons living there. The tomb discovered in James's Southminster Cathedral has undeniable similarities to the discovery circumstances of the de Sheppey tomb and the former location of the Lowe tomb; it also resembles the Lowe tomb strongly, though only a researcher or a visitor to Rochester would know this – strangely, no image of it has appeared in print before or since Thorpe's edition of *Custumale Roffense* in 1788.[30]

28 Hope, *Architectural History*, 111–20.

29 Hope, *Architectural History*, 129–30.

30 John Thorpe, *Custumale Roffense, from the Original Manuscript in the Archives of the Dean and Chapter of Rochester: to which are added, Memorials of that Cathedral Church* (London: Nichols, 1788).

When added to the many details already present in James's text via his Dickensian interests, these architectural details gain a cumulative force and encourage us to open ourselves to the possibility of even further influences. Mr. Worby's prominence in the story, for example, is more explicable when we learn that during the nineteenth century Rochester Cathedral had no more than two vergers at any given time (whereas others had as many as eight or ten). One of the longest serving of these was William Miles (1815–1908), who, like Worby, spent nearly all his life in its service – as a chorister (1826–34), lay clerk (1839–44), and then variously sexton, sub-sacrist, porter, barber, and organ-blower; he was appointed head verger in 1847, an office he held until his retirement in 1900 at the age of eighty-four.[31] Miles is widely accepted to have been the model for Mr. Tope, the verger in *Edwin Drood*, but the dates and activities of his life are also very close to those of Mr. Worby, whose biographical details are given by James with peculiar precision; both Tope and Worby play the showman by design, which seems to have been Miles's wont.[32] At least two more characters' names appear to have been imported from histories of the cathedral as well: G. H. Palmer, author of the Rochester's guide in the Bell's series,[33] whose surname is given to the mason directed to fill up the crack in the uncovered tomb, and Sir Joseph Ayloffe, a co-founder of the Society of Antiquaries who merited a full-page dedicatory engraving in Thorpe's 1769 survey,[34] and whose name

31 Philip Barrett, *Barchester: English Cathedral Life in the Nineteenth Century* (London: SPCK, 1993), 106–10.

32 "Death of 'Mr. Tope,'" *The Musical Times* (1 April 1908): 239. Miles, a friend of Dickens, died in March 1908, just over a year before James's Syndicate visit.

33 G. H. Palmer, *The Cathedral Church of Rochester: A Description of its Fabric and a Brief History of the Episcopal See*, 2nd edn. London: Bell, 1899). This guide is certainly the "little book in the series" which Worby mentions to Mr. Lake. Palmer tells his readers that "photographs of three drawings by Mr. Gunning, made in 1842, are preserved in the chapter room, and show this east end [i.e., the Choir and its transepts], and the two sides of the organ screen, as they were before Scott's alterations" (87); it is possible that these inspired the pre-renovation drawing of the choir which Worby shows Lake in his rooms while narrating the Episode, though a similar device is used in "The Stalls of Barchester Cathedral" (the latter story mentions the Bell's series and Gilbert Scott by name).

34 John Thorpe, *Registrum Roffense: or, a Collection of Antient Records, Charters, and Instruments of Divers Kinds, Necessary for Illustrating the Ecclesiastical History and Antiquities of the Diocese and Cathedral Church of Rochester* (London: Richardson, 1769). The dedication is motivated by Ayloffe's having helped John Thorpe *fils* see into posthumous print this work begun by his father, John Thorpe *père*.

M. R. James, Joseph Ayloffe, and Sir William Hope shared the experience of witnessing the opening of royal tombs: James and Hope were both present at the examination of Henry VI, and Ayloffe that of Edward I. Moreover, Ayloffe and Hope both published their accounts in the Society of Antiquaries' journal – Ayloffe when it was a fledgling publication ("An Account of the Body of King Edward the First, as it Appeared on Opening his Tomb

is imported for the elderly canon whose protest against the removal of the Southminster pulpit anticipates his own painful demise. And most persuasively of all to us is the simple sense of profound restfulness and intimacy to Southminster which accords very well with Rochester – a peacefulness which helps the lurking menace dilate among the populace just as Worby's night-time spectacle with Lake "adds to the size and heighth" of the cathedral. Both of these effects are appropriate to a relatively small church like Rochester, but lose their relevance in more massive structures.

Thus, while commentators may be pleased to repeat James's assertion about his cathedrals being blends of other known structures, we in fact find ourselves at the all-too-familiar critical loggerheads between intention and reception. No, Southminster is *not* Rochester, but infinitely less so is it any of the three other sites he names. Neither is it Cloisterham – when he wanted to, James was quite capable of setting action in a real place (St. Bertrand de Comminges) or of using the name of a fellow writer's fictional one (Trollope's Barchester). The information we possess about James's interest in Rochester, combined with such a powerful variety of verbal evidence, make us confident in asserting Rochester as a very important – and previously unrecognized – inspiration, and the diversity of reference leads us to conclude that James responded to the *Drood* problem through the architectural history of its model; his natural persistence would not allow him to let the enigma of *Edwin Drood* rest unexamined, but his own aesthetic would equally not allow him to join the lists of those who penned continuations in a Dickensian style (as he himself said in the preface to *A Thin Ghost*, "sequels are, not only proverbially, but actually, very hazardous things"). This point of decorum helps us demarcate the boundary of James's complicated identity as a self-identified "antiquary" living among the first generation of professional medievalists: just as he could not countenance the restoration of church structures by Gothic Revivalists, he responded to the fragmentary nature of a received text by recapitulating it in a mode of his own design.

Staging a Mystery

A cathedral's meaning is created in the accumulation of its local history as it moves forward through time, and in the same manner we gain insight into James's "cathedraly" story by understanding how the episodes of revival and restoration at Rochester connect to their fictional counterparts in Southminster. Given the presence of Dickens's novel in his story we might seriously

in the Year 1774," *Archaeologia* 3 [1786]: 376–413), and Hope 125 years later ("The Discovery of the Remains of King Henry VI in St. George's Chapel, Windsor Castle," *Archaeologia* 62.2 [1911]: 533–43).

wonder if James had the word "mystery" in mind when crafting his tale, for, as we will argue in this section, the genre of the medieval mystery play is powerfully invoked at the climax of the story. Moreover, the evolution of medieval drama within church architecture (and in particular the academic framing of the history of drama in James's lifetime) is a key context for understanding both the literal nature of the empty tomb and the figural significance of its inhabitant.

To make this case, it is important to review several key points found in James's very careful descriptions of the cathedral and its haunting, beginning with that rather inexplicable object at the center of the tale, a hidden altar tomb (perhaps partly to be understood as a palimpsest of the two Rochester tombs, as we have suggested), "rather awkwardly placed" on the north side of the choir, with no name attached to it, and, even more strangely, completely empty.[35] We must try for a moment to consider this object as a very literal *tabula rasa,* for the expectations of horror fiction may easily lead us astray: many readers since James's day have no doubt assumed that the tomb's corpse has been removed or reanimated in supernatural fashion, or that the tomb has been constructed or adopted to cage the horror that emerges from it in the story. Either way, we might easily imagine that the wooden panels boxing in the tomb were first put there to help imprison a rogue supernatural creature. And yet these assumptions make very little sense in terms of the precise details James supplies. For instance, would it be too naïve to question how the wooden shell of a pulpit should suffice for centuries to contain unnoticed the ferocious malevolency of a creature which, at the tale's climax, smashes with ease through the locked outer door of the north transept?[36] What is more, the description of the tomb's former covering suggests careful efforts to preserve the tomb itself from damage, much more than it implies panicked fear of what lies within: "The structure had been most carefully boxed in under the pulpit-base, so that such slight ornament as it possessed was not defaced."[37] Upon closer inspection, then, the original object of this careful encasement seems curiously to have been to *preserve* the tomb rather than to bottle up a threat.

35 James, *A Thin Ghost*, 79.

36 The case is made by Martin Hughes ("Murder of the Cathedral: A Story by M. R. James," *Durham University Journal* 87.1 [1995]: 73–98), who asserts that the evil represented by the entombed creature "is contained by being organized into the system which is dominated by the Name and presence of God. In 'An Episode' the disease-bearing demon is trapped beneath the great pulpit – '*ibi cubavit lamia*' – harmless under the weight of rational preaching until the Revivalists release it" (80).

37 James, *A Thin Ghost*, 87.

Nor is it clear why the creature no longer runs amok in the narrative present, though we do know that by the time of Worby and Lake's night expedition the haunting is long over: Worby assures his companion that he has no fear of entering the cathedral alone at night.[38] We also know when it left: the boy Worby is witness, if not eyewitness, to its departure as it emerges from the tomb and, knocking over Dean Burscough, flees the cathedral. Worby and most of the others at the scene fail to actually see the creature because they are distracted by a baffling commotion on the other side of the choir, which is heard – inexplicably – just *before* the creature emerges from the tomb: "there come a most fearful crash down at the west end of the choir, as if a whole stack of big timber had fallen down a flight of stairs."[39] Later inspection reveals no sign of anything having fallen, leading some critics, naturally if unconvincingly, to posit the presence of two separate entities acting together: "one in the tomb and one wandering the country-side seeking to free its mate from its imprisonment."[40] The idea receives some further support from an allusion one of the cathedral canons makes to Isaiah 34:14, where we read that "the satyr shall cry to his fellow," a reference that has led James's most recent editor to look even beyond this story to locate the entombed creature's mate.[41] This line of interpretation seems to suggest that we can only parse the story's climactic moment of horror through some fairly tangled explanations which (once again) rely on the mythology of the lamia – and even then the moment is deeply unsatisfying because it is not even consciously experienced by the arrogant Dean Burscough, the obvious target of James's contempt. In any other Jamesian tale of supernatural come-uppance we would expect to relish a moment where the monster embraces or presses upon his victim with terrifyingly proximity, "the linen face [. . .] thrust close into his own."[42] In this story, though, the linens are left harm-

38 James, *A Thin Ghost*, 79.

39 James, *A Thin Ghost*, 103.

40 As Joshi, ed., *Haunted Dolls' House*, 274, summarizes the argument of Bill Read, "The Mystery of the Second Satyr," *Ghosts & Scholars* 31 (2000): 46–7. As Read points out, "Unless the occupant of the tomb had remarkable powers of telekinesis, this diversion was a remarkable coincidence. However, if there was a second creature already at liberty in the cathedral, then it is an obvious suspect" (47). As we argue below, there is no need to assume a second creature or a coincidence.

41 James, *A Thin Ghost*, 92. In M. R. James, *Collected Ghost Stories*, ed. Darryl Jones (Oxford: Oxford University Press, 2011), 452, Jones wonders if the creature in "An Episode" is calling after a fiend from one of James's first stories, "Canon Alberic's Scrap-book," published in an earlier volume of tales: "Could 'Canon Alberic' 's demon be the fellow to whom this satyr cries, 'as if it were calling after someone that wouldn't come?'" Jones further seems to imply that these two monsters may be mates: "Thus, importantly, 'Cathedral History' 's demon is *female* (as opposed to its male counterpart in 'Canon Alberic')" (452).

42 M. R. James, *Ghost-Stories of An Antiquary* (London: Edward Arnold, 1905), 223.

lessly on the floor of the tomb, while the dean remains blissfully unaware of what hit him. It is indeed a very strange scene.

But it is also oddly familiar, and by pursuing its staged familiarity rather than its esoteric mythology we arrive at a much more coherent and rich interpretation of the climax. The key is to consider the many ways in which this final supernatural event appears crafted to echo the Resurrection narrative of the New Testament. Although hitherto unnoted by commentators on this tale, the empty tomb fairly gapes with scriptural significance, even were it not for the discovery inside of two scraps (a bit of paper and the torn piece of a dress), eerily similar to the *linteamina posita et sudarium quod fuerat super caput eius*, "the linen cloths lying and the napkin which had been upon his head" which Peter saw in the sepulcher.[43] The dean orders the tomb sealed and professes worry about the the superstitious "arrant nonsense" easily accepted by "Southminster people" (*et dicant plebi surrexit a mortuis et erit novissimus error peior priore*, "and they will say to the people that he has risen from the dead and the last error will be worse than the first").[44] The opening of the Southminster tomb produces consternation consonant with that of the soldiers scattered by Christ's rising, but more importantly the inexplicable commotion at the other end of the choir now makes perfect sense – not through the explanation of a hypothetical "second satyr," but in terms of biblical precedent and what happens at the moment when the sepulcher is opened and the rising is revealed: *et ecce terraemotus factus est magnus*, "and behold there was a great earthquake."[45]

The opening of the Southminster tomb is one of the most theatrical moments in James's fiction, and in more than one sense. The thunderous "fearful crash" at the tomb's opening erupts like a sound effect in a staged reenactment of the Resurrection, and there is much evidence to link the mystery of this moment to the medieval genre of mystery plays, popular performances that retold biblical events in the vernacular. Performed in cycles with individual episodes produced by craft guilds or "mysteries" (Latin *ministeria*), such plays focused on key moments of salvation history, such as the Resurrection – which was a dramatic moment indeed, with soldiers awakening to a supernatural din:

> Awake! awake!
> Hillis gyn quake,
> And tres ben shake

43 John 20:6–7, *Biblia sacra iuxta vulgatam versionem*, 3rd edn., edited by Robert Weber, 2 vols., paginated consecutively (Stuttgart: Deutsche Bibelgesellschaft, 1983), 1695.

44 Matthew 27:64 (*Biblia sacra*, 1573).

45 Matthew 28:2 (*Biblia sacra*, 1573).

Ful nere a too.
Stonys clevyd,
Wyttys ben revid [deprived],
Erys ben devid [made deaf] –
I am servid soo.[46]

In at least one early dramatization of the Resurrection, this clamor was produced by knocking sticks together: "the which one bare the Parte of a wakinge Watcheman who (espiinge Christ to arise) made a continual noyce like to the sound that is caused by the Metinge of two Styckes."[47] Such stagecraft closely recalls the clattering disturbance in "An Episode."

Emphasizing the affinities of the story's climax with the mystery-play tradition allows us to make sense of a haunting that is distinctively theatrical. In setting the scene, James has Worby recall the exact placement of the principal players in striking detail, positions carefully blocked out with reference to liturgical east, west, south, and north: "we heard the verger that was then, first shutting the iron porch-gates and locking the south-west door, and then the transept door [. . .]. Next thing was, the Dean and the Canon come in by their door on the north, and then I see my father, and old Palmer, and a couple of their best men, and Palmer stood a talking for a bit with the Dean in the middle of the choir."[48] Worby and his boyhood friends in the triforium, of course, can see all this because they have balcony seats for a very staged fright: "and the Dean he gave a kind of sniff and walked straight up to the tomb, and took his stand behind it with his back to the screen, and the others they come edging up rather gingerly. Henslow, he stopped on the south side and scratched on his chin, he did."[49] The spectacle is so carefully blocked that when the shock comes, Worby is too overwhelmed to explain the movements of all the principal actors: "Well, you can't expect me to tell

46 James Orchard Halliwell, *Ludus Coventriæ: A Collection of Mysteries* (London: Printed for the Shakespeare Society, 1841), 348 (glosses ours). Wherever possible, we have thought it most appropriate to cite from editions available before 1913, the year "An Episode of Cathedral History" was first read, though doubtless James would also be familiar with these plays in manuscript.

47 Cited in Alfred Heales, "Easter Sepulchres: Their Object, Nature, and History," *Archaeologia* 42 (1868): 280. The anecdote comes from Witney in Oxfordshire, less than ten miles east of Burford, the setting of what may well have been the rough draft of "An Episode of Cathedral History" – see below, n. 77. Heales, 283, notes another recorded performance in which "commeth sodenly a flash of fire wherewith they are all afraid and fall downe; and then up startes the man, and they begin to sing 'Alleluia' on all hands."

48 James, *A Thin Ghost*, 101.

49 James, *A Thin Ghost*, 102.

you everything that happened all in a minute."[50] He is able to tell it, though, transferring the visual memory into a narrative: the four investigators (the dean, Palmer, Henslow, and Worby senior), like the traditional four guards of the tomb, are thrown into stylized confusion, something like a painted or carved tableau of the Resurrection, with each figure variously "tumbled over," "making off down the choir," or "sitting on the altar step with his face in his hands."[51] The one figure we never see is the "resurrected" creature itself, though we understand it must have hurried west up the choir before departing "out through the north door."[52]

There are strong clues that this dramatic element of the tale is quite specific, closely tied to James's familiarity both with liturgy and with mystery-play conventions. One of the clearest indications of this comes prior to the climax, when, like Pilate and the Pharisees securing the tomb against a false resurrection, the dean and chapter order workmen to set about *signantes lapidem*, "sealing the stone."[53] The efforts of James's craftsmen are no more successful than per usual in mystery-play slapstick:

> It appears Palmer'd told this man to stop up the chink in that old tomb. Well, there was this man keeping on saying he'd done it the best he could, and there was Palmer carrying on like all possessed about it. "Call that making a job of it?" he says. "If you had your rights you'd get the sack for this. What do you suppose I pay you your wages for? What do you suppose I'm going to say to the Dean and Chapter when they come round, as come they may do any time, and see where you've been bungling about covering the 'ole place with mess and plaster and Lord knows what?" "Well, master, I done the best I could," says the man; "I don't know no more than what you do 'ow it come to fall out

50 James, *A Thin Ghost*, 103.

51 James, *A Thin Ghost*, 103. In *Encyclopedia of Medieval Church Art*, ed. Edward G. Tasker and John Beaumont (London: B. T. Batsford, 1993), 67, Tasker and Beaumont note: "In the thirteenth century there appeared a representation of the Resurrection in Western art which became universal in the fifteenth century. Christ with the cross staff in His left hand and His right hand raised in blessing, steps out of a chest tomb onto a prostrate soldier. This form may reflect the influence of the Mystery Plays and the Easter Sepulchres some of which, as at Hawton, had the sleeping soldiers at their base and some of which were actual tombs." Hundreds of paintings of this moment from the fifteenth century alone (the best known of which include those by Piero della Francesca, Mantegna, Bellini, Raphael, Perugino, and Dieric Bouts), as well as glass and sculptural programs involving it, can be found across Europe.

52 As the dean subsequently follows in its footsteps: James, *A Thin Ghost*, 104.

53 Matthew 27:66 (*Biblia sacra*, 1573).

> this way. I tamped it right in the 'ole," he says, "and now it's fell out," he says, "I never see."[54]

The eye dialect confusion of these craftsmen recall countless such scenes in the mystery-play cycles, perhaps none more famous than the York Crucifixion, in which soldiers, bickering in the vernacular, strain to fit Christ's body on a recalcitrant rood: "I hope [think] þat marke a-misse be bored," one complains, while his companion rejoins, "Why carpe ȝe so? faste on a corde, / And tugge hym to, by toppe and taile."[55] Mystery plays of Christ's burial and resurrection feature similarly clueless attempts to resist the supernatural, as when Annas and Pilate set about sealing the tomb:

> *Annas.* Loo! here is wax fful redy dyght,
> Sett on ȝour sele anon ful ryght,
> Than be ȝe sekyr [secure], I ȝow plyght—
> He xal [shall] not rysyn ageyn.
> *Pilatus.* On this corner my seal xal sytt,
> And with this wax I sele this pytt;
> Now dare I ley he xal nevyr flytt
> Out of this grave, serteayn.[56]

But when the seal inevitably fails, Pilate's underling soldiers receive the blame, in a tongue lashing that recalls Palmer's frustrated repetitions: ("What do you suppose I pay you your wages for? What do you suppose I'm going to say to the Dean [. . .]?"):

> *Pilatus.* What! what! what! what!
> Out upon the [thee], why seyst thou that?
> ffy [fie] upon the, harlat,
> How darst thou so say?
> Thou dost myn herte ryght grett greff!
> Thou lyest upon him, fals theff;
> How xulde [should] he rysyn ageyn to lyff,
> That lay deed in clay?[57]

Mystery plays are noted for their relish of such dramatic irony – and Dean Burscough's comic cluelessness fits this role admirably, whether ordering the

54 James, *A Thin Ghost*, 94.
55 Lucy Toulmin Smith, *York Plays: The Plays Performed by the Crafts or Mysteries of York* (Oxford: Clarendon Press, 1885), 352.
56 Halliwell, *Ludus Coventriæ*, 341 (glosses ours).
57 Halliwell, *Ludus Coventriæ*, 349 (glosses ours).

tomb sealed like a second Pilate, out-heroding Herod as he storms from the cathedral, or tumbling down like the astonished soldier over whom Christ clambers in the Chester Resurrection.[58] The dean's dismissal of the two "scraps" in the tomb ("no interest whatever") is not only foolish in terms of this ghost story, it is an ironic reversal of the biblical narrative and the disciple's reaction: *vidit et credidit*, "he saw and he believed."[59] Indeed, in early liturgical drama, these objects are *angelicos testes, sudarium et vestes*, "angelic witnesses, the head-cloth and the shroud."[60] In the Wakefield mystery play of the Resurrection, Pilate asks Caiaphas what he makes of this miracle and the priest admits his ignorance: "Sir, and I couth oght by my clergys, / ffayn wold I say" ("Sir, if I knew anything [about this] through my education, I would willingly say so"[61]). In this light, the dean's dismissal outdoes even biblical arrogance as he storms from the cathedral: "Another time perhaps you'll take the advice of an educated man."[62] The typical villain of the mystery plays is, in David Bevington's words, a "self-blinded worldling" who fails to recognize the grand narrative of which he is a part.[63] James's dean, in like fashion, never even realizes he is in a ghost story.

Critics, likewise, have heretofore not realized that they are, in a sense, "in a mystery play" at this moment in the tale, and we believe the perspective explains a great deal about the dramatic situation James has layered onto the architectural history of Rochester. His ghostly parody of the mystery play focuses specifically on the Resurrection, and yet its significance is not christological but rather architectural and literary-historical. This is a crucial point. In James's day, the predominating academic understanding of medieval drama was framed in terms of metaphors of evolutionary biology – it was frequently argued that all mystery plays developed gradually out of liturgical drama, and in turn that all of liturgical drama evolved specifically out of Easter plays of the Resurrection and those ultimately from cathedral ceremonies known as the *Visitatio sepulchri* or *Quem quaeritis*.[64] The *Quem quaeritis*

58 The soldier complains, "He sett his foote upon my backe, / That everye lith beganne to crake; / I would not abyde suche another shake / For all Jerusalem." *The Chester Plays: A Collection of Mysteries*, ed. Thomas Wright (London: Printed for the Shakespeare Society, 1847).

59 James, *A Thin Ghost*, 104; John 20:8 (*Biblia sacra*, 1695).

60 From the *Visitatio Sepulchri* as edited and translated in David Bevington, *Medieval Drama* (Boston: Houghton Mifflin, 1975), 37.

61 *The Towneley Plays*, ed. George England, Early English Text Society, Extra Series 71 (Berlin: Asher & Co., 1897), 322 (translation ours).

62 James, *A Thin Ghost*, 104.

63 Bevington, *Medieval Drama*, 240.

64 For example, in the influential work of E. K. Chambers, *The Mediaeval Stage*, vol. 2 (Oxford: Clarendon Press, 1903), 10, we read: "In the Easter *Quem quaeritis* the liturgical

(short for the query, *Quem quaeritis in sepulchro, o Christicolae?* "Whom do you seek in the tomb, O Christians?") was a ceremony performed during the Easter services in which clergy played the roles of the women discovering the tomb empty of Christ's body; the body was often represented by a large metal cross which, on Good Friday during the rite of the *Depositio crucis,* had been wrapped in cloth and "entombed" amid great ceremony and chanting, along with, at times, the sacred host.[65] A whiff of these rites is perhaps to be caught in the details of James's haunting, as when "a bit of a candle" is lit to inspect the tomb, for it is well attested that the lighting of the "Sepulcre-candell" formed a prominent part of these ceremonies.[66] The rolled scrap of a music sheet might also be thought appropriate, given the central role of antiphonal chanting in the ceremony, while the dean's startled exclamation "Good God!" serves as an ironic variation on the traditional words of praise shouted at the moment the resurrection is revealed: "*Alleluia! Resurrexit Dominus!*"[67] In this key scene, then, James is in effect staging not simply an adapted version of the Resurrection but a haunting reenactment

drama was born." Chambers and many others sought to map out a line of development from the "germ" of this Easter ceremony to dramatic forms of ever-increasing complexity. Some critics went further to argue that even early modern popular drama could be traced to the same evolutionary roots. For instance, John Addington Symonds, *Shakespeare's Predecessors in the English Drama* (London: Smith, Elder, & Co., 1884), 7, discusses how the "evolution of our Drama through three broadly marked stages follows the law of growth which may be traced in all continuous products of the human spirit." Since James's day, the assumptions underlying such evolutionary models have been repeatedly called into question, so that Bevington (*Medieval Drama*, 31) concludes: "The evidence seems to contradict a once well-established scholarly hypothesis of dramatic growth, which assumed that the *Visitatio* grew first into a complex Resurrection play and then served as a model for the subsequent development of other kinds of drama."

65 Note that near the beginning of the story James reports that "a metal cross of some size" is the "solitary feature of any interest" found on the tomb (*A Thin Ghost*, 79). Only at the end of the story do we gain illumination as to its origin: it was fixed there, along with the phrase from Isaiah, by Canon Lyall after the opening ceremony has taken place (for which, see below).

66 Heales, "Easter Sepulchres," 273 and passim.

67 Chambers, *Medieval Stage*, vol. 2, 14. The boys' use of a music sheet "rolled up [. . .] small" (95) is a tantalizing detail in this context, given the etymology of the word "role" in the sense of a part in a play (note that Worby's friend Evans remarks, "Give me that roll," before shoving it into the tomb). As Bernard Bischoff (*Latin Paleography*, trans. Dáibhí Ó Cróinín and David Ganz [Cambridge: Cambridge University Press, 1990], 32) remarks, the use of individual rolls or *rotuli* for actors learning their lines is the origin of this word, and in fact some of the best early examples of such roles/parchment rolls are from medieval dramas including, Bischoff notes, "the roll of the fourth guardian of the sepulchre" from a south Italian Easter play. Karl Young (*The Drama of the Medieval Church* [Oxford: Clarendon Press, 1933], 701) notes that this roll of the sepulcher play, known as the "Sulmona fragment," was published separately in 1887 and 1889.

of the liturgical dramatization of that event. In this sense, it is the cathedral's ritual past that has come back to life in a latter-day mystery.

These connections to an Easter ceremony may seem slight enough until we revisit the significance of the strangely plain and unmarked altar tomb, the *tabula rasa* which, Worby notes, has no recorded occupant: "we don't own any record whatsoever of who it was put up to."[68] As a tomb, this object makes very little sense, but in relation to both the *Quem quaeritis* ceremony and English architectural history its significance is plain. James's tomb is best taken as the structural core of what is called an Easter Sepulcher: an elaborate liturgical prop used in the *Quem quaeritis* rite to represent Christ's tomb.[69] The typical features and position of such sepulchers match James's description of the haunted tomb with the kind of precision with which we are by now familiar. Here is Alfred Heales's description of Easter Sepulchers in an article from 1868 that M. R. James may very well have read:

> There can be little or no doubt that it [the typical Easter Sepulcher] was a temporary wooden structure, framed so as to be easily put up when required, and afterwards removed, and that it stood on the north side of the choir or chancel. There are, however, numerous high or altar tombs set in a recess in the like position, which were probably inclosed within the framework, and served as the "sepulchre" itself.[70]

Compare the description of James's tomb, which is a "plain altar-tomb" that stands "on the north side of the choir."[71] The location of the tomb is again carefully pinpointed in a later passage, placing it "standing at the east end of the stalls on the north side of the choir, facing the bishop's throne."[72] Except in extraordinary circumstances such as that specified by the will of Bishop Lowe of Rochester, this is the precise location where we would expect to find an empty tomb that is not really the tomb "of anybody noted in 'istory," but rather the architectural remains of the ceremony of the sepulcher. As we read

68 James, *A Thin Ghost*, 80.

69 As is characteristic of James's style, gentle fun is made of the antiquary Lake who says of the tomb, "'unless it's the tomb of some remarkable person, you'll forgive me for saying that I don't think it's particularly noteworthy'" (*A Thin Ghost*, 79). We are indeed expected to forgive Lake his error, for he is wise enough to offer respect to the opinion of the local amateur, Worby.

70 Heales, "Easter Sepulchres," 288.

71 James, *A Thin Ghost*, 79.

72 James, *A Thin Ghost*, 84. James describes Worby and Lake walking "down the choir aisle" westwards on the way out of the cathedral, so it is doubly clear and indeed emphasized by James that the tomb is imagined as situated at the east end of the choir, on the north side (*A Thin Ghost*, 80).

in the *Rites of Durham* for Good Friday: "two Monkes did carrye [the cross] to the Sepulchre with great reverence, which Sepulchre was sett up in the morninge, on the north side of the Quire, nigh to the High Altar."[73] Worby and Lake agree the tomb dates to the fifteenth century, and it so happens that just such a sepulcher tomb was erected in 1485 at Stanwell, Middlesex, under the direction of Thomas Windsor's will:

> My body to be buried on the north side of the quire [. . .] before the image of Our Lady, where the Sepulchre of Our Lord standeth, whereupon I will that there be made a plain tomb of marble of competent height, to the intent that it may bear the blessed body of Our Lord, and the Sepulchre at Easter to stand on the same.[74]

So James's "plain altar-tomb," like the "plain tomb of marble" Windsor orders placed over his grave, is likely not an "Easter Sepulchre" proper, but rather the base for one. Francis Bond notes that "hundreds of such tombs remain [. . .] it must, however, be borne in mind that many are only pedestals on which the temporary wooden framework of an Easter sepulchre was placed."[75] So, it would seem that the peculiar and empty altar tomb, "on the north side of the choir, and rather awkwardly placed," makes perfect sense both architecturally and in the context of the haunted mystery-play revival that James stages around it. Once we begin to look for them, such connections seem all but inevitable, though James's famous commitment to "reticence" perhaps led him to hide this pattern in plain sight, to the point that it has been wholly overlooked by critics.[76] Another small indication of this is that a very early version of the story has plans for the restoration work set during the Easter season (though James has exchanged early spring for early fall in the final draft, perhaps to avoid too overt a paschal link).[77]

73 Cited in Chambers, *Medieval Stage*, vol. 2, 310.

74 Cited in translation in Francis Bond, *The Chancel of English Churches* (London: Humphrey Milford, 1916), 236. Heales, "Easter Sepulchres," 289, notes of this sepulcher: "This tomb was only removed (quite unnecessarily) at a recent date."

75 Bond, *Chancel of English Churches*, 236.

76 As James, *Some Remarks on Ghost Stories*, 10, famously wrote, "Reticence may be an elderly doctrine to preach, yet from the artistic point of view I am sure it is a sound one. Reticence conduces to effect, blatancy ruins it, and there is much blatancy in a lot of recent stories."

77 A thorough engagement with the abandoned story draft in James's hand, Cambridge University Library, Add. Ms. 7484.1.28 (i–ii), must await another occasion. There we read that Mr. Green (the restoring architect) will complete plans for church renovations while young Mr. Cave (the son of the Dean Burscough figure in this draft, who has "a strong taste for Gothic architecture as it was then understood") returns to Oxford "for the Easter term." Note also that the owner of the tomb in this very early version is named "Lenthall," a figure

James is also quite reticent in revealing the nature of the tomb's encasement, which as we have noted was done "most carefully [. . .] so that such slight ornament as it possessed was not defaced." The Easter Sepulcher, along with the *Quem quaeritis* ceremony itself, was a notable casualty of the Reformation, so that the wooden structures were either destroyed ("given to the poor for firewood") or repurposed ("of others were made cupboards, biers, hencoops, steps, and necessities").[78] Chambers writes, "I have suspicion that the wooden so-called 'watcher's chamber' to the shrine of St. Frideswide in Christ Church, Oxford, is really a sepulchre. It is in the right place, off the north choir aisle, and why should a watcher of the shrine want to be perched up in a wooden cage on the top of a tomb?"[79] James's tomb, too, is in the exact "right place" and, as we began this discussion by noting, the description of its own repurposing, as the base of a wooden pulpit, suggests that those who boxed it in wished to preserve it "most carefully" in an effort, we can only assume, to preserve it from Reformation zeal.[80] It is an irony, then, that the pulpit's sounding-board is itself repurposed by the Gothic Revivalists "as a table in a summer-house in the palace garden."[81] The shadow of de Sheppey in Rochester Cathedral looms large here, for that painted tomb, as we have noted, is a striking example of a tomb preserved from defacement by being walled up during the Reformation, only to be triumphantly rediscovered by the forces of the Revival. In James's tale, though, the painted effigy of de Sheppey has been replaced with something much less dramatic – much more like the shifted Lowe altar tomb – yet still harboring great historical

James apparently modeled closely after Sir John Lenthall (1624–81), but whose surname also invokes the Easter season; it is also set in the Oxfordshire village of Burford, near Witney, the source of the often-quoted noisy resurrection play (see above, n. 47). The draft is undated but is probably c. 1900; it shares some features with "The Ash-Tree," which appeared in James's first collection in 1904, and it seems sensible to assume that this draft inspired that story. It also clearly anticipates "An Episode of Cathedral History," though the moral and social ambitions of the published story are much farther-reaching. The draft was christened "Speaker Lenthall's Tomb" by Rosemary Pardoe, but only half of it appears in her transcription (printed as if in full in Roden and Roden, eds., *A Pleasing Terror*, 449–52); the entire draft is some two and a half times the length printed there.

78 Bond, *Chancel of English Churches*, 220.

79 Chambers, *Medieval Stage*, vol. 2, 23 n. 6.

80 Compare this conclusion to what is perhaps the more common assumption that the pulpit's original function was to contain and conceal a threat. See, for example, Read, "Second Satyr," 46: "The purpose of the pulpit was clearly to keep the creature in." See also Michael A. Mason, "On Not Letting Them Lie: Moral Significance in the Ghost Stories of M. R. James," *Studies in Short Fiction* 19 (1982): 254, where it is explained that the story "has a very obscure foundation in the fifteenth century, when considerable trouble since lost to history must have been experienced."

81 James, *A Thin Ghost*, 87.

(and supernatural) significance. The dean's zealous demolition crew do not betray any knowledge of this history when they "disclosed to view, greatly to the exultation of the restoring party" an Easter Sepulcher, which itself had been preserved only by concealing it from the notice of ancient reformers. In fact, it is tempting to see here a less literal significance of Isaiah 34:14 ("the satyr shall cry to his fellow"[82]), if the disruption of the creature is taken as more or less the direct manifestation of that which "smote the Cathedral" in 1840. That is, the two entities most obviously "crying" out to each other, across the centuries, are those kindred external forces of Reformation and Restoration that have imposed their will on the cathedral, the fabric of which had otherwise evolved internally to fit its community ("all comfortable and furnished-like," in the words of Worby).

These contexts, then, provide a solid foundation on which we might construct a reading of the story. For instance, our sense that it is the local community that is furnished with authoritative, if ineffable, access to the meaning of the cathedral is most clearly seen in the figure of the "oldest of the body," Dr. Ayloff, whose very claim to a doctorate seems based in habitual courtesy: "for thirty years I've been known as Dr. Ayloff, and I shall be obliged, Mr. Dean, if you would kindly humour me in that matter."[83] But although James would have us smile fondly at the dignity of "Doctor" Ayloff and the pride of the "Head Verger" (as Worby conceives his own capitalized role in the cathedral), it is also clear that these men have a kind of understanding that outsiders do not. Ayloff, exasperated by the dean's stubborn plan to remove the pulpit, tells him, "if you'd only listen to reason a little, and not be always asking for it, we should get on better." There is reason, and then there is a kind of felt institutional instinct: "all I'll say is, I *know* you're doing wrong in moving it." Ayloff, aloft for thirty years preaching from the pulpit, has a feel for the building equal to that of Worby who, like Dickens's "Stony" Durdles, taps on walls to determine "the flavour of what you might call Saxon masonry."[84] Even if Worby's opinion is groundless, Lake has the good sense to defer to the verger even in matters that most concern antiquarian expertise. But of course Ayloff is proven resoundingly right in his instinct about the pulpit, and we need not attribute this wisdom to supernatural clairvoyance. On the contrary, Ayloff may well be the conduit of a lingering institutional memory, so that the eldest canon has a sense of the residual sacredness of this area of the cathedral, once home to the Easter Sepulcher ceremony. Heales notes that in many cathedrals following the Reformation, "A deep feeling of respect for the spot on which the sepulchre

82 As cited by Worby in the tale: James, *A Thin Ghost*, 92.
83 James, *A Thin Ghost*, 86.
84 James, *A Thin Ghost*, 80.

was accustomed to be placed continued in many minds for some time after the ceremonies had ceased to be observed."[85] Such a deep feeling of a cathedral's history can only reside with those who have lived lives within its walls.

As we asserted in the introduction to our essay, this perspective may also offer clues for understanding the nature of the supernatural beast that emerges from the tomb – *if* we stress that the most salient cause of this haunting is not some unexplained demonic infestation from the past, but rather the mischief produced by a sudden disruption of "comfortable and furnished-like" structures that have evolved to fit the congregational needs of the present.[86] The climax of this haunting comes in the peculiar form of a parody of medieval drama, a scholarly subject that was dominated in James's day by the application of Darwinian evolutionary models to its development.[87] So it does not seem out of place to note that, while critics have often observed the bestial tendencies of Jamesian ghosts – Lovecraft characterized them as "hellish night-abomination(s) midway betwixt beast and man"[88] – the creature in "An Episode" has a particularly Darwinian feel, described as "A thing like a man, all over hair" with "two legs, and the light caught on its eyes."[89] The atavistic hints here are confirmed when we note that critics have overlooked a missing link between the two canons who first discuss "the crying" of the creature: "it was Mr. Henslow that one, and Mr. Lyall was the other." Michael Cox notes that this could be a tribute to two "eminent Victorians," John Stevens Henslow (1796–1861) and Alfred Lyall (1795–1865), a philosopher. Henslow, as Cox notes, was a "botanist and naturalist on the *Beagle*, who presided over the celebrated debate on

85 Heales, "Easter Sepulchres," 307.

86 James, *A Thin Ghost*, 84.

87 These widespread metaphors are discussed at length in O. B. Hardison, Jr., "Darwin, Mutations, and the Origin of Medieval Drama," chapter 1 of *Christian Rite and Christian Drama in the Middle Ages* (Baltimore, MD: Johns Hopkins University Press, 1965), 1–34. Of particular note is the influential article by John M. Manly, "Literary Forms and the New Theory of the Origins of Species," *Modern Philology* 4.4 (1907): 1–19, which was published just prior to the time James is thought to have written "An Episode of Cathedral History." Manly, a leading authority on medieval drama in James's day, both challenged aspects of Darwinian analogies to medieval drama and strongly reinforced them in advocating for an updated model of dramatic evolution, one that would draw freely from "zoölogical theory" and Darwinian metaphors wherever useful (15). Manly also confirmed what Chambers and many others would argue: "we may feel a high degree of confidence that in studying the origin of the Visit to the Sepulcher – i.e. of the Easter trope, 'Quem quaeritis is sepulchro?' – we are studying the origin of the drama in mediaeval Europe" (7).

88 H. P. Lovecraft, *Dagon and Other Macabre Tales* (Sauk City, WI: Arkham House, 1965), 433.

89 James, *A Thin Ghost*, 106.

Darwin's *Origin of the Species* at the British Association in 1861."[90] In that light, however, a more natural selection for his counterpart would be Charles Lyell (1797–1875), who, along with Henslow, was an influential mentor to Darwin. The emphasis on gradual instead of cataclysmic change in Lyell's *Principles of Geology* (1830–33) helped set the stage for Darwin's theories, and so James's pairing of a "Henslow" with a "Lyall" seems a fairly clear allusion to evolution in this context. A constructive way to interpret such an allusion would be in light of the tale's patent disgust for sudden, catastrophic reforms and restorations. When Dean Burscough, "very set on the Gothic period," attempts to replace what has naturally evolved in the cathedral's long history with a romanticized anachronism – well, the results are predictably hairy.

And yet it is clear that the cathedral is able to absorb these disruptions, so that the haunting becomes simply another "episode" in cathedral history (one that, as Worby notes, "we don't tell to our visitors"). All along, the damage done by the monster is directed toward local victims dwelling in the "immediate neighborhood" of the cathedral, visiting illness and death on "house after house" by night. In the Easter context, the creature's nocturnal visitations inevitably recall those of the Passover *percussor*, "destroyer" (or "angel of death"),[91] but we should not be tempted to pursue too far the implications of these scriptural echoes (though a demonic reversal of the Resurrection – or, more precisely, Resurrection drama – is certainly a striking choice for a ghost story).[92] Nor is it wise, as we began this essay by observing, to parse too closely the demonology of the creature, whether or not we would identify it as a lamia, a vampire, or something else. It is what the creature represents – the disruption of a cathedral's relationship to a community – that really counts, and the community we find will not be delivered until a dark version of the ritual of the sepulcher has been acted out in a performance involving all levels of cathedral hierarchy, from the dean "tumbled over on the floor" to the angelic choirboys perched in the triforium – at once witnesses to and actors in the drama. Ultimately it is the communal performance of history that drives the monster off and clears the tomb, "repossessing" it by restoring the cathedral's past as a space for the living. Here, perhaps, is the more important significance of the lamia quotation, if we read it in its larger context in Isaiah which warns of the coming desolation of the Kingdom of Edom:

90 Cox, "Casting the Runes," 330 n. 219.

91 Exodus 12:13 ff.

92 The choice resonates with much of the anti-typological playfulness of the mystery plays themselves: Mak's sheep in the *Second Shepherd's Play* comes to mind.

> [F]rom generation to generation it shall lie waste; none shall pass through it for ever and ever. But the cormorant and the bittern shall possess it; the owl also and the raven shall dwell in it: and he shall stretch out upon it the line of confusion, and the stones of emptiness. They shall call the nobles thereof to the kingdom, but none shall be there, and all her princes shall be nothing. And thorns shall come up in her palaces, nettles and brambles in the fortresses thereof: and it shall be an habitation of dragons, and a court for owls. The wild beasts of the desert shall also meet with the wild beasts of the island, and the satyr shall cry to his fellow; the screech owl also shall rest there, and find for herself a place of rest.[93]

Franz Delitzsch, a contemporary of James, called the prophecy of God laying waste to Edom "the negative reverse of building,"[94] an apt description for what those forces of reform and restoration, crying out to each other across cathedral history, have carried out. In the face of such forces it is communal resilience that James seems most to stress, the inheritance and attentive stewardship by the living of structures from the past. To borrow a metaphor from *Edwin Drood*, he depicts an ultimate unification of the "live breath" of the local contemporary community with the "dead breath" of the past, all of it mediated for the antiquarian visitor by the sturdy voice of Mr. Worby – a witness to just one more episode in the history of a cathedral.

93 Isaiah 34:10–14, King James translation. The problems with verb tense and the rendering of biological and mythological nouns are discussed at the beginning of this essay.

94 Franz Delitzsch, *Biblical Commentary on the Prophecies of Isaiah*, trans. James Martin (Edinburgh: Clark, 1867), 72.

Rodin's *Gates of Hell* and Dante's *Inferno 7*: Fortune, the Avaricious and Prodigal, and the Question of Salvation

Aida Audeh

Introduction

Among the artists and illustrators in nineteenth-century France inspired by Dante's *Divine Comedy*, Auguste Rodin (1840–1917) is unique for the attention he accorded the seventh canto of *Inferno*.[1] The numerous drawings

1 Within the major illustrated editions published in France during this period representation of the events and figures in canto 7 is inconsistent and none is complete. Flaxman illustrates Dante and Virgil's initial encounter with Plutus; Etex includes an image of Dante and Virgil observing the Wrathful in the Styx as described in the last lines of canto 7 and treated fully in canto 8; Doré includes images of Plutus gnawing his hands (much like Carpeaux's statue of Ugolino) and of a group of sinners pushing what appear to be boulder-size bags of coins up a hill in Sisyphean fashion; D'Argent includes a minor illustration in the form of an in-text vignette of a fallen Plutus. Of the more than 200 works of art (including paintings, sculptures, drawings, engravings, and miscellaneous *objets d'art*) exhibited at the Paris salon between 1800 and 1900, none addresses the incidents or characters of *Inferno* 7. On Dante's reception in French art, c. 1750–1900, see the author's publications, especially "Dante in the Nineteenth Century: Visual Arts and National Identity," in *Dante in France*, ed. Russell Goulbourne et al. (Florence: Le Lettere, forthcoming); "Dufau's *La Mort d'Ugolin*: Dante, Nationalism, and French Art, ca. 1800," in *Dante in the Long Nineteenth Century: Nationality, Identity, and Appropriation*, ed. Aida Audeh and Nick Havely (Oxford: Oxford University Press, 2012), 141–63; "Gustave Doré's Illustrations for Dante's *Divine Comedy*: Innovation, Influence, and Reception," in *Studies in Medievalism XVIII: Defining Medievalism(s) II*, ed. Karl Fugelso (Cambridge: D. S. Brewer, 2010), 125–64; "Images of Dante's Exile in 19th-century France," *Annali d'Italianistica* 20 (2002): 235–58. On Rodin's interpretation of Dante's *Divine Comedy* see the author's publications, especially "Rodin's *Gates of Hell* and Dante's *Divine Comedy*: The Literal and Allegorical in the Paolo and Francesca Episode of *Inferno* 5," in *Dante in the Nineteenth Century: Reception, Portrayal, Popularization*, ed. Nick Havely (Bern: Peter Lang,

Rodin created as he read Dante's poem in preparation for his monumental sculpture, the *Gates of Hell* (Fig. 1), are remarkable for their treatment of the canto's primary figures. These figures' prominent placement in significant relief on the Gates suggests that the artist grasped the importance of canto 7 not only within the *Inferno*, but also in relation to the entire *Divine Comedy*. While ostensibly concerned with the punishment of the Avaricious and the Prodigal, central to *Inferno* 7 is the question of free will in relation to man's changing circumstances as administered by the goddess Fortune. Rodin came to Dante through the lens of nineteenth-century France and its interpretation of the poet's work, however, suggesting that his understanding of the issues raised by canto 7 was affected by the advent of the modern age and its skepticism.[2] And while Dante ultimately affirms man's ability to

2011), 181–98; "Rodin's Gates of Hell: Sculptural Illustration of Dante's *Divine Comedy*," in *Rodin: A Magnificent Obsession* (London: Merrell Holberton Publishers, 2006), 93–126; "Rodin's Three Shades and their Origin in Medieval Illustrations of Dante's *Inferno* XV and XVI," *Dante Studies* 117 (1999): 133–69; "Rodin's Gates of Hell and Aubé's Monument to Dante: Romantic Tribute to the Image of the Poet in 19th-century France," *The Journal of the Iris and B. Gerald Cantor Center for Visual Arts at Stanford University* (continuation of *The Stanford University Museum of Art Journal*) 1 (1998–99): 33–46. The author discusses Rodin's engagement with *Inferno* 7 to some extent in her dissertation and in her essay in *Rodin: A Magnificent Obsession*.

2 See, for example, Baudelaire's *Les fleurs du mal* in which the poet presents in "La mort des pauvres" the Prodigal wishing for death as his only salvation. Rodin illustrated *Les fleurs du mal* in the 1880s while working on the *Gates of Hell*, applying to Baudelaire's poetry many of the same forms he first developed for his interpretation of Dante's *Commedia*. Rodin's own engagement with Baudelaire is a fruitful area for further study, particularly in light of both artists' dialogue with Dante. On Rodin's illustrations for *Les fleurs du mal*, see Victoria Thorson, *Rodin Graphics: A Catalogue Raisonné of Drypoints and Book Illustrations* (San Francisco: The Fine Arts Museum of San Francisco, 1975). On Baudelaire's interest in Dante see James S. Patty, "Baudelaire's Knowledge and Use of Dante," *Studies in Philology* 53:4 (October 1956): 599–611; Mark Musa and John Porter Houston, "Dante, 'La Béatrice', and Baudelaire's Archaism," *Italica* 42:1 (March 1965): 169–74; Peter Collier, "Baudelaire and Dante," *Studi francesi* 34:102 (1990): 417–35. The Miser, of course, is best known in Molière's seventeenth-century play *L'avare*, the popularity of which has continued well into the present day. The Prodigal Son, particularly, proved highly adaptable to eighteenth-, nineteenth-, and even early twentieth-century motifs of alienation in the modern world. See, for example, David Steel, "The Return of the Prodigal Son: Gide, Millet and 'les marches du perron,'" *Word & Image* 17:4 (October–December 2001): 379–88; Joan E. Holmes, "Rodin's Prodigal Son and Rilke's *Malte*," in *Rilke and the Visual Arts* (Lawrence, KS: Coronado Press, 1982), 19–25; Dragos Gheorghiu, "Brancusi's 'Prodigal Son,'" *The Burlington Magazine* 138:1125 (December 1996): 822–26. On Dante's reception in the nineteenth century see *Dante and the Long Nineteenth Century*; on the recast Middle Ages during the period see *Consuming the Past: The Medieval Revival in fin-de-siècle France*, ed. Elizabeth Emery and Laura Morowitz (Burlington, VT: Ashgate, 2003). On Dante's reception in the arts generally, see Jean-Pierre Barricelli, *Dante's Vision and the Artist* (New York: Peter Lang, 1992); *Dante on View*, ed. Antonella Braida and Lusa Calè (Burlington, VT: Ashgate, 2007); *Dante, Cinema and Television*, ed. Amilcare

choose his course in response to the challenges in life wrought by change, where Rodin ends on the issue of free will and the possibility of salvation within the context of the modern world is left ultimately in question on his *Gates of Hell*.[3]

Inferno 7

Among the most subtle and complex of the poet's creations, *Inferno* 7 concerns Dante's encounter with the Avaricious and the Prodigal. Lodged between the Gluttons and the Wrathful (treated in cantos 6 and 8, respectively), these sinners in the fourth circle of hell are guilty of excessive concern for material possessions and wealth manifested in miserly hoarding (the Avaricious) or reckless squandering (the Prodigal). Framing this are Dante's brief encounter with the guardian figure Plutus, who attempts to block his entrance to this circle of hell, and Virgil's exposition on the nature of Fortune, who is described, significantly, as among the angelic intelligences ordained by God. Canto 7 ends with the pilgrim and his guide's initial encounter with the Wrathful in the marshy Styx as they transition to hell's sixth circle.

The apparent choppiness of the narrative and the Pilgrim's relatively detached manner throughout belie canto 7's internal coherence in service of the larger issue of Fortune's role in relation to Divine Providence and to man's proper response to both.[4] Contextualizing this discourse is the place of Pride/Greed as foundation for all sin treated in hell, represented here in microcosm by the Avaricious, the Prodigal, and Plutus. To communicate his meaning, Dante bends, transforms, and sometimes abandons chronological time and sequential narrative in favor of a descriptive mode emulating the qualities of divine revelation.[5] Dante achieves this through repetition of certain words and phrases within and between cantos and canticles of

A. Iannucci (Toronto: University of Toronto Press, 2004). None of these last sources treats Rodin's interpretation of Dante's works, however, nor is French reception in art or otherwise treated in most existing scholarship on the poet.

3 The complexity of Dante's exploration of the concept of man's free will in the *Commedia* is explored in John Freccero, "Dante's Firm Foot and the Journey without a Guide," in *Dante: The Poetics of Conversion*, ed. Rachel Jacoff (Cambridge, MA: Harvard University Press, 1986), 29–54. For an overview of the issue see Warren Ginsberg's entry on "Will" in *The Dante Encyclopedia*, ed. Richard Lansing (New York: Garland, 2000), 883–85.

4 Kenneth John Atchity, "*Inferno* VII: The Idea of Order," *Italian Quarterly* 12:47–48 (Winter–Spring 1969): 5–62. See also Barbara Newman, *God and the Goddesses: Vision, Poetry, and Belief in the Middle Ages* (Philadelphia: University of Pennsylvania Press, 2003). Newman explores the imbrication of classical deities and Christianity, including the goddess Fortuna as treated by Boethius.

5 Christopher Kleinhenz, "Dante and the Bible: Intertextual Approaches to the Divine Comedy," *Italica* 63:3 (Autumn 1986): 225–36.

the *Divine Comedy* and through displacement of action out of sequential time.[6] Similarly, Rodin rejects the use of ordered systems of perspective and chronological narrative on the Gates in favor of a nonlinear mode emulating Dante's poetic technique.[7] Where Dante repeats words and phrases, Rodin works in repetition of gesture and form throughout the Gates, thereby capturing the sense of resonance of meaning within and between cantos of *Inferno* and throughout the *Divine Comedy*. Sequentially, canto 7 begins with Dante's encounter with Plutus, moves on to the description of the Avaricious and Prodigal, and concludes with Virgil's exposition on Fortune. However, Fortune is truly the controlling principle of canto 7 and its primary tie to the rest of the *Commedia*.

Fortune

Departing from the pagan conception of a fickle and irrational goddess and from Christian ideology which recast her in somewhat less arbitrary terms, Dante describes Fortune as a vital performer of Divine Providence, of God's will.[8] Spoken through Virgil as the personification of the highest level of human reason, the poet's exposition on Fortune is the first lengthy theoretical digression of the *Divine Comedy*, marking its significance as a controlling aspect of the poet's larger belief system.[9] As such it is worth laying out in its entirety as the words given to Virgil explain most clearly the poet's innovative conception of the goddess:

> He whose wisdom transcends all, made the heavens and gave them guides, so that every part shines to every part, equally distributing the light. In like manner, for worldly splendors He ordained a general minister and guide who should in due time transfer the vain goods from race to race, and from one to another blood, beyond the prevention of human wit, so that one race rules and another languishes, pursuant to her judgment, which is hidden like the snake in the grass. Your wisdom cannot withstand her: she foresees, judges, and pursues

6 Atchity, "*Inferno* VII," esp. 9–19.

7 On Rodin's early creative process regarding the form of the Gates in relation to Renaissance precedent see Albert Elsen, *The Gates of Hell* (Stanford, CA: Stanford University Press, 1985), 35–55.

8 Howard R. Patch, *The Goddess Fortuna in Mediaeval Literature* (New York: Octagon Books, 1967), esp. 18–20; Vincenzo Cioffari, *The Conception of Fortune and Fate in the Works of Dante* (Cambridge, MA: Dante Society of America, 1940); and *Fortune in Dante's Fourteenth Century Commentators* (Cambridge, MA: Dante Society of America, 1944).

9 Robin Kirkpatrick, "Dante's Fortuna: *Inferno* VII," in *Dante Soundings: Eight Literary and Historical Essays*, ed. David Nolan (Dublin: Irish Academic Press, 1981), 4–27.

> her reign, as theirs the other gods. Her changes know no truce. Necessity compels her to be swift, so fast do men come to their turns. This is she who is much reviled even by those who ought to praise her, but do wrongfully blame her and defame her. But she is blest and does not hear it. Happy with the other primal creatures she turns her sphere and rejoices in her bliss. (*Inf.* 7.73–96)[10]

In this description, Dante, speaking through Virgil, contrasts the pagan conception of the fickle goddess, whose reason seems to those ignorant of her divine nature "hidden like the snake in the grass" and who therefore "wrongfully blame her and defame her," with the recast vision of a beatified intelligence who acts as a "general minister and guide" distributing "the vain goods" in the earthly realm according to God's wisdom which "transcends all." She is oblivious to man's protests and "rejoices in her bliss."

Dante's divinely ordained Fortune caused his earliest commentators and modern scholars alike to interrogate implications of determinism. Ultimately, these critics settled on an interpretation which not only affirms the existence of free will in Dante's theology, but credits the challenges posed by Fortune's turning of her sphere and thus her constant redistribution of material wealth as a necessary condition for its exercise in the form of choice to adhere to or stray from the "straight way" (the path of goodness, toward God).[11]

Central to this interpretation are the numerous references to Fortune throughout the *Divine Comedy*. Particularly relevant are those which tie the poet's conceptualization of Fortune expressed by Virgil in canto 7 to questions of free will, destiny, and his own historical condition of exile.[12] This association is announced in *Inferno* 1 as Dante begins his journey as a pilgrim lost in the "dark wood," having strayed from the right path. As he attempts to regain the "straight way" he is pushed back by three beasts, the most threatening of which, the wolf ("lupa" – a name Virgil also uses in canto 7 to describe Plutus), is emblematic for greed and covetousness. The poet's pronouncements on Fortune throughout the *Commedia* are intensely personal as he struggled to find the workings of God's order within the events of his life which resulted in his banishment from Florence.

10 All English quotations used in this essay are from Dante Alighieri, *The Divine Comedy: Inferno*, translated and with commentary by Charles S. Singleton (Princeton, NJ: Bollingen/Princeton University Press, 1989).

11 Kirkpatrick, "Dante's Fortuna."

12 Kirkpatrick, "Dante's Fortuna," esp. 5–6; Amilcare A. Iannucci, "*Inferno* XV.95–96: Fortune's Wheel and the Villainy of Time," *Quaderni d'Italianistica* 3:1 (1982): 1–11; Vincenzo Cioffari, "Lectura Dantis: *Paradiso* VIII," *Dante Studies* 90 (1972): 93–108.

Within iconographic traditions related to literary and visual depiction of Fortune, pagan and Christian conceptions mingled and joined over centuries, with certain elements consistent and characteristic of her representation.[13] And while certain elements are, in a sense, standard, there are aspects of Dante's description of Fortune which are absolutely unique: most important, his conception of Fortune as a divine intelligence completely subservient to God's will.[14]

This brings us to Rodin's understanding of Fortune evinced by the large and well-defined figure of the goddess on the *Gates of Hell* (Figs 2 and 3). Note the following significant aspects of the figure of Fortune on the Gates: the figure is clearly represented as female; she is positioned horizontally over a closed tomb-like architectural feature; her body is draped; she is blindfolded and winged; she holds in her right hand a wheel; and, finally, she is doubled (seen most clearly in Fig. 3) as just behind her and a bit lower down is a twin form whose nude shoulders and uplifted chin are most visible and whose eyes are covered by the primary figure's wing and blindfold. Rodin arrived at this final conception of Fortune on the Gates through a series of working drawings created as he read Dante's poem with close attention to her significance.

First, Rodin's sketch (Fig. 4) depicts an elegant female form, loosely draped to expose only partially her young and beautiful body, while her eyes are softly closed in accord with a hint of a blissful smile. She holds an object in her left hand which resembles, alternatively, a wheel or a sickle. This drawing suggests Rodin's attention to several significant aspects of Fortune as Dante defines her in the *Divine Comedy* generally and in *Inferno* 7 specifically.

Her softly draped body, beauty, elegance, and soft smile, carried through to the sculpted version, recall Virgil's description of her blessed state: "Happy with the other primal creatures she turns her sphere and rejoices in her bliss" (*Inf.* 7.95–96). Her closed eyes, elaborated in the sculpted version through use of the more obvious draping blindfold, recall the iconographic tradition for representation of Fortune (both pagan and Christian views of her) which refers to her distribution of wealth with no attention to the merit of the favored/disfavored.

However, in Dante's conception the reference to Fortune's "blindness" has additional meaning in the sense that it relates to her existence as an angelic intelligence.[15] Virgil explains that because Fortune is blessed, she does not

13 Patch, *The Goddess Fortuna*, esp. 42–48; Newman, *God and the Goddesses*.

14 Patch, *The Goddess Fortuna*, esp. 18–20; Christopher Kleinhenz, "The Visual Tradition of *Inferno* 7: The Relationship of Plutus and Fortune," *Lectura Dantis* 22–23 (Spring–Fall 1998): 247–78.

15 Atchity, "*Inferno* VII," 26–29.

hear man's curses and complaints (in Italian, "non ode"). He also explains that to those who are ignorant of God's will working through Fortune, her judgment (in Italian, "lo giudicio") is hidden "like the snake in the grass" (in Italian, "occulto come in erba l'angue"). Rodin's notation on the upper left corner of the page, "le [sic] volonté," transcribed from this passage in the French translation with which he worked ("dont la volonté est cachée comme le serpent sous l'herbe"), clearly indicates he had in mind this aspect of the sinners' perception of Fortune as he created this drawing.[16]

Thus, in Dante's conception, from the point of the view of the Avaricious and Prodigal working through their limited knowledge and material senses – those who curse Fortune most loudly in this round and who in life attempted to circumvent her rule through hoarding and squandering – the goddess's actions are unjust and nonsensical. From the perspective of God, however, Fortune's actions represent perfect order – symbolized by the perfect circle of her wheel and its rotation. It is, in fact, the Avaricious and Prodigal who are "blind" and "deaf" to Fortune and to God's larger order. Their *contrapasso*, in which they turn in incomplete half-circles for eternity, embodies the imperfection and limitation of their understanding. Thus, the metaphor of blindness refers not only to Fortune's eternal turning regardless of the merit of those on the rim of her wheel who are uplifted or downcast but, in the context of canto 7 and the *Commedia* more generally, also to the separation between the conditions of the blessed (Fortune) and the damned (all those in hell and, specifically in this context, the Avaricious and Prodigal). Further, canto 7 makes clear that Fortune herself does not exist within hell, or even within the earthly realm of life. She exists in canto 7 only through Virgil's exposition which is, in itself, a remarkable example of clarity of discourse glowing between moments of darkness and coarseness of language: the framing motifs of Plutus (who "clucks" nonsense at Virgil and Dante as they enter the fourth circle) and the Avaricious and Prodigal

16 While there remains some question as to which of many nineteenth-century French translations of Dante's *Commedia* available to Rodin the artist used, those of Rivarol and Artaud de Montor are repeatedly suggested as likely. Rodin's particular choice of words on this and other drawings suggests that, at least as it concerns his engagement with canto 7 of *Inferno*, he used Artaud's translation. Further, Artaud offers an extensive footnote concerning Virgil's exposition of Fortune which quotes directly Ginguené's *Hist. litt. d'Italie*, emphasizing the uniqueness and beauty of Dante's conception: "On ne trouve dans aucun poëte, un plus beau portrait de la Fortune. [. . .] Dante a profité d'une idée de l'ancienne philosophie, adoptée par le christianisme, de cette idée d'une intelligence secondaire chargée de présider à chacune des sphères célestes [. . .]. C'est un de ces morceaux de Dante qui sont rarement cités, mais que relisent souvent ceux qui ont une fois vancu les difficultés et goûté les beautés sévères de ce poëte inégal et sublime." Dante Alighieri, *La divine comédie*, trans. Artaud de Montor, 3rd edn. (Paris: Librairie de Firmin Didot Frères, 1846), 29.

(who yell insults at one another resulting in nothing more than a general cacophony) at the opening of the canto, and the wrathful in the Styx (who burble and moan in a murky swamp) which closes it.[17]

Thus, in this drawing, and on the Gates, Fortune is separated from the damned around her through her blindness to their state and their blindness to hers; her vision is celestial and eternal while theirs is material and limited. Significantly, Fortune is the only figure among the hundreds present on the Gates who is draped. This draping of her form separates her from the naked damned and indicates that, as typical of similarly draped angels and beatified figures in medieval Last Judgment scenarios, she exists in the realm of the blessed. And although a few small figures on the Gates are winged, none is given the prominent position and serene countenance of Fortune as she is presented here.

The object resembling a wheel or a sickle is an interesting detail in the Philadelphia sketch which suggests Rodin's understanding of the significance of the figure of Fortune beyond this passage in canto 7 of *Inferno*. Both objects – wheel and sickle – are traditionally associated with Fortune.[18] The wheel, obviously, represents the turning of favor in both pagan and Christian traditions. In Christian tradition, however, the circular form as metaphor for the perfection of God's order (also the concept of the rota/rosa expressed through Fortune/Rose windows in many Gothic cathedrals in France) is added to the pagan conception.[19] The sickle, traditionally associated with both farming trade (and thus the turning of the seasons of the year, harvest, passage of time as referenced through Saturn/Cronos, etc.) and with death (more often portrayed as the larger scythe held by the "Grim Reaper" but also associated with Saturn as devourer of his own children), refers in the context of the *Divine Comedy* to an important reference to Fortune in association with time/death which appears in *Inferno* 15.[20] Here Dante converses

17 Atchity, "*Inferno* VII," esp. 18–19 and 26–29.

18 Patch, *The Goddess Fortuna*, see 115–20 on Fortune's relationship to Time/Death and 147–77 on Fortune's wheel.

19 On the Rota/Rosa and its relationship to Dante's Fortune and the *Commedia* see John Leyerle, "The Rose-Wheel Design and Dante's *Paradiso*," *University of Toronto Quarterly* 46 (1977): 280–308. Leyerle demonstrates that the rose window in many Gothic cathedrals functions toward the interior of the church structure (thus in the spiritual realm) as a representation of both the heavens (the rosa) and Fortune's wheel (as God sees the turning of Fortune's wheel as manifestation of his divine plan) operating in eternal and timeless harmony, while to the exterior (the earthly realm) only Fortune's wheel (the rota) as bringer of temporally ruled change is visible. Rota/Rosa windows are found at Beauvais and Amiens; Rodin is sure to have known these structures as they are included in his book recounting his travels to France's churches, *Les cathédrales de France* (Paris: Librairie Armand Colin, 1914).

20 Iannucci, "*Inferno* XV.95–96"; Amilcare A. Iannucci, "Saturn in Dante," in *Saturn from*

with his mentor, Brunetto Latini (condemned to hell for sodomy), who in a long discourse warns his former student of his impending political troubles and exile. Dante indicates his readiness to accept the future, come what may, including his exile as "predicted" by Latini, concluding, "let Fortune whirl her wheel as pleases her, and the yokel his mattock" (*Inf.* 15.88–96). This passage underscores the personal nature of Dante's concern with Fortune and its relation to his painful experience of exile; Dante's task throughout the *Commedia* is to reconcile his own shortcomings and those of his fellow man, among them many that he loved and respected in life such as Brunetto Latini, with what he considered God's infinite justice and order.

Thus, Rodin retains the reference to both the wheel held in the sculpted Fortune's right hand (significantly, it is the only material object included among the figures on the Gates) and the passage of time and inevitability of death implied by the sickle through the goddess's placement on the Gates atop what appears to be a closed tomb. Rodin communicates the personal nature of Dante's concern for Fortune in relation to God's order through the prominence he allows the goddess in relation to the Thinker as Dante/Poet/Everyman on the Gates in the location traditionally given to Christ in Last Judgment tympanum sculpture (clearly a model for Rodin's Gates). As I have argued elsewhere, Rodin utilizes differences of scale and relief as a physical replication of Dante's literary device of "spotlight" figures or characters throughout the *Commedia* whereby individuals are removed from the anonymous masses Dante encounters through momentary suspension of their place within the allegory of punishment (as it concerns *Inferno* or *Purgatorio*) or of blessedness (as it concerns *Paradiso*).[21] Rodin's horizontal placement of Fortune in such large scale and her prominent relief (which would be at about eye level of a viewer standing before the Gates) just over the conspicuous tomb structure put her in immediate dialogue with other "spotlight" figures on the Gates – most obviously the Thinker who gazes down below to Fortune and the damned around her.

Rodin's sketch (Fig. 5) depicts again a lovely young female form, partially draped. She appears to stand on what is clearly shown as a wheel and is surrounded by figures of infants. Fortune's association with carnal love through the presence of cupid-like forms is common to traditional iconography, as is her position standing on a wheel or sphere rather than holding one.[22] Similarly, in the sculpted version just below Fortune's wheel, adjacent to the tomb structure, we see infants. Ostensibly relatable to the mothers and

Antiquity to the Renaissance, ed. Massimo Ciavolella and Amilcare A. Iannucci (Toronto: University of Toronto Italian Studies, 1992), 51–67.

21 See Audeh, "Dante in the Nineteenth Century."

22 Patch, *The Goddess Fortuna*, 90–98.

infants included in Limbo as described in canto 4 where virtuous heathens and unbaptized children are found, these babes in relation to Fortune within traditional iconography are references to love through association with Venus. Dante makes clear throughout the *Commedia* that love is the driving force of all God's actions and underlies man's behavior, both good and bad. Right love compels man toward harmony with God; perverse love compels him to sin as in the case of the Avaricious and Prodigal who wrongly direct their love toward material possessions and wealth. Fortune's perfection, exemplified by her beatitude and her eternally turning sphere/wheel, is a manifestation of divine love, while Venus-ruled carnal love, according to medieval Christian thought, is often confused for the divine by man.[23]

Rodin's understanding that Dante's reference to love goes beyond that associated with Venus to the divine associated with God is further suggested by his inclusion of an infant in his sketch (Fig. 6) to the right of the primary female form sketched darkly in the foreground. This primary form is shadowed by another female form, lightly sketched, just behind her. This doubling of Fortune is again within iconographic traditions of both the pagan and Christian conceptions, referencing her dual nature as providing both good and bad fortune to earthly beings.[24]

Plutus

Another figure, apparently male, is presented as collapsed beneath the more prominent of the two female forms (his head appears between her feet while he seems to clutch at her right foot with his right hand). This male form suggests a reference to Fortune's antithesis in canto 7 – Plutus. Plutus, in his raging and babbling in the opening lines of this canto, in his role as pagan god of wealth, and under the similar name of Pluto (the god of the underworld), represents excessive pride through reference to the incoherence of Nimrod and the Tower of Babel. He is emblematic of both the Avaricious and the Prodigal in their excessive concern for material goods.[25]

23 Cioffari, "Lectura Dantis: *Paradiso* VIII." See also Newman, *God and the Goddesses*, 182, regarding Dante's treatment of love.

24 Patch, *The Goddess Fortuna*, 42–49.

25 On the relationship of Plutus to Nimrod and the Tower of Babel, see Atchity, "*Inferno* VII," esp. 30–40. On the relationship of Saturn and Fortune in literary and visual iconographic traditions, see Kirkpatrick, "Dante's Fortuna," esp. 17–23; Kleinhenz, "The Visual Tradition of *Inferno* 7"; Kleinhenz, "Plutus, Fortune, and Michael: The Eternal Triangle," *Dante Studies* 98 (1980): 35–52.

Plutus tries but is wholly unable to stop Dante and Virgil from entering this round when rebuked by Virgil:

> "Pape Satàn, pape Satàn aleppe!" Plutus began with a clucking voice; and that gentle sage who knew all, said, to reassure me, "Do not let your fear harm you; for, whatever power he have, he shall not keep us from descending this rock." Then he turned back to that bloated visage and said, "Silence, accursed wolf! Consume yourself inwardly with your own rage. Not without cause is this journey to the depth; so is it willed on high, there where Michael avenged the proud rebellion." As sails swollen by the wind fall in a heap when the mainmast snaps, so fell that cruel beast to the ground. (*Inf.* 7.1–15)

Dante's description of Plutus emphasizes a sense of inflation masking a central hollowness ("bloated visage"; "as sails swollen by the wind") as metaphor for the excessive importance accorded essentially empty material wealth (the "vain goods" which Fortune transfers among people and nations) so coveted in life by those condemned to this circle of hell. Thus, the reference in Rodin's sketch to a fallen Plutus groveling at the feet of a doubled Fortune captures the essential relationship between the imbalanced souls who, in defiance of Fortune, chase material wealth and power through hoarding or squandering, and the goddess herself who distributes these "vain goods" with knowledge and acceptance of her role in God's order. These Avaricious and Prodigal, symbolized by Plutus, are ultimately held to account for their attempt to circumvent God's order as enacted by Fortune and are thus condemned to hell, among the "fallen."

Rodin's attention to Plutus is also found in a drawing (Fig. 7) which portrays a male figure, bloated in a manner similar to the depiction of the Avaricious and Prodigal in Figure 10, falling backwards. The bloated figure appears to be supported as he falls by two other male figures. Rodin's notation, barely visible in the lower section of the drawing, reads "le transport de Plutus," clearly identifying the subject. The image of Plutus falling backwards in response to Virgil's scolding is also found in the earliest manuscript illustrations of the *Divine Comedy*, so Rodin is well within tradition. While Dante does not describe "helpers" assisting or transporting Plutus, Rodin here may be referencing Plutus' role as guardian figure and emblem of the Avaricious and Prodigal in this circle of hell: Plutus – as embodiment of their excessive concern for material wealth and of the sins of Avarice and Prodigality – is metaphorically "sustained" in a position of power by them. The Avaricious and Prodigal elevate this false god, this antithesis of God's Fortune, in place of the divinely ordered distribution of wealth they try to defeat by their sinful means of hoarding and squandering.

While Rodin does not represent him directly on the *Gates of Hell* as an individual figure, Plutus is referenced there through the presence of Fortune as his opposite and through the overall ordering of the Gates in the manner of a Last Judgment. As discussed above, Virgil rebukes Plutus, described in the final line of canto 6 as "the great enemy" ("il gran nemico"; *Inf.* 6.115), with a stern speech in which the Archangel Michael's quelling of the rebel angels is mentioned as a symbol of God's greater power against those of excessive pride. As pride and greed are the roots, in Christian theology, of all sin – most particularly the sin of the first man, Adam, whose fall led to the original sin which stains all mankind – the ultimate judgment in which Michael aids Christ as the blessed are separated from the damned for eternity is implicated in Virgil's reference to the Archangel in these first lines of canto 7.[26] Rodin's original plans called for the placement of Adam and Eve as freestanding figures just before the Gates in reference to original sin; the Thinker on the Gates takes the position usually occupied by Christ within Last Judgment scenes such as that at Saint-Lazare Cathedral at Autun and, most obviously, Michelangelo's fresco of the subject in the Sistine Chapel.[27] Plutus, as representative of that essential greed and pride, nemesis of Fortune, and in Virgil's lines also of Michael, is thus also embodiment of the Antichrist himself as enemy of Christ and ultimately God. Damnation, the subject of the *Gates of Hell*, references in its entirety the larger presence of evil embodied by Plutus and Lucifer such that Rodin need not represent them as individual figures.

Avaricious and Prodigal

The maritime imagery referenced in Plutus' fall ("As sails swollen by the wind fall in a heap when the mainmast snaps, so fell that cruel beast to the ground"; *Inf.* 7.13–15) is continued in the poet's encounter with the Avaricious and Prodigal and is also traditionally associated with Fortune.[28] Thus,

26 Kleinhenz, "The Visual Tradition of *Inferno* 7"; Kleinhenz, "Plutus, Fortune, and Michael."

27 Michelangelo's engagement with Dante has been explored by Bernardine Barnes, "Metaphorical Painting: Michelangelo, Dante, and the Last Judgment," *Art Bulletin* 77 (1995): 65–81. Rodin's own engagement with Dante in relation to his admiration for Michelangelo is ripe for exploration given the complexity of each artist's views on art and spirituality but is, unfortunately, beyond the scope of this essay.

28 On Fortune's relationship to maritime imagery see Patch, *The Goddess Fortuna*, esp. 82–83 and 101–7; see also Kleinhenz, "The Visual Tradition of *Inferno* 7." On maritime imagery in relationship to the entire canto see Kirkpatrick, "Dante's Fortuna," esp. 8–9.

leaving Plutus who falls in a heap in response to Virgil's harsh words, Dante sees and describes the Avaricious and Prodigal:

> Ah, justice of God! who crams together so many new travails and penalties as I saw? And why does our guilt so waste us? As does the wave, there over Charybdis, breaking itself against the wave it meets, so must the folk here dance their round. Here I saw far more people than elsewhere, both on the one side and on the other, howling loudly, rolling weights, which they pushed with their chests; they clashed together, and then right there each wheeled round, rolling back his weight, shouting, "Why do you hoard?" and "Why do you squander?" Thus they returned along the gloomy circle on either hand to the opposite point, shouting at each other again their reproachful refrain; then, having reached that point, each turned back through his half-circle to the next joust. (*Inf.* 7.19–35)

Among the briefest of descriptions given in *Inferno* of the *contrapasso* of a group of sinners, it packs great complexity which is reflected in Rodin's efforts to work through its meaning. On the Gates Rodin treats the Avaricious (Fig. 8) and Prodigal (Fig. 9) separately, yet expresses their essential unity as driven by one and the same sin through use of gesture and association. Rodin arrived at this elegant solution for their representation through his working drawings which fall into three categories of representation: both groups of sinners together; Avaricious alone; Prodigal alone.

Rodin produced only one drawing representing the Avaricious and Prodigal together (Fig. 10). In the upper right corner of the sketch Rodin has noted "avares et prodigues" making very clear the association with canto 7 of *Inferno*. Rodin has placed Dante and Virgil in the center of the circle (noting "Dante" on the back of the larger of the two figures). While canto 7 describes the sinners as "rolling weights, which they pushed with their chests" ("voltando pesi per forza di poppa"; *Inf.* 7.27), Rodin does not illustrate literally the undefined "weights" ("pesi"). Rather, the artist has understood the metaphor Dante employs here – that these are not literal weights but spiritual ones which represent the burden exerted upon their souls by their excessive concern for material possessions in life – and, seen, rightly, in tandem with the references to the hollowness of Plutus' power (his "bloated" visage, his falling like "swollen" sails suddenly devoid of their mainmast), seems to bloat these nude figures as if this emptiness is carried within themselves. Similar to his depiction of a bloated Plutus falling backwards (see Fig. 7), in this sketch the legs, arms, and chests of the sinners are inflated, as balloons, contrary to the figure of Dante in the center whose back and buttocks are well defined and muscular. As in the text, where no sinner is identified individually, Rodin's Avaricious and Prodigal are subsumed by their desires and become the sin itself.[29]

The sinners are represented in circular formation as described, with Dante and Virgil in a position however *not described* in the text; rather, Rodin seems to combine the reference to the circularity of their endless toil with the reference later in the canto to Fortune's "wheel" or "sphere," also endlessly turning. In this, Dante and Virgil take the place of the wheel's hub – the central axis upon which all turns – while the sinners occupy the wheel's rim as in traditional representations of Fortune where figures on the rim would signify those in various stages of receiving favorable/unfavorable events. As Fortune's wheel, forever turning in perfect circular formation, reflects the eternal and perfect turning of God's ordered cosmos, the sinners' "turning" is incomplete, yet constant in this imperfection, as perfect punishment for their imbalance and lack of measure in life. In Rodin's drawing, then, Dante and Virgil's placement at the center of the circle – the hub of the wheel – represents right measure or balance in harmony with God's order and Fortune's just actions.[30] Typical of his working practice, Rodin did not directly transcribe the overview of the *contrapasso* represented in this sketch to the *Gates of Hell*. Rather, it becomes the basis for further exploration of the natures of the Avaricious and the Prodigal as separately defined yet essentially equivalent sins.

Returning to the figure of the Avaricious on the Gates (see Fig. 8), Rodin presents a nude male figure clutching a nude female figure. Two drawings relate to this final sculptural expression of the sin. The first (Fig. 11), represents a lone male figure, hunched inward as he apparently lurches forward while looking over his shoulder at some unseen threat. Rodin has noted in the upper central portion of the page "ombre avare," specifying his sin. The Avaricious clutches an object which Rodin defined in quick strokes of dark ink as a coin bag upturned and spilling its contents to the ground between the sinner's legs.

In this drawing Rodin refers to the familiar form of the Miser, common in Romanesque and Gothic cathedral sculpture throughout France, who came to personify from the thirteenth century onward the sin of Avarice.[31] In

29 Atchity, "*Inferno* VII."

30 Leyerle, "The Rose-Wheel Design."

31 For discussion of the development of concern for and iconography related to Avarice and its personification in the Miser see Adolf Katzenellenbogen, *Allegories of the Vices and Virtues* (New York: W. W. Norton, 1964); Richard Newhauser, *The Early History of Greed* (Cambridge: Cambridge University Press, 2000). See also Priscilla Baumann, "Miser and Userer Iconography in Romanesque Auvergne: Variations on a Theme," *Les arts profanes du*

traditional iconography the Miser most often clutches a money bag which sometimes hangs about his neck (Dante reserved this specific imagery for the sin of Usury, described in canto 17, which in medieval imagery was often conflated with the figure of the Miser and the sin of Avarice). Alternatively, the Miser may be shown with a treasure chest, sitting on it or otherwise holding down its lid to prevent escape or loss of its contents. The central idea conveyed by traditional imagery is the Avaricious's futile grasping for the material possession he covets, empty of the spiritual value he should seek in God. Rodin's "avare" attempts to fill the emptiness of his heart and soul, emphasized by his contorted position forming a reversed letter "C", by clinging desperately to the wealth he continually loses. His frowning face and sidelong glance betray his despair and fear of loss which control him: the denial of, and attempt to escape from, the inevitable turning of Fortune's wheel is the essential nature of his sin.

Retained in the sculptural version on the Gates is the sense of desperate grasping, as Rodin replaces the inanimate coin bag with the body of a nude woman. In this Rodin also references traditional iconography, frequently found in medieval imagery, associating the figure of the Miser and the sin of Avarice with the sin of Lust or Luxuria personified in female form: these sins – Avarice and Lust – were conceptualized as gendered results of the root vice of cupidity or greed.[32] Both represent desire to possess and retain against the passage of time and actions of Fortune things of earthly rather than spiritual value: the male wishes to retain his wealth while the female wishes to retain her beauty. By virtue of its awkward placement, the nude female form on the Gates, grasped by the male figure, appears headless (the head is actually present but largely hidden beneath the male's overly muscled and extended right arm), emphasizing her lack of individual identity. She has become only an object to be possessed while he has become only desperate misguided desire.

Another drawing concerning Avarice (Fig. 12) is truly remarkable in demonstrating Rodin's close study and understanding of Dante's poem. Rodin again captures the essential nature of Avarice as desperate grasping. The human figure, rather ambiguously gendered this time, echoes the gesture of the "avare" in the Musée Rodin drawing. Absent, however, is the money bag, the traditional iconographic accessory and symbol of the Miser. By

moyen âge 5:2 (1996): 151–60, and Pamela Berger, "Avarice, Money, and Judgment Day," in *Secular Sacred: 11th–16th Century Works from the Boston Public Library and the Museum of Fine Arts* (Chicago: University of Chicago Press, 2006), unpaginated.

32 On the association of Avarice and Luxuria see Katzenellenbogen, *Allegories*, 58–59; Newhauser, *The Early History*, 81–82; and Alfred A. Triolo, "Ira, Cupiditas, Libido: The Dynamics of Human Passion in the *Inferno*," *Dante Studies* 95 (1977): 1–37.

removing the money bag and de-emphasizing obvious maleness, Rodin has referenced the figure and gesture of Eve, a sculpted freestanding form before the Gates (Fig. 13), as ultimate sign of cupidity (desire, in Eve's case, for power, thus considered an aspect of Pride/Superbia which is root of all sin).[33] In a sense, then, Rodin combines male and female forms into one image in this drawing, embodying the linked figures of Avarice and Lust as they are expressed on the Gates in sculpted form.

Most importantly, Rodin has placed the figure in the drawing in a blue wash of color, from its feet up to its waist, signifying water. Noted in the upper left corner is just one word which reveals Rodin's intent: "Charybe" (sic), referencing the French word "Charybde" found in the translation of Dante's text likely used by the artist.[34] It originates in this line describing the *contrapasso* of the Avaricious and Prodigal: "As does the wave, there over Charybdis, breaking itself against the wave it meets, so must the folk here dance their round" (*Inf.* 7.22–24). Dante uses maritime imagery throughout canto 7 to tie together its seemingly disparate sections devoted to Plutus, the

33 On Cupidity as associated with Adam and Eve's fall, see Newhauser, *The Early History*, esp. 92–94.

34 In this it is certain that Rodin used Artaud de Montor's translation rather than Rivarol's: Rivarol omits entirely the use of the word "Charybde," referring instead to the rock, Scylla, associated with it: "comme on entend les hurlemens de Scylla, quand le flot qui jaillit, heurte le flot qui s'engoufre." Dante Alighieri, *L'enfer*, trans. Antoine de Rivarol (Paris: Chez Cussac, 1788), 93. Artaud, however, translates the passage thus: "comme les ondes amenées par des courants opposés, se heurtent avec fracas, près de l'écueil de Charybde." Dante Alighieri, *La divine comédie*, 27. That neither Rivarol nor Artaud included in the notes to this canto any explanation of the reference to Scylla or Charybdis suggests that they assumed their readers were familiar with the metaphor beyond its use in this passage of *Inferno* 7. French dictionaries of the eighteenth and nineteenth centuries reflect the understanding that Charybdis and Scylla represent two nearly unavoidable dangers. For example, from the *Dictionnaire de l'Académie française* (6th edn., 1835): "CHARYBDE. s. m. (On prononce Carybde.) Nom que les anciens donnaient à un gouffre situé dans le détroit de Sicile, vis-à-vis d'un écueil appelé Scylla. On le rapporte ici à cause de son emploi dans cette phrase proverbiale et figurée, Tomber de Charybde en Scylla, En voulant éviter un mal, tomber dans un autre." Further, Artaud's use of the word "écueil" to describe Charybdis actually captures the geographic materiality of Scylla, while at the same time referring to moral danger. Again, according to the *Dictionnaire de l'Académie française* (6th edn., 1835): "ÉCUEIL. s. m. (On prononce Ékeuil.) Rocher dans la mer. Dangereux écueil. Naviguer dans une mer pleine d'écueils. Éviter un écueil. Donner sur un écueil. Ce vaisseau s'est brisé contre un écueil. Ce port est fermé par des écueils. Il se dit, figurément, Des choses dangereuses pour la vertu, l'honneur, la fortune, la réputation, etc. Le monde est plein d'écueils. Il faut éviter cela comme un écueil. C'est un écueil où les plus avisés font naufrage." Thus, Victor Hugo used the metaphor to describe the barricades of June 1848 in *Les misérables* in the chapter titled "La Charybde du Faubourg Saint-Antoine et La Scylla du Faubourg du Temple."

Avaricious and Prodigal, and Fortune. More specifically, however, Dante here refers to a particular geographic location in the Straits of Messina. Known since antiquity for the whirlpool created by the clashing of the Tyrrhenian and Ionian seas at that location on the one side and the massive rock known as Scylla on the other, the name "Charybdis" ("Cariddi" in the original Italian) was synonymous with Avarice in Dante's era.[35] Conceptualized as a massive vortex akin to the insatiable devouring desire for material possession characteristic of Avarice, Charybdis together with Scylla came to symbolize the extremes of hoarding and squandering, respectively – the dangers awaiting those who are unable to achieve right measure and balance in the face of Fortune's turning wheel. Thus, occasional manuscript illustrations of the *Commedia* place the Avaricious and Prodigal in or near water.[36] Further, traditional iconography sometimes presents Fortune in or near waves, near a rock in water, or on or near a ship navigating between these two extremes. Good Fortune was often portrayed as a ship with full sails, Bad Fortune with a sinking vessel.[37] As the sailor must find, through careful and measured navigation, the stillness in the eye of a storm, the good Christian in harmony with God must find the balance in the center and avoid both the "rock and the hard place," collision with which (one or the other) results in destruction of the soul. From the perspective of the sinner, the waves, vortex, and rock appear chaotic and impassable, just as the pushing of unmanageable weights in continually incomplete half-circles appears from the limited perspective of the sinners in canto 7 meaningless and haphazard. From the view of Dante and Virgil, allowed by divine will to suspend the normal order of hell to witness the workings of God's justice there, the eternal nature of the sinners' imperfect half-circles is in itself a perfect and complete expression of this divine will and order.[38]

Dante's use of the metaphor is not limited to Avarice, but applies equally to both types of sinners, though he does, in canto 7, indicate his abhorrence of greed as a particular affliction of clerics, popes, and cardinals (see *Inf.* 7.36–48). And while "Charybdis" traditionally referenced Avarice, the sin of Prodigality was considered in Dante's time as subsidiary to and indeed connected closely to it in that, operating in turn, squandering is the result of over concern for other material pleasures attained through wealth. This

35 Gino Casagrande and Christopher Kleinhenz, "*Inferno* VII: Cariddi e L'Avarizia," *Aevum* 54 (1980): 340–44; Michele d'Andrea, "Dinamica della Pena di Avari e de Prodighi," *Collana di cultura* 42 (1985): 169–90.

36 Kleinhenz, "The Visual Tradition of *Inferno* 7," 248.

37 Patch, *The Goddess Fortuna*, 101–7 and 131–32.

38 Atchity, "*Inferno* VII," 24–26.

squandering then leads to poverty, which in turn leads to desire to acquire more wealth and to hoard it, then again disperse it in wasteful spending as a symbol of its power and social status.[39] Closely connected to the rise of the capitalist money-driven economies of Europe in the twelfth and thirteenth centuries, the rise of concern for Avarice as a sin also related to advocacy of the Franciscan ideal of saintly poverty as a mode of purification and salvation.[40] Thus, prodigality, as opposed to the ideal of saintly poverty, was considered part of a vicious cycle driven primarily by the greed and concern for material possession (its acquisition and its display) at the root of Avarice.

Turning then to the Prodigal on the *Gates of Hell* (see Fig. 9), we find two expressions of this sin placed very near the figure of Avarice (joined with the female figure of Lust/Luxuria) just over the tomb structure on the lower right panel. We recall that on the lower left panel, just opposite these figures of the Avaricious and the Prodigal, we find the horizontally positioned figure of Fortune. All of these figures are placed at eye level to the viewer standing before the Gates and are described in strong relief so as to be easily distinguishable from numerous adjacent figures of varying size. The figure of the Prodigal on the left of the image is a lone male, emaciated, on his knees, reaching with both arms upwards. The figure of the Prodigal on the right is in similar attitude – floating with knees bent, reaching upwards – but this time the body of a nude female is shown escaping his grasp. Like the figure of the Avaricious, the primary gestural expression is one of grasping. While the Avaricious's grasp is held tightly to his body, the Prodigal's grasp is away from it – a gesture which signifies both reckless dispersion and indiscriminate desire simultaneously. This complex expression of the condition of the Prodigal can be traced through multiple working drawings; Rodin created numerous versions of figures in similar attitudes as he worked out his understanding of the sin and its essential characteristic. Two drawings exemplify Rodin's approach.

The first is a drawing which represents the Prodigal in his iteration within the biblical parable of the Prodigal Son (Fig. 14). As the Franciscan ideal of saintly poverty was celebrated by Dante in the *Commedia*, the Prodigal Son embodies, in a sense, the wrong kind of poverty – a poverty brought on by wasteful squandering in pursuit of sensual pleasures. The parable of the Prodigal Son was among the most frequently portrayed in Romanesque

39 Newhauser, *The Early History*, 79–85.

40 Nick Havely, *Dante and the Franciscans: Poverty and Papacy in the "Commedia"* (Cambridge: Cambridge University Press, 2004). See also by the same author, "Poverty in Purgatory: From *Commercium* to *Commedia*," *Dante Studies* 114 (1996): 229–43.

and Gothic imagery, particularly in France, and was the subject of countless prints, paintings, and sculpture in the eighteenth and nineteenth centuries.[41] That Rodin was familiar with the traditional iconography associated with the narrative is certain.

The parable itself, at Luke 15:11–32, describes the journey of a young man from the safety and comfort of his father's home to the perils and temptations of the city. The youth is at his lowest point when, reduced to tending swine in a yard, he resolves to repent and return to his father. Dressed now only in rags, he stands outside his father's house where he is forgiven and embraced by the patriarch, who has the son reclothed in finery and feted with the killing of the fatted calf enjoyed at a banquet. Conflict arises when the older of the patriarch's sons, who never disobeyed or strayed, expresses anger at the younger son's feting. The father exclaims that the celebration is just as the son was "dead and is now again alive, was once lost is now found." The parable is one of salvation through repentance and forgiveness and is positioned in Luke just after the related parables of the lost coin and the lost sheep (Luke 15:1–10). It appears in proximity to the parable of Lazarus and Dives (Luke 16:19–31) which treats the avarice of the rich man who finds himself condemned in the afterlife in relation to the poverty of Lazarus who is saved. Thus the related concepts of squandering and hoarding, the Prodigal and the Avaricious, are presented by these parables and echoed by their pairing in the *Commedia*.

Scholars of the Prodigal Son parable and its representation in art have remarked that the father's home represents the church or divine realm, and the city, the place of temptation and sin (frequently elaborated in imagery much beyond the biblical text to include several scenes in brothels and taverns in which the Prodigal is shown dissipating his wealth through whoring, drinking, and gambling).[42] Each narrative moment of the parable

41 On the representation of the Prodigal Son parable in the Middle Ages, see Wolfgang Kemp, *The Narratives of Gothic Stained Glass* (Cambridge: Cambridge University Press, 1997); Don Denny, "Some Narrative Subjects in the Portal Sculpture of Auxerre Cathedral," *Speculum* 51:1 (January 1976): 23–34; Gerald B. Guest, "The Prodigal's Journey: Ideologies of Self and City in the Gothic Cathedral," *Speculum* 81:1 (January 2006): 35–75. On its popularity in early modern and modern periods see Ellen G. D'Oench, "Prodigal Sons and Fair Penitents: Transformations in Eighteenth-Century Popular Prints," *Art History* 13:3 (September 1990): 318–43; also by the same author *Prodigal Son Narratives 1480–1980* (New Haven, CT: Yale University Art Gallery, New Haven, CT and Davison Art Center, Wesleyan University, Middletown, CT, 1995). See also Frances Rustin, "From the Prodigal Son to the *Rake's Progress*: Hogarth's Forerunners," *Apollo* 438 (August 1998): 15–16.

42 Guest, "The Prodigal's Journey."

has significance along these lines: the farmer who hires the Prodigal to tend his swine symbolizes Satan, and the Prodigal's forlorn moment with the swine is his furthest distance from God and thus his moment of repentance; his return to the father whose acceptance is marked by the embrace represents his return to God and thus his salvation. The embrace of the father is additionally significant when we consider that it is the antithesis of the embrace of the prostitute in the brothel scenes and could be seen in reference to the treacherous embrace of Christ by Judas (and thus the sin of Avarice, with which Judas was associated in the Middle Ages); the gesture of embrace of the Prodigal (the sinner) by the forgiving Father (God) is thus singularly significant in capturing the parable's ultimate message that Christian salvation is possible given God's grace and the sinner's preceding act of penitence.[43]

Thus, without acknowledgment of sin, the Prodigal cannot attain the salvation he seeks and is granted, symbolically, through the forgiving embrace of the Father upon his return home.[44] Rodin presents in this drawing the traditional embrace of repentant Prodigal in the arms of the Father. Typical of such representations, the son's youthfulness is communicated through his smaller stature and his approach to the Father in a manner of supplication to higher authority communicated through his kneeling or half-kneeling gesture (a pose reportedly originated by Albrecht Dürer's engraving of the half-kneeling Prodigal with swine – thus originally associated with repentance and then transferred to the moment of embrace in many later representations of the parable).[45] Rotating 180 degrees the page upon which this drawing appears (Fig. 15), we find that Rodin sketched in very lightly the Prodigal on his knees, alone, in repentance – most likely a reference to the previous moment relayed in the parable when he finds himself tending the

43 On the use of "paired antitheticals" in depiction of the Prodigal Son parable see Kemp, *The Narratives*, esp. 32–41. On the association of Judas with Avarice, see Berger, "Avarice."

44 Catholic and Protestant views differ on the necessity of the Prodigal's penitence in achieving salvation. Catholics emphasize the need for the sinner's penitence while Protestants assert that salvation is due only through the grace of God. There is some disagreement, however, as to whether these differences are apparent in the iconographic traditions related to the parable. On this issue, see Barbara Haeger, "The Prodigal Son in Sixteenth and Seventeenth-Century Netherlandish Art: Depictions of the Parable and the Evolution of a Catholic Image," *Simiolus: Netherlands Quarterly for the History of Art* 16:2–3 (1986): 128–38.

45 On Dürer's Prodigal Son and the development of iconography in relation to it see Christopher Witcombe, "Dürer's Prodigal Son," *Source: Notes in the History of Art* 17:3 (Spring 1998): 7–13; Campbell Dodgson and Werner Weisbach, "Two Versions of the Prodigal Son by Dürer," *The Burlington Magazine for Connoisseurs* 74:434 (May 1939): 228–29, 233.

swine and realizes the error of his ways. Thus, on this page Rodin presents both the penitent and forgiven Prodigal.

But, as we see on the Gates, Rodin's final sculpted version retains only the upreaching gesture of the Prodigal and the reference to the position of kneeling. Absent is the Father. We see then in the second drawing (Fig. 16), much closer to the final sculpted versions on the Gates, how Rodin has developed the figure of the Prodigal Son, who returns home to his Father and to God, into the lone figure of the Prodigal who is without this salvation. In this drawing, and others like it, the youth's figure is exaggerated and elongated as he reaches endlessly upwards with outstretched and empty arms. He is no longer on his knees but now fully extended to empty and silent space, enveloped in darkness. The Prodigal without the embrace of the Father becomes then the eternal sinner who, simultaneously, dissipates his wealth (the inheritance squandered in acquisition of prostitutes, drink, and general debauchery in the city's taverns and brothels as he lives, momentarily, the life of the wealthy man as if he is at the top of Fortune's wheel enjoying her favors) and thus his spiritual integrity, and seeks something (the spiritual integrity he lacks) through misguided desire for earthly pleasures that are ultimately empty (as does the Avaricious). The Prodigal without the Father is still dead, still lost, as are all the damned who are condemned exactly because they do not see the mistake of their ways and do not repent; Dante treats those who repent, we should recall, in *Purgatorio* (the Avaricious and Prodigal specifically in *Purgatorio* 19–21).

The sculpted figure on the left resembles most closely this second drawing, as he reaches alone toward emptiness. The sculpted figure on the right, however, could be seen to represent the Prodigal of the taverns and brothels, much like the figure of Avarice with Lust, who, in pursuit of material pleasures at the expense of his soul's goodness, seeks to embrace the sexualized female form rather than the forgiving Father as represented in the first drawing. That this same grouping of the Prodigal and the female form when positioned differently on the Gates is referred to as Fugit Amor and considered a representation of the sinners guilty of Lust, Paolo and Francesca, as described in *Inferno* 5, contributes to this reading. As we have seen, the connection between Lust/Luxuria and Avarice, and therefore the Prodigal, was well established from Dante's era on. Both figures retain the reference to kneeling, but in this case, without genuine repentance and then forgiveness, it represents the Prodigal's abased condition, weighed down by earthly preoccupations which prevent his spiritual uplifting. As in the *contrapasso* described by Dante, the Prodigal is occupied eternally with the "weight" of material concern for the "vain goods" at the expense of his own soul.

That this fate is eternal for both the Avaricious and the Prodigal, and as Rodin represents them on the *Gates of Hell*, is explained by Virgil:

> They will come forever to the two buttings; these will rise from the grave with closed fist, and these with cropped hair. Ill-giving and ill-keeping have robbed them of the fair world and set them to this scuffle – what this is, I spend no fair words to say. Now can you see, my son, the brief mockery of the goods that are committed to Fortune, for which humankind contend with one another; because all the gold that is beneath the moon, or ever was, would not give rest to a single one of these weary souls. (*Inf.* 7.55–66)

Autobiography, the Last Judgment, and Salvation

Finally, coming full circle to the autobiographical nature of Dante's engagement with Fortune, and thus with those out of harmony with her, the Prodigal in the Middle Ages was often juxtaposed with the image of the poet/jongleur in association with what was considered the artist's itinerant and somewhat debauched lifestyle.[46] Autobiographical interpretations in art and literature developed as a result, with Dante among those who positioned himself, particularly given his condition of exile, as the wanderer in rags seeking salvation.[47] The *Commedia* is, ultimately, the story of Dante's fall, repentance, and return to the Father whose embrace he seeks and finds. And while Dante approached the question of sin with the firm conviction of a believer in God and thus in the possibility of salvation through right action, we have no such assurance with Rodin.

That Rodin had a personal stake in the question of salvation is suggested not only by his twenty-year engagement with the commission for the *Gates of Hell*, but also by his inclusion of a self-portrait at the very base of the massive sculpture (Fig. 17).[48] Rodin presents himself nude, in a position of thought, much like the Thinker above, while a muse in female form hovers near his head. Across the base of the Gates, opposite his self-portrait, Rodin's muse appears again (Fig. 18). This time, however, the muse, much like Eve in traditional representations, is presented as a lone figure offering the artist a fruited branch which suggests both temptation and expulsion.

We recall that Rodin has placed the Thinker, simultaneously Dante and Everyman, in the place of Christ in medieval Last Judgment tympanum sculpture. Where Christ acts as fierce judge, the Thinker, as a mortal and

46 Kemp, *The Narratives*, 136–44.

47 On Dante's self-representation in the *Commedia* as the Prodigal Son, see Peter S. Hawkins, "Virgilio cita le scritture," *Dante e la Bibbia* (Florence: Olschki, 1988), 351–59.

48 See Albert Alhadeff, "Rodin: A Self-Portrait in The Gates of Hell," *Art Bulletin* 48:3–4 (September, December 1966): 393–95.

fallible individual having achieved in the modern world a position of unprecedented autonomy and power, seems neither to judge nor to act. Rather, he sits hunched over, melancholy, turning inward upon himself as he gazes blankly past the wreckage of hell below him, oblivious to those behind him who are soon to fall into the abyss. While Dante rests the possibility of salvation on man's capacity for choice, the Thinker on the *Gates of Hell* seems to remain uncommitted, choosing no path, in tension between the straight way and the dark wood as Fortune turns her wheel, blissfully unaware of his plight.

Figure 1. Auguste Rodin (1840–1917) *The Gates of Hell.*

Figure 2. *Fortune*, detail of *The Gates of Hell* (lower left panel).

Figure 3. *Fortune*, detail of *The Gates of Hell* (lower left panel).

Figure 4. Auguste Rodin (1840–1917) *Standing Female Nude with Drapery.*

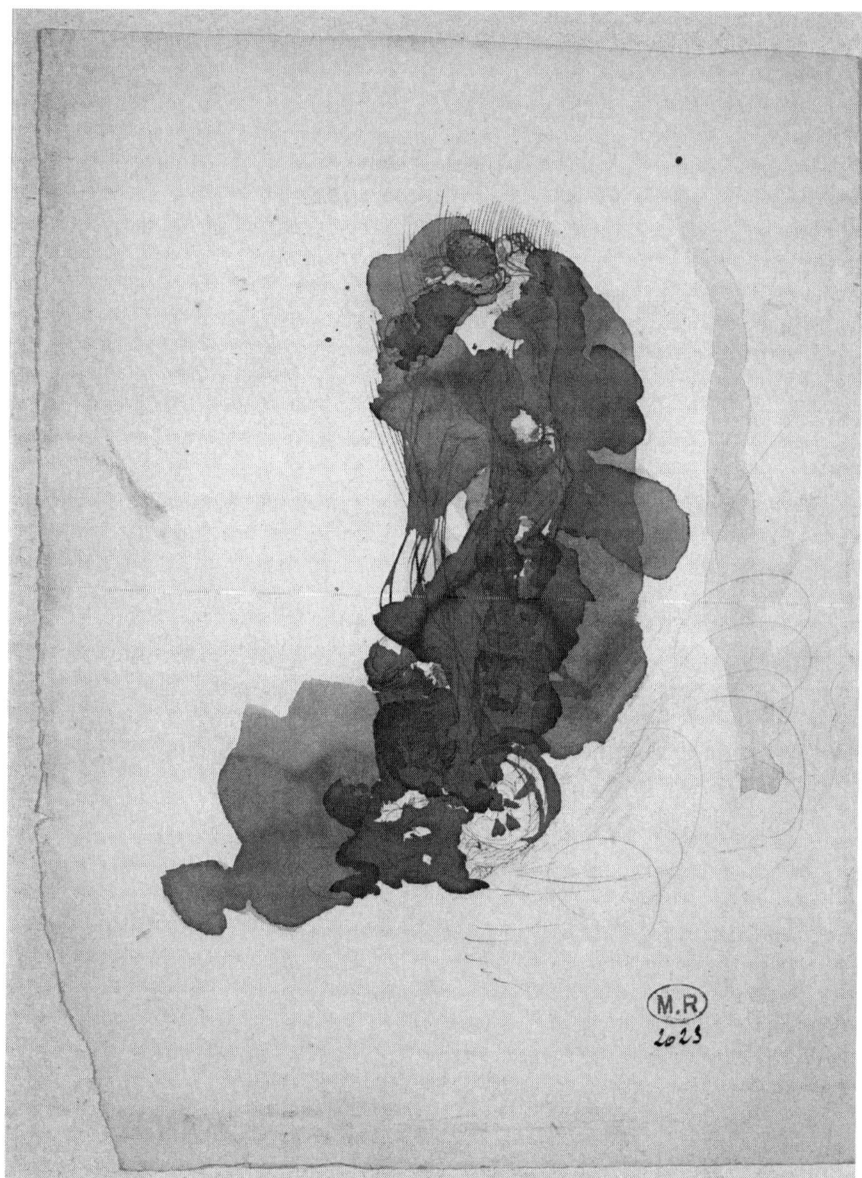

Figure 5. Auguste Rodin (1840–1917) *Amours et roue de la fortune* (*Putti and wheel of fortune*). © 2013 Artists Rights Society (ARS), New York/ADAGP, Paris.

Figure 6. Auguste Rodin (1840–1917) *La Fortune* (*Fortune*).

Figure 7. Auguste Rodin (1840–1917) *Plutus* ?

Figure 8. *Avarice and Lust*, detail of *The Gates of Hell* (lower right panel).

Figure 9. *The Prodigal*, detail of *The Gates of Hell* (lower right panel).

Figure 10. Auguste Rodin (1840–1917) *Dante parmi les avares et les prodigues* (*Dante among the avaricious and the prodigal*).

Figure 11. Auguste Rodin (1840–1917) *Ombre d'un avare* (*Shade of an avaricious*).

Figure 12. Auguste Rodin (1840–1917) *Charybe/Eve.*

Figure 13. *Eve*, detail of *The Gates of Hell.*

Figure 14. Auguste Rodin (1840–1917) *L'enfant prodigue* (*The prodigal son*).

Figure 15. *Penitent figure*, detail of *L'enfant prodigue* (rotated).

Figure 16. Auguste Rodin (1840–1917) *Ombre* (*Shade*).

Figure 17. Rodin's "self-portrait," detail of *The Gates of Hell.*

Figure 18. Rodin's "muse," detail of *The Gates of Hell.*

Film Theory, the Sister Arts Tradition, and the Cinematic *Beowulf*

Nickolas Haydock

This essay contributes to a larger discussion on the relationships between medieval studies and medievalism that has occupied an increasing number of scholars in recent years.[1] Concerning the sub-field of movie medievalism, how can we put into productive relation the all-too-obviously disparate projects of writing a critical essay on *Beowulf* and adapting the poem for the silver screen? This essay revisits the question of homologies between scholarly and cinematic approaches to *Beowulf* by posing the question in another register – that of inter-media comparisons as informed by what is commonly known as "the Sister Arts Tradition." My working thesis is simply this:

1 Even a representative bibliography of the extent of such work would fill dozens of pages, not only by dint of increasing and intensifying activity in this area but also because, as I put it in an earlier essay: "The point is to avoid the temptation to define medievalism as error and to recognize that in the long view medieval studies is a sub-set of medievalism [. . .]. The differences between popular medievalism and academic medieval studies are those of degree – not of kind – and these differences of degree erode quite precipitously with the passage of time," Nickolas Haydock, "Medievalism and Excluded Middles," in *Studies in Medievalism XVII: Defining Medievalism(s)*, ed. Karl Fugelso (Cambridge: D. S. Brewer, 2009), 17–30 (19). The line between philology and medievalism within the corpus of writers such as J. R. R. Tolkien or Umberto Eco is especially blurry. In the case of Tolkien, explored below, the essay "Beowulf: The Monsters and the Critics" serves not only as a touchstone for much subsequent scholarship on the poem, but also has a great deal in common with Tolkien's fantasy medievalism and his artwork. Let us content ourselves, then, with citing only three influential books to serve as emblematic of a rising trend: Carolyn Dinshaw, *Getting Medieval: Sexualities and Communities, Pre- and Postmodern* (Durham, NC: Duke University Press, 1999); John Ganim, *Medievalism and Orientalism: Three Essays on Literature, Agriculture and Cultural Identity* (New York: Palgrave Macmillan, 2005); and the anthology of essays edited by Eileen A. Joy et al., *Cultural Studies of the Modern Middle Ages* (New York: Palgrave Macmillan, 2007).

inter-arts comparisons occupy the borderland between these two different realms, where the crossovers and continuities between traditional scholarship and movie medievalism are most readily apparent. Such a project offers an example of how scholars of medievalism might begin to move beyond the parochial tendencies of a sub-discipline – one that typically overemphasizes medievalism's exotic, egregious departures from original sources – into a more open, level field of play. Specifically, I provide evidence of interactions between scholarship and popular culture that are anything but one-sided or unidirectional; rather, scholarship can be seen taking its cues from cinema, and cinema decoding scholarly approaches to texts and then encoding them in nuanced, subtle ways. Such filiations between scholarship and popular filmmaking have not always been registered by academics who tend to focus on dialogue and plot to the virtual exclusion of any concern with how images and their collocations function in film.[2]

Comparisons among different media are perhaps as old as criticism itself: Aristotle's anatomy of tragic drama and its interrelationships with epic, lyric, music, dance, and mime; Horace's famous comparison *ut pictura poesis*; Lessing's influential discussion of plastic and poetic arts in depictions of Laocoön; down through recent film, media, and cultural theory in which

2 Any study of movie medievalism should begin with Kevin Harty, *The Reel Middle Ages: American, Western and Eastern European, Middle Eastern and Asian Films about Medieval Europe* (Jefferson, NC: McFarland, 1999). Some of the problems with the fidelity approach to this mode were outlined in my *Movie Medievalism: The Imaginary Middle Ages* (Jefferson, NC: McFarland, 2008), where I offer psychoanalytic and philosophical alternatives (chiefly those offered by Lacan, Žižek, and Deleuze) to the Real/Reel Middle Ages distinction. My introduction to the edited collection of essays *Hollywood in the Holy Land: Essays on Film Depictions of the Crusades and Christian/ Muslim Conflicts*, ed. Nickolas Haydock and E. L. Risden (Jefferson, NC: McFarland, 2009) demonstrates at some length the inter-implication of scholarly, filmic, and mass-media discourses in framing public-policy debates on the relevance of the Crusades to modern interventions in the Middle East. Also recommended are Laurie Finke and Martin B. Shichtman, *Cinematic Illuminations: The Middle Ages on Film* (Baltimore, MD: Johns Hopkins University Press, 2010), inspired in part by an attempt to read the juxtaposition of medieval book and modern cinema "illuminations." A similar approach, undertaken with rigor and pizzazz, is Richard Burt, *Medieval and Early Modern Film and Media* (New York: Palgrave Macmillan, 2008). Also see Burt's fascinating introduction to a special issue of *Exemplaria*, "Getting Schmedieval: Of Manuscript and Film Prologues, Paratexts, and Parodies," *Exemplaria* 19.2 (2007): 217–42. Stephanie Trigg's essay, "Transparent Walls: Stained Glass and Cinematic Medievalism," *Screening the Past* 26 (2009): www.latrobe.edu.au/screeningthepast/current/issue-26.html, accessed 29 August 2012, represents perhaps the most thoroughgoing attempt to read medieval and modern images in productive relation. Books on medievalism in film which employ the more widespread strategy of comparing movies with medieval history are: John Aberth, *A Knight at the Movies: Medieval History on Film* (Jefferson, NC: McFarland, 2003) and Andrew B. R. Eliot's *Remaking the Middle Ages: The Methods of Cinema in Portraying the Medieval World* (Jefferson, NC: McFarland, 2010).

the translations across an increasing array of media platforms have become an emergent, if not the dominant, paradigm. The sister arts paradigm likewise informs the development of film theory from Sergei Eisenstein and the Russian formalists down through thinkers as diverse as Erwin Panofsky, André Bazin, Siegfried Kracauer, and Gilles Deleuze. Inter-art comparisons and analogies have also served as the basis for a number of now-classic essays on *Beowulf* by Alain Renoir, John Leyerle, Fred C. Robinson, and Gillian R. Overing, among numerous others (see below for further discussion and citations). The present essay reviews the role of sister arts comparisons in the work of J. R. R. Tolkien and Alain Renoir, highlighting some issues in what W. T. J. Mitchell has recently called the "pictorial turn" in postmodern culture, before returning to the mutually implicated topics of *Beowulf* as an object of cinematic analysis and as a product of recent films.[3]

Alain Renoir's inter-arts criticism on *Beowulf* seems almost genetically determined. He was the grandson of the impressionist painter Pierre-Auguste Renoir, and the son of the *auteur* Jean Renoir, on whose films Alain worked as an apprentice and assistant cinematographer between 1938 and 1941. During these years his father Jean directed two films often mentioned in reverent terms by film scholars and cineastes alike, *The Human Beast* (1938; Apprentice Cameraman: Alain Renoir) and *The Rules of the Game* (1939; Second Assistant Cameraman: Alain Renoir). These films are celebrated for a realistic style that allows meaning to emerge within a single, long take, as a function of mise en scene, deep focus, and, especially, the spatial relationships and movements of actors within and through the frame, rather than chiefly as the production of montage. These years saw a crucial break with the tenets of classical cinema toward a modernist form, perhaps most evident in the work of Renoir and a young Orson Welles. For these influential directors – and for the French New Wave and Italian Neorealism more generally – the shot, not the image or the cut, became the chief element of film composition.

The son of Jean Renoir became a professor of comparative literature at Berkeley, and his work deserves recognition as an important, though under-acknowledged forerunner of media and cultural studies. Alain Renoir *compared* not only texts written in different languages, but made numerous, sustained, and richly elaborated inter-media comparisons as well. The scholarship for which he is best known applied oral-formulaic theory to poems written in medieval Germanic languages, like *Beowulf* and *The Nibelungenlied*, down through the survivals of oral formulism in works of the alliterative revival such as *Sir Gawain and the Green Knight*. To simplify somewhat,

3 W. J. T. Mitchell, *Picture Theory* (Chicago: University of Chicago Press, 1994).

Renoir worked within traditional comparisons between painting and poetry, greatly influenced by Lessing's preference for poetry's greater capacity to express movement and change, but he also tapped into vibrant debates in film theory that sought to situate the new art form in relation to painting and written language. The result was a revolutionary thesis about oral-formulaic texts and their acute visualization of specific details, which compared the appositive style of alliterative poetry to cinematic montage. Renoir's revolution, however, was premature. The outlandishness of his claims provoked little more than a ripple in Anglo-Saxon studies,[4] which was more accepting of less anachronistic sister arts comparisons, such as those of John Leyerle, Fred C. Robinson, and Gillian R. Overing. Leyerle identified a "parallel" in the intricately woven designs of plastic arts in the north of Britain, as evidenced in productions such as the Lindisfarne Gospels or Franks Casket, which he dubbed the "interlace style" of *Beowulf*.[5] Robinson stressed the poem's "appositive style," linking its paratactic diction to larger juxtapositions of imagery, episodes, and overall structure.[6] And, more recently, Overing turned to Charles Sanders Peirce's semiotic categories to compare swords in the poem with surviving weapons of the period, noting that the final significance of such objects is never established but rather differed, met again in later contexts where it is interwoven with different themes and takes on new connotations.[7]

I

The work of these scholars – as they themselves were happy to affirm – can be seen as attempts to elaborate Tolkien's magisterial, elegiac argument about the essence of the poem: "It is essentially a balance, an opposition of ends and beginnings [. . .] a contrasted description of two moments in a great life, rising and setting; an elaboration of the ancient and intensely moving contrast between youth and age, first achievement and final death."[8]

4 The influence of Renoir's visual stylistics was greater in subsequent scholarship on Middle English alliterative poetry. See, for instance, Sarah Stanbury, *Seeing the Gawain Poet: Description and the Act of Perception* (Philadelphia: University of Pennsylvania Press, 1991).

5 John Leyerle, "The Interlace Structure of *Beowulf*," *Beowulf: A Verse Translation, Authoritative Text, Contexts, Criticism*, trans. Seamus Heaney, ed. Daniel Donoghue (New York: Norton, 2002), 130–51. Originally published in *University of Toronto Quarterly* 37 (1967): 1–17.

6 Fred C. Robinson, Beowulf *and the Appositive Style* (Knoxville: University of Tennessee Press, 1987).

7 Gillian R. Overing, *Language, Sign, and Gender in* Beowulf (Carbondale: Southern Illinois University Press, 1990), 33–67.

8 J. R. R. Tolkien, *The Essays of J. R. R. Tolkien: The Monsters and the Critics and Other Essays*, ed. Christopher Tolkien (New York: HarperCollins, 2006), 28.

If we look at Tolkien's essay with something like the loving stewardship he lavished on the Anglo-Saxon poem (following his practice of moving to the center what has traditionally been found marginal or unworthy of notice) what we find is an argument buttressed at every stage by inter-arts comparisons. For Tolkien, the diction of the poem should not be confused with the subtle harmonies of quantitative verse favored in southern climes; rather, it is "more like masonry than music"; in fact, its "verse-kind approaches rather to sculpture or painting. It is a composition not a tune."[9] In the famous allegory of the poem's composition and reception, Tolkien likens *Beowulf* to a tower, with stone quarried from an older ruin, from the top of which its owner could look out upon the sea. Generations of historians and archeologists have knocked down this tower, scrambling over the chaotic ruin they themselves created, attempting to reconstruct the older building from which its stones derive, and even digging beneath it for clues to earlier civilizations. So goes perhaps the most famous demolition of a scholarly orthodoxy in the history of medieval studies.

Yet if Tolkien insisted upon restoring the balanced architecture of the poem, the way in which this famous allegory is developed throughout the essay has received considerably less attention. The more extensive critical allegory at work throughout the piece concerns not simply architecture but artistic perspective – an allegory elaborated to chastise critical views for their failure to respect the poet's vision, whose panoramic vistas we can learn to appreciate though never fully share. The dominant comparison throughout the essay is with painting – modern, not Anglo-Saxon painting – urging us toward recognition of a three-point perspective in which depth of field and point of view serve to allegorize historical differences and distances. The "scene" of the poem, as Tolkien repeatedly calls it, resembles nothing so much as a romantic landscape painting, with a distant figure in a makeshift tower rapt in contemplation of a horizon that recedes from his view, even as he recedes from ours.[10] Tolkien encourages modern audiences to identify

9 Tolkien, *Essays*, 30.

10 Ted Nasmith, in tracing the development of his own style in illustrating Middle-Earth, makes a similar point: "I came to recognize that since a work like *The Lord of the Rings* was basically anachronistic thematically (that is, set in a mythical past age), as well as stylistically related to nineteenth-century adventure novels and fairy tales, paintings that could capture its feeling and complement its grandeur ought to look back to what I saw as the corresponding golden era of detailed landscape painting," Ted Nasmith, "Similar but Not Similar: Appropriate Anachronism in My Paintings of Middle-Earth," in *Tolkien's Modern Middle Ages*, ed. Jane Chance and Alfred K. Siewers (New York: Palgrave Macmillan, 2005), 189–204 (193). This represents both an insightful use of inter-arts comparisons as well as a window into Nasmith's creative process, but it elides the influence of Tolkien's own indebtedness to nineteenth-century landscapes and the rather more direct influence of his artistic style

with the poet's elegiac response toward the world represented in the poem, wherein we are urged to sympathize with the poet's sense of loss from our own even more distant point of view. The poem is designed to "give that sense of perspective, of antiquity with a greater and yet darker antiquity behind." What Tolkien calls "this impression of depth" results – like three-point perspective – from an "illusion," that of "surveying a past, pagan but noble and fraught with deep significance – a past that itself had depth and reached backward into a dark antiquity of sorrow [. . .] mostly darker, more pagan, and desperate than the foreground."[11] While from this perspective *Beowulf* does not present an "actual picture" of fifth-century Scandinavia, it is "on a general view a self-consistent picture, a construction bearing clearly the marks of design and thought."[12] The repetition of the word "picture" in different senses – photograph and painting – is typical of Tolkien's style of argument; it juxtaposes documentary with aesthetic approaches, even as it insists upon the poet's deliberate construction of a deep and progressively more obscure perspective.[13]

This "impression of depth" is also richly evident in Tolkien's paintings. Many of his most oft-reproduced drawings and watercolors recede from the viewer into intricate depths of tantalizing complexity. Numerous examples of

on Nasmith's illustrations – abundantly clear, for instance, in the latter's version of *Rivendell* (1984).

11 Tolkien, *Essays*, 27. Tolkien's fondness for perspectival metaphors and inter-arts comparisons is also abundantly on display in the essay on *Sir Gawain and the Green Knight*: "Antiquity like a many-figured back-cloth hangs ever behind the scene. Behind our poem stalk the figures of elder myth, and through the lines are heard the echoes of ancient cults, beliefs and symbols remote from the consciousness of an educated moralist (but also a poet) of the late fourteenth century. His story is not *about* these old things, but it receives part of its life, its vividness, its tension from them" (Tolkien, *Essays*, 73). In fact, the *Gawain* essay seems to offer a less elaborate version of the "allegory" familiar from "Monsters and Critics" in order to make a similar point: "Out of whatever more ancient stones may have been built the gleaming but solid magnificence of this castle (Hautdesert), whatever turn the story may take, whatever details may be discovered that the author inherited and overlooked or failed to accommodate to his new purpose, this much is clear: our poet is bringing Gawain to no haunt of demons, enemies of human kind, but to a courteous and Christian hall" (Tolkien, *Essays*, 78).

12 Tolkien, *Essays*, 27.

13 Tolkien's call for a recognition of the "impression of depth" in *Beowulf* scholarship also resonates with his essay "On Translating *Beowulf*": "your language must be literary and traditional: not because it is now a long while since the poem was made, or because it speaks of things that have since become ancient; but because the diction of *Beowulf* was poetical, archaic, artificial (if you will), in the day the poem was made" (Tolkien, *Essays*, 54). The survival of usages like *beorn* (bear) and *freca* (wolf) for "warrior" in traditional poetic diction are the philological equivalent of receding pictorial compositions, words (if you will) that contain their own dark history and provide remnants, "when much else of the ancient diction had perished" (54), of the tantalizing links between language, myth, and tale.

the style might be adduced, such as the painting of *Rivendell III* (6)[14] seen only as a distant prospect at the end of a long crevice. Nearer rock formations and vegetation are sharply realized, while the ostensible topic of the painting, Rivendell, sits tucked away behind trees on a plateau between a sheer rock face and the bending river Bruinen, with Lonely Mountain as an even more distant prospect. Indeed, one of the many pleasant surprises of *The Lord of the Rings* film trilogy was to find Tolkien's picture of Rivendell rather carefully rendered via CGI in a painterly shot within *The Fellowship of the Ring.* As has often been remarked, the technology of computer graphic imaging brings movies into a more intimate relation with painting than ever before. Frodo's distant perspective of Mount Doom in the film version of *The Return of the King* seems similarly inspired by Tolkien's artistic and intellectual style. Frodo looks up from the dangerous position of Shelob's cave through a deep crevice to the tower in the distance, shining with the searchlight eye. The distant light thus represents at once a beacon, lighting the way to his goal, and the sign of a malevolence that continues its unblinking search for *him.* In this scene and in an earlier one where Aragorn is about to enter through a deep crevice "the paths of the dead," Peter Jackson also repeatedly employs a shot invented by Alfred Hitchcock in *Vertigo*, produced by a zooming lens in conjunction with a camera tracking backwards, to suggest the vertiginous feelings that such gazes into the unknown provoke, their frisson of desire and fear. In Jackson's films such shots subjectify depth perception: we gaze with Frodo and Aragorn into the abyss and it looks back at us. The unsettling visual effect combines in a distinctly Lacanian way the combination of aversion and attraction in the gaze, the means through which objects of the gaze look back at the viewer.[15]

Tolkien's impressionistic pictures in pencil, crayon, and watercolors, such as *The Front Gate* (16), *The Doors of Durin and Moria Gate I* (22), *Helm's Deep and the Hornburg* (26), *Dunharrow* (29), or *Gondolin and the Vale of Tumladen* (35), illustrate what he christened "*ishness*," a quality that seems at least partially a function of recessive compositions. Paradigmatic in this regard is the drawing *The Elvenking's Gate II* (12), in which the ostensible topic of the composition is merely a tiny square placed at the center, though the picture itself is dominated by the curving tree-lined path in the fore-

14 Tolkien's artwork has been widely reproduced and marketed in art books and calendars, etc. Hereafter, references are keyed to the numbered illustrations in the edition by Christopher Tolkien, *Pictures by J. R. R. Tolkien*, ed. Christopher Tolkien (Boston: Houghton Mifflin, 1992). Also see, *J. R. R. Tolkien: Artist and Illustrator*, ed. Wayne G. Hammond and Christina Scull (Boston: Houghton Mifflin, 1995).

15 James Elkins, *The Object Stares Back: On the Nature of Seeing* (New York: Simon and Schuster, 1996).

ground that leads (our gaze) to the gate. Likewise, in the crayon drawing *The Doors of Durin and Moria Gate I* (22) the doors comprise a tiny, fingernail-size center of a picture featuring enormous rock faces and the intervening lake. Even Tolkien's interiors, such as the drawings *Beorn's Hall* (10) or *The Hall at Bag End, Residence of B. Baggins Esquire* (20), share this extreme depth of field. *The Hall at Bag End* has at its center Bilbo's open portal, leading the viewer's gaze ever onward to the outside world and the long road that awaits an initially reluctant traveler. Further evidence of the style exists even when the artist intentionally breaks with his own conventions, as in *Glaurung Sets Forth to Seek Túrin* (38), where the dark and pale mountains open at a tunnel – reminiscent of Three Cliffs Bay in Swansea, Wales – from which a dragon lunges in lurid colors beyond the borders of the painting to confront its viewers head on.

Tom Shippey's *J. R. R. Tolkien: Author of the Century* proffers the intriguing suggestion that the painting described in *Leaf by Niggle* may well serve to allegorize Tolkien's own career, and that the *ekphrasis* of "this great picture" in the story can be seen as the gradual unfurling of Tolkien's imagined worlds:

> How good a painter is (Niggle)? This is one of the two main questions raised in paragraphs two to five of the story, and the answer is fairly complex. He is certainly "Not a very successful one," partly because "He was the sort of painter who can paint leaves better than trees." But the "one picture in particular which bothered him," while it started as a leaf caught in the wind, soon became a "tree" indeed a "Tree," while behind it "a country began to open out; and there were glimpses of a forest marching over the land, and of mountains tipped with snow." If one translates this from Niggle to Tolkien, it makes good sense. Tolkien began with short poems like the 1914 "Lay of Earendel" (leaves, so to speak); they grew into explanatory narratives [. . .] as he wrote "a country began to open out" … and there were indeed glimpses in it of a "forest marching" (the Ents) [. . .]. Niggle's "great picture," existing only in the mind, was something like a completely finished and integrated version of the whole history of Arda from Creation to the end of the Third Age.[16]

What emerges across Tolkien's art, his fiction, and his scholarship, then, is a remarkably abiding concern with perspectives in depth, attentive to spatial and temporal relationships, as any moment a single image or ancient object becomes the leaf from which a mighty "Tree" (and an even mightier world)

16 Tom Shippey, *J. R. R. Tolkien: Author of the Century* (Boston: Houghton Mifflin, 2000).

can spring abundantly forth. This philosophy of deep perspectives informs Tolkien's art and his fiction, just as it informs his philology and his appreciation of *Beowulf* – in all of which spatial depth serves as a figure for historical distance and the fantastic. Indeed, one might call "the impression of depth" the key to Tolkien's perspective in his paintings, in his fascination with fairy tales, and in his approach to *Beowulf*. At the dead center of such concerns is that which is typically furthest from view; his sublime is a function of this rule of depth, but it is also a standing invitation to close distances and penetrate obscurities, like the door in *Bag End* that opens onto the road beyond or the imagined painting of a leaf that burgeons into a variegated landscape. In similar fashion, what emerges in the *Beowulf* essay is not simply an allegory of poetic and critical perspectives, but the *ekphrasis* of an imagined picture like that described in *Leaf by Niggle*, which – had Tolkien painted it in watercolors rather than in words – would have necessitated a style in close accord with Niggle's greatest creation.[17]

Tolkien also utilized the analogy of painting to distinguish *Beowulf* from the musical hexameters of ancient epic verse like that of Virgil's *Aeneid*, with which the Old English poem had often been unfavorably compared. Not only a picture, *Beowulf* is a painting of a specific kind, allowing the illusion of depth and employing chiaroscuro effects which cast the heroic age of Germanic paganism in semi-darkness. Tolkien's distinction between Greco-Roman and Anglo-Saxon resembles that made by Erich Auerbach in *Mimesis*: Homer like the sun shines on everything alike; while the Book of Genesis is rather more like a searchlight, illuminating specific details while leaving so much else in shadow and inscrutable.[18] It is only with Alain Renoir, however, that sister arts comparisons are fully marshaled to distinguish the different styles of visualization in ancient and Old English epic. Renoir's essays read like a calculated response to Tolkien's *ut pictura poesis* comparisons, and they draw the distinction between the visual poetics of Old English and Latin just as definitively as Auerbach did for Greek and Hebrew. Renoir contrasts Virgil's static, painterly style with what might well be called the *cinematic Beowulf*, characterized by "a mobility of point of view" and shifts in scale – techniques of visualization that Renoir contends are central to oral-formulaic poetry.[19] Traditional source study had attempted to relate the descriptions of the underworld in the *Aeneid* and *Beowulf* through the identification of

17 For a discussion of themes and structures common across Tolkien's oeuvre, see Jane Chance, *Tolkien's Art: A Mythology for England*, rev. edn. (Lexington: University Press of Kentucky, 2001), 142–46.

18 Erich Auerbach, *Mimesis: The Representation of Reality in Western Literature*, trans. Willard R. Trask (Princeton, NJ: Princeton University Press, 1968): chapter one, "Odysseus' Scar."

19 Alain Renoir, "The Terror of the Dark Waters: A Note on Virgilian and Beowulfian Tech-

similar details. Renoir's work moves in the opposite direction – a truly critical and comparative mode – which attends to contrasting styles of visualization, and leaves little doubt which of the two styles he thinks the more effective.

"The Terror of the Dark Waters" makes a rather direct reply to Tolkien's insistence that the poem resembles not a photograph but a painting. Instead, Renoir judges Virgil's description of Avernus akin to "a simple photograph" and calls the similar scene in *Beowulf* "a motion picture."[20] The approach to Grendel's mere for Renoir features a "quasi-cinematic motion" by which means "the audience [. . .] is irresistibly swept toward the mounting terror of the scene," just as a tracking camera mounted on a plane might film the shot.[21] Upon arrival at the banks of this other world, the poem's visual style guides our perspective, drawing the gaze of the audience steadily upwards from the tarn seething with swamp-gas fires, to the hunted stag frozen motionless on its banks, to the waves vaulting upward toward the darkening heavens. In particular note that Renoir's analysis of the description of the tarn reads like a shot schedule: an establishing shot of the "general area," followed by a tracking shot approaching the pond, "a close up of the stag on the shore," panning down again to the frightening water and then following the arc of the waves heavenward.[22]

Another essay, "Point of View and Design for Terror in *Beowulf*," analyzes Grendel's approach to Heorot, in which Renoir finds a tour de force of subjective camera and mise en scene, whereby, as the night-stalker glides ever nearer, he takes up ever more of the frame, until the whole shot is composed only of "two dots of fire against a veil of blackness."[23] These tightening shots also function to increase the monster's imagined proximity to the *audience* of the poem, allowing us to share the mounting suspense within the scene by aligning our point of view with that of the night-stalker's potential victims. When Grendel finally arrives at the doorway, a radical shift in perspective makes the audience share the monster's point of view as he touches open the door and approaches the sleeping thanes within. Finally though, as Grendel bolts the flesh of Handscio, our perspective shifts for a third time as we observe the ugly light from his eyes glowing like fire in the dark hall through the half-open eyes of Beowulf, whose viewpoint both combines and reverses

niques," in *The Learned and the Lewd: Studies in Chaucer and Medieval Literature*, ed. Larry D. Benson (Cambridge, MA: Harvard University Press, 1974), 147–60 (155).

20 Renoir, "Terror," 154.

21 Renoir, "Terror," 159.

22 Renoir, "Terror," 154.

23 Alain Renoir, "Point of View and Design for Terror in *Beowulf*," in *The* Beowulf *Poet: A Collection of Critical Essays*, ed. Donald K. Fry (Englewood Cliffs, NJ: Prentice Hall, 1968), 154–66 (164). Originally published in *Neuphilologische Mitteilungen* 63 (1962): 154–67.

that of the potential victims and the stealthy hunter in the night. Thus, Renoir concludes, "the terror which the scene so powerfully evokes in the audience is entirely the result of masterfully selected visual details consistently presented from the most immediately effective point of view."[24]

Had we but space enough and time, we could well extend Renoir's cinematographic approach, following it down into the mere with Beowulf. While a complete analysis of the episode is impracticable here, I will illustrate with a few examples how such an analysis might proceed, focusing especially on changes in point of view and the cuts between them.[25] At the center of the poem, in a striking montage of shots analogous to many a self-conscious thriller, the poet "cuts on the cut." Beowulf hacks off Grendel's head ("þa heafde becearf," 1590b), followed immediately by a jump cut to a very different mise en scene, back to the warriors (about whom we had perhaps quite forgotten) waiting on shore:

> Sona þæt gesawon snottre ceorlas,
> þa ðe mid Hroðgare on holm wliton,
> þæt wæs yðgeblond eal gemenged,
> brim blode fah. Blondenfeaxe,
> gomele ymb godne, ongeador spræcon
> þæt hig þæs æðelinges eft ne wendon
> þæt he sigehreðig secean come
> mærne þeoden; þa ðæs monige gewearð
> þæt hine seo brimwylf abroten hæfde.
> ða com non dæges. Næs ofgeafon
> hwate Scyldingas; gewat him ham þonon
> goldwine gumena. Gistas setan
> modes seoce ond on mere staredon,
> wiston ond ne wendon þæt hie heora winedrihten
> selfne gesawon. (1591–1605a)

> Soon the wise men saw,
> those who with Hrothgar gazed on the water,
> that the wave-turmoil was all mingled,
> the lake stained with blood. The gray-haired
> old ones spoke together concerning the good man
> that they did not expect again that nobleman,
> triumphing in victory, to come seeking

24 Renoir, "Point of View," 166.

25 A fuller version of this analysis will be available in a book on *Beowulf* films I am co-writing with E. L. Risden for McFarland, forthcoming 2013.

> the famous king. Then it seemed certain to many
> that the she-wolf had slain him.
> Then came the ninth hour of the day; the brave Scyldings
> abandoned the headlands. The gold-friend of men
> departed thence home. The guests sat
> sick at heart and stared at the mere.
> They wished but did not expect that they would see him,
> their friend-lord.[26]

This cross-cutting from the tarn bottom to shore side represents a masterful stroke, so formidably brilliant in its strained continuities with the prior segment, so plangent in its elegiac tone, so devastating in undermining this tone, and, finally, so decisive in introducing a series of distinctions. All those on shore seem to misinterpret the sign of blood, a mistake emphasizing the difference between their perceptions and reality. Yet the old Danes and young Geats also respond differently to what they see: the latter return home muttering to themselves, while the former stay on desperately trying to keep hope alive. Subjective camera makes the audience assume the point of view (POV) of the "snottre ceorlas," but we seem to look over their shoulders in a long shot at the churning waves. Gore oozes in the surf as dusk settles in, but we also understand how short-sighted are the understandings of these "wise" and "brave" gray-beards who give up and go home. Knowing what we know, the extended vigil of the youthful Geats testifies to their perseverance, though we will also come to understand that these same Geats – or others like them – will flock to the forest fifty years hence when Beowulf is finally in desperate need of their support. Indeed, such cross-cuttings from intense combat to the restricted, compromised perspectives of the internal audience is crucial to the style of the poem: the Danes quivering in terror from the relative security of the outbuildings during the first fight mistake what they hear (783b–788a); the differing reactions of Danes and Geats at the apparent sign of Beowulf's death in the middle episode; down to the last episode's band of *hand-gesteallan* (2696) cowering in the woods when their failing lord finally does need a hand.

Twice- and even thrice-told tales constitute a hallmark of the poem, so much so that the depiction of momentous and violent action from multiple viewpoints must be said to be a distinctive feature of its recursive style. All three of the monster fights are narrated directly and then retold – and

26 This and subsequent translations are from *Beowulf: A Student's Edition*, trans. E. L. Risden (Troy, NY: Whitston, 1994).

sometimes retold again, as is the case with the Grendel episode, which is first narrated, then woven into the riding scop's song including the comparison with Sigemund, then chillingly recalled as the hero searches for Grendel's corpse in the tarn, and then narrated again as part of the larger story upon Beowulf's return to Gotland. Note as well how the swimming match with Breca is twice recounted, first by Unferth and then retold by Beowulf in a way which uncovers the hidden proof of strength and endurance that Unferth's account glossed over. Something similar is at work in the second episode, where the Danes in general likewise mistake a triumph for a failure, because, like Unferth, they are mislead by superficialities, while the truth of what has occurred in the subaqueous hall is unfathomable to them.

This segment from line 1591 occupies the exact midpoint of the 3182 lines of the text in modern editions; the uncertainties and ambivalence of the scene tie it inextricably to the funerals that begin and end the poem. James W. Earl suggests that "*Beowulf* is an act of cultural mourning," "a literary form invented as the culture's way of mourning the recent loss of its past."[27] Earl's insight also allows us to remember that the first half of the poem is more about renewals, unexpected resurgences, metaphorical and metaphysical rebirths, than it is about mourning a lost past. The past continues to be prologue, and that motivates the poem's intricate structure as well as its apocalyptic closure. Premature reports of Beowulf's death are both immediately ironic and ultimately tragic – as Mark Twain's quip recognizes – but in Earl's terms it also invites us to treat the present too as something already lost, so that we can begin mourning Beowulf long before he dies, throughout the final half of the poem.

A second radical jump cut returns us at midline to the hall in the mere, but to a starkly different mise en scene – an extreme close-up on the marvel of the melting sword:

þa þæt sweord ongan
æfter heaþoswate hildegicelum,
wigbil wanian; þæt wæs wundra sum,
þæt hit eal gemealt ise gelicost,
ðonne forstes bend fæder onlæteð,
onwindeð wælrapas, se geweald hafað
sæla ond mæla; þæt is soð metod.
Ne nom he in þæm wicum, Weder-Geata leod,

27 James W. Earl, *Thinking About Beowulf* (Stanford, CA: Stanford University Press, 1994), 133–34.

maðmæhta ma, þeh he þær monige geseah,
buton þone hafelan ond þa hilt somod
since fage. Sweord ær gemealt,
forbarn brodenmæl; wæs þæt blod to þæs hat,
ættren ellorgæst se þær inne swealt. (1605b–1617)

Then that sword began,
from the battle-blood, the war-blade to dissolve
into battle-icicles; that was a certain wonder
that it all melted most like ice
when the father loosens the bond of frost,
unwinds winter-fetters, who has the power
over season and time: that is the true god.
Nor took he from that place, man of the weather-Geats,
more precious possessions, though he saw many there,
than the head and the hilt together,
adorned treasure; the sword had melted before,
the wave-patterned blade burnt up. Too hot was the blood
of the poisonous alien-spirit who died therein.

Continuity editing in film tends to place fewer demands upon an audience than disorienting, jump cuts like those suggested here. The suspense of Beowulf's fight with the tarn-hag was driven along by seamless manipulations of perspective, requiring little in the way of interpretation in order to be appreciated. These "invisible cuts," as they are sometimes called, work to stitch the viewer into the scene and to encourage vicarious excitement with the action, thoroughly in keeping with the Hollywood style of films made to be watched rather than looked at. Once the fight concludes, however, radical montage and the deep-focus texturing of shots more commonly associated with auteurist cinema work to complicate appreciably the meaning of this central episode in the poem. In lines 1591–1605a, the cut from the beheading of Grendel to the warriors' view of the gore-plashed whitecaps troubles continuities even as it affirms them. For Eisenstein, intellectual montage creates an idea out of the juxtaposition of images, such as when shots of strikebreaking in *Strike* (1925) are counterpoised with inset shots of a bull being butchered in a slaughterhouse. For Renoir, meaningful juxtapositions can also be achieved more realistically within a single, extended take. In *The Rules of the Game*, a wife watches through binoculars her husband's passionate conversation with another woman. (The husband has decided that he loves his wife and must break off the affair, which he is in fact doing, as his wife watches from afar.) Yet his wife imagines that she is witnessing the beginning of a seduction, the intensity of which suggests that her husband cannot love her, and she quickly demands a divorce.[28] The visual poetics of the Old English poem work in analogous ways, deploying both "intellectual" montage as well as emotionally complicated and ironically textured shots in deep focus. The light shining from the giant sword and the bloodstained waters juxtapose hope and despair, a lord who shows the way even in the dark places of the world to those who do his work, over against those in no danger giving into gloom and doom at the garish remnants of a bloodbath. Though equally misled by what they have seen, the Danes and the Geats go their separate ways, and the tone and meaning of the scene modulate from ironic distance to a trenchant focus on loyalty and its opposite, pride.

As Beowulf's Danish support melts away, the second radical cut presents an extreme close-up of the liquefying sword: "þa þæt sweord ongan / æfter heaþoswate hildegicelum, / wigbil wanian" (1605b–1607a). The focus on the sodden blade thus serves as an objective correlative for the waning of hope above the tarn. Yet, with the simile of the spring thaw (in film terminology this would be analogous to a match cut inset, juxtaposing the melting blade and icicles), the meaning of the image is transformed as well. Beowulf's victory, however doubtful it may have seemed to those on the bluffs, was – because God willed it – as inevitable as the coming of spring. The simile, in distancing the poem's audience for a moment both physically and emotionally from the carnage in the tarn-hall, provides a much broader context and a glimpse of transcendence. However, the wider meanings of this morphing image have only begun to accrue, arguably becoming complete only when Hrothgar glosses the sword-hilt for Beowulf in his famous speech. The hilt memorializes the obliteration of the race of giants who broke faith with God; he destroyed them with a flood and his power can still be seen in the changing seasons, freeing the world from freezing cold (as from the enormous giants) and opening the seas to men. The hilt, then, functions with something like the deadpan irony of Piers the Plowman's pardon. It is neither a curse nor a magic talisman; rather a remarkably durable sign that God will destroy those whose pride makes them break their troth – a terrible fate to which by the end of the poem both Geats and Danes will have fallen victim.

The final shot in the sequence seems anti-climactic, but it closes the circle adeptly and also contains tantalizing contradictions worthy of consideration:

28 Note Jean Renoir's juxtapositions of mayhem committed within an interior with external crowd scenes in films such as *La Chienne* (1931; a prostitute is murdered while revelers sing songs beneath her window), *La Bete Humaine* (1938; the murder of a woman is cross-cut with a dance). See Katherine Golsan, "Murder and Merrymaking: The 'Seen' of the Crime in Renoir's 1930s Cinema," *Film Criticism* 32:2 (2007): 28–47.

Sona wæs on sunde se þe ær æt sæcce gebad
wighryre wraðra, wæter up þurhdeaf.
Wæron yðgebland eal gefælsod,
eacne eardas, þa se ellorgast
oflet lifdagas ond þas lænan gesceaft.
Com þa to lande lidmanna helm
swiðmod swymman; sælace gefeah,
mægenbyrþenne þara þe he him mid hæfde.
Eodon him þa togeanes, gode þancodon,
ðryðlic þegna heap, þeodnes gefegon,
þæs þe hi hyne gesundne geseon moston.
Đa wæs of þæm hroran helm ond byrne
lungre alysed. Lagu drusade,
wæter under wolcnum, wældreore fag. (1618–31)

Soon was he swimming; he who had known in struggle
the fall of the enemy quickly swam up through the water.
The surging waves were all cleansed,
a vast area, since the alien-spirit
relinquished life-days and this transitory world.
The protector of seafarers then came to land,
swimming stout-hearted, rejoiced in sea-plunder,
in the might-burden of that which he had with him.
They went to him together, gave thanks to god;
the trusty troop of thanes rejoiced for their leader
because they were able to see him sound.
Then from the strong one helmet and byrnie
were quickly loosened. The lake grew still,
water under the clouds, stained with slaughter-blood.

The stages of Beowulf's return to shore are carefully demarcated in three increments: from the long swim ("Sona wæs on sunde [. . .] wæter up þurhdeaf"), to the hero's arrival on shore ("Com þa to lande") and his reception by the Geats ("Eodon him þa togeanes"). Nevertheless, the joyous welcome of the retainers is sharply undercut by a caustic reminder of those no longer there: "þæs þe hi hyne gesundne geseon moston." Moreover, though stained with gore in the prior segment, the whitecaps have now been thoroughly cleansed ("eal gefælsod," 1620). Beowulf used the verb when he promised Hrothgar that he would "Heorot fælsian" (433). Twice after he made good this boast the purge was confirmed in the same terms ("Hæfde þa gefælsod [. . .] sele Hroðgares," 825–26 and "Heorot is gefælsod," 1176b) – but that was before Grendel's mother emerged to resume the feud and befoul the hall once more. Here in the tarn the lapse into contamination is about to recur yet again. Beowulf is quickly disarmed with the help of his retainers, yet the camera-eye lingers at the scene for a final glimpse of the tarn. Two changes have taken place in a brief span. The waves have ceased churning; instead, the lake seems to drowse ("drusade"), and the waters supposedly cleansed by Beowulf's victory are once more awash with gore ("wældreore fag") beneath an overcast sky.[29] The direction of the shot has not changed; rather the location has itself been transformed (for a second time). A recurrent topos in the poem – that of danger lurking on the outskirts of peace – has been eerily reiterated. Our first sight of these gore-splashed waters occurred on the morning after the first fight, when the warriors followed Grendel's bloody tracks back to the tarn. Then, too, there was cause for celebration, though blood called out for blood and that same night Grendel's mother took her revenge. This final transformation within a scene celebrating the monster-slayer's glorious return functions much as the stereotyped open endings in horror films – it threatens a sequel, which of course the third part of the poem supplies, albeit in a different locale. Has the evil hosted by the tarn really and truly died, or is it only sleeping ("drusade"), waiting like the monsters that woke after the flood ("onwocon," 111) to be born again?

We can draw a number of specific conclusions from this analysis of visual styles, especially as regards deliberate manipulations of POV and changes within the mise en scene. The sharpest, most radical cut in the episode comes at the precise moment when Grendel's head is struck off, transporting the audience back up to the shore, where an audience within the poem watches waves churning gore, which they mistakenly conclude is the hero's. A subsequent jump cut juxtaposes the shot in depth of the bloody tarn and the Danes abandoning the watch with a tightly framed shot on the melting sword. The effect of the cut is highly surreal, but the resultant concatenation of images represents a dense interweaving of metonymic and metaphoric images of blood. The synecdoche of the blood in the water is misinterpreted as a sign of Beowulf's death. The blood on the sword marks his victory in the tarn, while the melting of the sword down to the hilt figures the melting away of support on shore down to the faithful stub of Geats. Of course it also intimates that there is something supernatural about the creatures' blood. They are hell fiends and reside in a hellish hole many fathoms beneath the earth, but their corrosive, flammable blood suggests that hell is also within them. The simile juxtaposing the images of the melting sword and melting

29 Compare an analogous moment in *Dream of the Rood* where the gory stains of Christ's wounds and precious jewels alternate back and forth at the four corners of the cross: "Geseah ic þæt fuse beacen / wendan wædum ond bleom; hwilum hit wæsmid wætan bestemed, / beswyled mid swates gange, hwilum mid since gegyrwed" (21b–23).

ice widens the context of Beowulf's achievement still farther, remixing, as it were, the blood and waves of the earlier image in the tenor and vehicle of a simile. Just as the burning blood dissolves the sword, God melts the ice, opening up the waterways for mankind, as the blood apparently does for Beowulf, who meets no further resistance from sea monsters on his return swim. Beowulf's victory is thus also God's, but the watery images within the last passage discussed juxtapose cleansed waves (like those in the simile) with the final lapse of the lake back into a stagnant, gore-choked pool – an image that seems at once to glance backward to God's rout of the giants and forward toward the tenuous, brief nature of Beowulf's achievements in Denmark and later among the Geats.

Certainly Renoir's inter-arts essays deserve more attention than they have received, but it is also necessary to point out an unexpected limitation of his approach. I mentioned earlier his work as a cameraman on some of his father's most important films, such as *The Human Beast* (1938) and *The Rules of the Game* (1939). The long takes in deep focus with people moving in and out of the frame that characterize the cinematography of these films opened auteur cinema and film theory to an approach that was in stark contrast to the intellectual montage championed in the films and theory of Sergei Eisenstein. As maintained by André Bazin, who was Jean Renoir's greatest champion, the shot, not the cut, constitutes the fundamental element of film composition: the relationships, contrasts, and tensions between actors and objects in an expansive environment move film art out of the cutting room into a sustained engagement with the rhythms of the world at large. Hence, the threshold of film is not an artificial frame cut off from any engagement with the real world, but rather directs attention beyond itself to the world at large, to continuities and possibilities not contained within a thoroughly artificial construct. In this openness to the world beyond the frame reside not only cinema's connection to reality, but also its access to the sublime. The meaning of film is composed on location in real time, a function of the continuous relation of elements within and beyond the film frame.

Yet, Renoir's cinematic analyses of *Beowulf* are chiefly informed by the montage theory of Eisenstein (to whom he refers repeatedly) rather than by his father's revolutionary conception of a cinema made out of inclusive long takes, moving camera, and depth-of-field. The reasons are not far to seek. Stark juxtapositions and the intercalating of radically different times and places are distinctive features of the poem's narrative style. If one sought to champion oral poetry as an art form that did not preclude complex design and a high degree of artistic self-consciousness, what better analogy for this than the popular medium of film? Nevertheless, a markedly dissimilar style of visualization does occur periodically in the poem, a style of the cinematic shot, not the cut, to which we should also attend. Take, for instance, the feast after the defeat of Grendel. Here the emotional and political complexities of the scene produce a style of visualization analogous to a long take in deep focus, as Wealhtheow circulates among the gleeful warriors, pouring mead into their cups, speaking privately to Beowulf about her son, and then addressing more formally the whole assembly. Just as in the layered, textured shots made famous by Jean Renoir's *The Rules of the Game*, competing agendas – collegiality and suspicion, present joy and apprehensions about the future – compete for our attention within a single frame, as Wealhtheow sits between Hrothgar and Hrothwulf, who are for the moment at least still faithful to one another, while the kin-killer Unferth reclines, part dog and part snake, at their feet. Within the festive celebration lurks a dynastic controversy simmering just beneath the surface. Wealhtheow's initial place seated between the king and Hrothwulf correlates with her insistence that the succession of her sons under the protection of Hrothwulf be maintained, despite the rumor that Hrothgar has decided to name Beowulf his heir. Next, she carries the cup of friendship over to the bench upon which Beowulf sits between her sons, Hrethric and Hrothmund. The hero's position is likewise correlative with the danger he represents in Wealhtheow's eyes. Ever the subtle politician, Wealhtheow publicly interprets Beowulf's situation as an expression of his support for her two sons. The torque she bestows is explicitly tied to the version of the fostering relationship between Beowulf and the boys that Wealhtheow is taking elaborate pains to establish: "Cen ðec mid cræfte, ond þissum cnyhtum wes / lara liðe" ("Prove yourself with skill, and to these boys be / kind in giving instruction," 1219–20a). Her instructions, couched in imperatives, are careful to distinguish what Beowulf's triumph means from what it does not: he has won everlasting fame, not the throne. The imperatives are draped in dignified, regal discourse, but they fail to hide her evident anxiety about the danger Beowulf's victory poses for her sons' future:

"Wes, þenden þu lifige,
æþeling, eadig! Ic þe on tela
sincgestreona. Beo þu suna minum
dædum gedefe, dreamhealdende!
Her is æghwylc eorl oþrum getrywe,
modes milde, mandrihtne hold;
þegnas syndon gehwære, þeod eal gearo,
druncne dryhtguman doð swa ic bidde." (1224b–1231)

"Be, while you live,
noble one, happy. I properly grant you
the wealth of treasure. Be to my sons

gracious in deeds, protective of happiness.
Here each man is true to the others,
mild of heart, loyal to the lord of men.
The thanes are united the nation quite ready;
having drunk, the retainers will do as I bid."

The scene is thus about places – both physical space and the power relationships of individuals occupying that space – which Wealhtheow, with elaborate politeness and subtle implication, struggles to fix and contain. Obliquely, she groups Beowulf among the loyal retainers to whom she passes the cup, enjoining the hero to be like them and do as she bids. Of course, further complexities also shadow the scene for audiences aware of the latter history of these Danes. The queen negotiates this political minefield with a graceful majesty, and the poet's camera-stylus tracks her throughout the scene as she attempts to weave peace in a hall rife with threats only reawakened by the death of Grendel.

II

If we turn now from the cinematographic styles of *Beowulf* to films adapted from the poem, we find not only the predictable lack of fidelity to the story, which has been widely adulterated with ideas drawn from novels by John Gardner and Michael Crichton, but also (and more egregiously in my view) a lack of attention to styles of visualization already extant in the poem itself.[30] Yet one does catch glimpses, even in popular cinema, of shot compositions and editing strategies that arguably descend from the poem's visual poetics. The purpose of this second section is to demonstrate specific examples of films *adapting*, not plot elements or dialogue from the original poem, but rather the very same visual strategies identified by scholars such as Tolkien and Renoir elaborated above.

A sterling example of the latter comes from Graham Baker's 1999 film, *Beowulf*. Set in a futuristic world, starring Christopher Lambert as an undead Beowulf, and featuring the Playboy centerfold Layla Roberts as Grendel's mother, no one has ever mistaken the film for a faithful adaptation of the poem. At the level of plot, the film's relationship to its source is tenuous at best, a kind of reverie we might imagine inspired by the distant memory of text finding expression in a genre film. Yet the visual strategies of the poem receive much more faithful translation. I outlined above the radical montage

30 John Gardner, *Grendel* (New York: Knopf, 1971) and Michael Crichton, *Eaters of the Dead* (New York: Knopf, 1976).

in the second monster fight where the poet "cuts on the cut," jumping from the hall within the mere to those waiting on shore and back again. Though it conceives the monster fights very differently, the 1999 *Beowulf* cleverly and rather exactly quotes this sequence of jump cuts. Beowulf's second fight in the film is a rematch with Grendel, which the hero contrives to stage within a flooded basement. He employs a spring-loaded, purpose-built hand blade, which multiplies the power of his punches manifold. As his uppercuts drive the wedged blade into Grendel's armpit, a radical cut takes us to Hrothgar and his Danes assembled in the dining room, who misinterpret the screams resounding through the castle and conclude that Beowulf is being killed. The collocation of shots thus combines the internal audiences of the first two fights in the poem: those who hear the screams of Grendel from the outbuildings and those who see the blood rising to the surface of the tarn in the second fight. A second radical montage returns us to the flooded basement with no apparent lapse of time – in fact, just in time to catch the severed arm splashing into the water on the floor. The passage in *Beowulf* masterfully employs a simile comparing the melting sword to melting ice, a comparison we likened to a form cut which juxtaposes similar objects in different frames. An analogous form cut occurs in the film at this point: the shot of Grendel's arm falling horizontally into water is juxtaposed with another shot of the arm, still soaking wet, falling horizontally onto the dining-room floor, where Beowulf has unceremoniously dumped it. The crash alerts the internal audience who remain along the wall listening for some sign of the outcome of the fight. Hopefully, there is no need at this point to insert the usual disclaimers: this is not a good film nor a faithful adaptation. However, it does contain a rigorously detailed imitation of one of the poem's most complex visual strategies, a quotation that reveals a remarkable appreciation of the poem's appositive style and what we might call its proto-cinematic use of radical montage.

One can also find in popular cinema significant uses of depth of field of the kind Tolkien valorized in his *Beowulf* essay. Take, for example, *The Thirteenth Warrior*. Early in the film (an adaptation of Crichton's 1976 novel *The Eaters of the Dead*) we have a long shot in deep focus, with that deepening of perspective that is crucial to the cinema of Jean Renoir, as well as to Tolkien's championing of the poem's darker background and its "impression of depth." The scene takes place on a riverbank at night and depicts the ship burial of a king. An undulating procession of mourners bearing torches shoulders the body to a ship loaded with treasure and sets it ablaze. Through the smoke and the pre-dawn haze we watch from a considerable distance as a young woman dressed in white is raised three times into the air. She and the mourners chant the prayer: "Lo there do I see my father, Lo there do I see my sisters and brothers, Lo there do I see the line of my people back to the beginning. Lo, they do call to me. They bid me take my place among them in the halls of Valhalla where the brave may live forever." These depth-of-field shots are intercut with eye-line matching shots from the POV of the Arab, Ahmed ibn Fadlan, his interpreter, and the Viking, Herger. The latter glosses the ritual for the foreigners in increasingly tighter shots, as the camera zeros in on the reactions of ibn Fadlan. The final shot in extreme close-up registers the reaction of this Arab ambassador, played by Antonio Banderas, as Herger narrates: "She will travel with him. You will not see this again, it is the old way." The alternation between tight and long shots in deep focus (in harmony with the simultaneous translation by Omar Sherif's Melchisidek of Herger's Latin) works to establish the obscurity, the incomprehensibility of a pagan culture even now receding from view. This scene in its mysterious, bleak perspectives, while not at all faithful to the ship burial which begins the Old English poem, is remarkably close to the poem's negotiation of Germanic paganism as Tolkien conceived it: "a past that itself had depth and reached back into a dark antiquity of sorrow" (2006, 27).

It would be misleading to suggest that either Michael Crichton's novel or its film adaptation pursues anything akin to Tolkien's insistence upon the depths of *Beowulf* or his aesthetics of "sub-creation," wherein richly imagined worlds are both internally self-consistent and philologically derived. Instead, Crichton invests in an imaginative response to evolutionary biology – to which, of course, the development of comparative philology owes a great deal – in its euhemeristic rationalizations of myths and monsters. The film version, directed by John McTiernan, rather cleverly evokes visual parallels between the funeral scene just discussed and the fight with the "dragon." First glimpsed by Edgetho through the branches of the tree he has made his lookout post, the *fyr-wyrm* glows like a giant red worm on the mist-shrouded mountain in the distance – a shot thoroughly in keeping with Tolkien's perspectival style in his art and criticism. Ahmed ibn Fadlan catches sight of a lost child wandering in a valley between the mountain and the fortress. As he rides out to rescue her, he discovers that the "fire-worm" is actually a line of a torch-bearing cavalry, snaking its way down the mountain and across the plain in tight formation. As ibn Fadlan reports the truth of this illusion to Herger, the Viking wistfully comments: "I rather prefer a dragon" – thereby giving voice to a sentiment shared by many in the film's audience. But while the shots of the undulating faux dragon clearly quote the earlier funeral procession, itself the vestige of a dying custom, the perspective of those within the film is here revealed as an illusion, a visual trick orchestrated by fog, night, and hundreds of remarkably well-drilled Neanderthal horsemen! (Later they organize their cavalry into the silhouette of a dragon in a remarkably intricate formation that would tax even the most accomplished marching band.) The thirteenth warrior thus serves as the film's rational stand-in and middleman, bridging modern and mythological perspectives. (He also discovers that the cannibals are men not monsters, as well as the location of their lair in the Thunder Caves.) Crichton's reimagining of the poem is thus in essence a fictionalization of the scholarly approaches Tolkien had so thoroughly routed in his essay: archeology and anthropology (however gerrymandered) uncover realities beneath or behind the poem, and, in doing so, destroy its carefully modulated view of the past.

The difference between an "illusion of depth" and depth as productive of illusions is an enormous one. Crichton's ibn Fadlan exposes the illusoriness of superstitions just as thoroughly as his counterpart Hank in Twain's *A Connecticut Yankee in King Arthur's Court.*[31] In fact, commonplaces in the scholarly history of the poem – oral transmission, "Christian coloring," the bear's son folktales, analogues from *Grettis Saga* and *Hrolfs Saga Kraka*, etc. – are leveraged in order to recast Tolkien's "perspective of antiquity with a greater and yet darker antiquity behind," on an evolutionary scale. The fight between monsters and men becomes a battle between competing sub-species of *genus homo* – a difference within phenotypic history that underlies ibn Fadlan's vacillation about their classification: "They are men, They are men!" (when he first examines a Vendol corpse); "I was wrong, these are not men" (later, when the extent of their cannibalism is appallingly revealed). He also reasons about the furtive strategies of these creatures of the mist, slowly recognizing that "They want us to think they are bears," thereby glossing the Neanderthal bear costumes as attempts to fool human beings into thinking they are under attack by a wholly different species.[32] This inter-species masquerade later aids the cause of the Vikings when one strolls up to the guarded cave mouth disguised as a Vendol in disguise as a bear.

The genealogies in the Old English poem that help to create its sense of depth are replaced in Crichton's novel by the immeasurably vaster time schemes of evolutionary genealogy. Neanderthals were once apex predators atop the food chain; they shared an evolutionary – and for perhaps 10,000 years in Europe a geographical – boundary with physically less powerful human beings.[33] The inference that *Homo sapiens* contributed to the extinc-

31 Cf. my discussion of the film's use of euhemerism in *Movie Medievalism*, 27–28.

32 See E. L. Risden, "The Cinematic Sexualizing of *Beowulf*," *Essays in Medieval Studies* 26 (2010): 109–15 (113): "Their patriarchal-matriarchal battle represents a struggle for power between the female-led primitives and the male-led defenders of civilization – one can hardly call it *civilization*, but at least the Norse represent humans moving toward human-ness and away from beastliness."

33 See J. F. Hoffecker, *A Prehistory of the North: Human Settlement in the Higher Latitudes* (New Brunswick, NJ: Rutgers University Press, 2005), 48: "One of the reasons why the Neanderthals are so difficult to understand is that they are not ancestral to modern humans, but rather the product of a parallel and separate line of evolutionary development. In some respects, they may be considered an alternative form of modern human. Just as they evolved

tion of *Homo neanderthalensis* in Europe some 30,000 years ago is an unsupportable conjecture. Another speculation erected atop this conjecture is that the fear of "monsters" living at the borders of human settlements might have originated from a war of natural selection fought between humans and their shorter but significantly stronger "relatives," descended from a common ancestor – a form of fantasy anthropology familiar from the Eloi and Morlocks in H. G. Wells's *The Time Machine*.[34] Thus Crichton rationalizes (if that is the right word) the descent of monsters from Cain, as well as tracing the origin of the feud to that first murder and the divergence of two parallel species sharing a common ancestry in Adam and Eve.[35]

III

Until critical reappraisals of the Old English poem's central episode beginning some forty years ago, Beowulf's fight with the tarn-female was overshadowed by those against Grendel and the dragon. Films such as the 1999 and 2007 free adaptations of the poem, as well as *The Thirteenth Warrior* – in their different ways – make the *aglacwif* the star of the monsters and her lair the showpiece of the film. In *The Thirteenth Warrior* the recursivity of feud in the poem is recast: "Slaughter them until you rot, you'll accomplish nothing. Find the root; strike the will. This is the mother of the Vendol, she they revere [. . .] she is the earth, seek her in the earth." The implicit assumption that Neanderthals were matriarchal is impossible to prove, but if one accepts Crichton's premise about the parallel existence of *homo neanderthalensis et homo sapiens* in Denmark, then the inference that Neanderthal societies retained matriarchal organization even after it died out

certain unique anatomical features, the Neanderthals probably developed some peculiar patterns of behavior that never appeared in modern humans and are unknown among earlier hominids. Their burial of the dead – without convincing evidence of ritual – could be an example of this."

34 Hoffecker, *A Prehistory of the North*, 51–52: "To the modern humans who eventually met up with them, the physical appearance of the Neanderthals must have seemed odd and perhaps grotesque. They possessed a long and low cranial vault with a low receding frontal bone and large brow ridge (*supraorbital torus*). Their brain volume nevertheless was large – comparable to that of modern humans – averaging slightly more than 1,500 cc. The back of the cranium projected outward to form an *occipital bun*. The face projected forward with inflated cheeks and a large nasal cavity. The front teeth were exceptionally large relative to the cheek teeth, and the jaw lacked a chin."

35 Hoffecker, *A Prehistory of the North*, 71: "In many ways the evolutionary origins of modern humans parallel those of the Neanderthals. Modern humans also evolved gradually from *Homo heidelbergensis* during the same broad interval of time (roughly 600,000 to 200,000 years ago)." The *Beowulf*-poet derives the evil progeny ("untydras") of orcs, giants, and elves from Cain (lines 111–13).

among *Homo sapiens* is plausible in terms of Tolkien's rules for sub-creation. The matriarchal womb of monsters – even of the "dragon" – in *Thirteenth Warrior* is the Thunder Caves, ultimately given, as are most marvels in the film, a thoroughly rational explanation. But the idea of a cave beneath the earth pregnant with forces of destruction set loose upon the world by an undying feminine malevolence also finds an echo in the paradigmatic first scene of *Aeneid*. There, Juno bribes Aeolus (with sex, what else?) to release the teeming winds that destroy the fleet of Aeneas and cast him upon Dido's shores. Though the Thunder Caves scene is set near the middle of the film, it is paradigmatic of the film in the same way the opening scene in *Aeneid* is paradigmatic.[36] It is the source of a feminine chaos that threatens to obliterate the Danes, just as Juno's "undying hate" sought to expunge forever the fugitive Trojans. As the "mother of the Vendol" and as a formidable warrior in her own right, as a sign of supernatural fertility and the equally fecund destructiveness of war, the film's earth mother is both source and root of monstrous evil in all its incarnations.

In the *catabasis* into the Thunder Caves, torches light the way for a team of explorers bent on finding the feminine "root" of evil, just as Beowulf sought the bed of Grendel's corpse in the poem. Their spelunking adventure in the caves thus translates Beowulf's journey into terms easily recognizable from lexicon of action-adventure cinema. Eye-line matches from the POV of the invaders survey pockets of Vendol warriors gathered around campfires. However, their descent also stages a journey back in time to an earlier point in human development when men too lived like bears in caves and competed with bears for control of this precious bulwark against enemies and the cold. Cinematically speaking, the most striking images in the film depict the Vendol at home in their lair, their elaborately painted bodies blending into the backdrop of similarly decorated cave walls. They seem to disappear chameleon-like into these backdrops, emerging from and fading into the cave paintings, just as they appear and disappear with the mists in the world above. The torch-bearing spelunkers soon discover the center of this nether world, a kind of altar overseen by an enormous, headless fertility statue with bulbous breasts and womb. Awe-struck, they raise their torches high to scan this impressive monument, but then – in a shift familiar from other action-adventures such as *Raiders of the Lost Arc* – they finally lower the torches to view the horror of what lies beneath. Piles of skulls and assorted bones pave the floor and have been fashioned into columns and dividing walls – an architectural feature not drawn from archeology

36 On the storm scene as a paradigm for the struggle against chaotic outbursts of fury that threaten the establishment of Roman order, see Viktor Poschl, *The Art of Virgil: Image and Symbolism in the* Aeneid (Ann Arbor: University of Michigan Press, 1962), chapter one.

of the Neanderthals but from Christian churches! Yet the idea that this is a shadow world fertile with death rather than life is, within the context of the film, what differentiates the species that must be utterly destroyed from that which must survive. That is, the matriarchal society represented by the archaic mother who permits no cut, the abject horror of a world without abjection.[37] At this late juncture ibn Fadlan concludes: "I was wrong, these are not men." The headless feminine statue, like the headless figurines found throughout the film and the soon-to-be-beheaded mother of the Vendol, signify a world not ruled by masculine reason.

In a combination of relevant elements from *Grettir's Saga* and *Beowulf*, the spelunkers next cross through a waterfall and then swim further toward the center of this cave, where who-knows-what-kind of a religious service is in progress, including chants and ritualized dancing. The Vikings emerge from the water to ambush the Neanderthal shamans giving thanks, perhaps, for the earth mother's favor in their war against humankind. They do not pray to demons like the backsliding Danes in the poem, rather they are themselves the race of demons whose *wig-weorþung* (war-like sacrifice to idols, 176) stacks human bones on the altar of a female god. The next shot in deep focus shows the band of species warriors standing up silently behind the Neanderthal congregants, rising to their feet as Beowulf does in the poem to turn the tide in his fight with the troll wife. This objective shot in deep focus perfectly exemplifies the evolutionary approach of Crichton and McTiernan to the matter of *Beowulf.* Like the ubiquitous textbook illustrations charting the descent of man from apes across generations of distinct species and sub-species, this shot parses differences and similarities in a group portrait containing both Neanderthals and humans. The Neanderthals are more physically powerful, but human beings are taller, stealthier, and more adept in the use of weapons. Those still illustrations of genetic filiations and the slow process of natural selection they represent thus become a still shot of the Vikings waiting behind the Vendol that soon becomes a moving picture of one species overtaking another. When, at the end of the film, Beowulf has killed the Grendel-like military leader of the Vendol, we get a final long shot in deep focus in which the remnant of the Vendol army quite literally disappears into the mist. This is not simply the fog of war; it is the wedding of visual strategies we have identified in the poem with a cinematic style that, in its fashion, is considerably more faithful to these visual strategies than to the plot of the poem. The Vendol evaporate, as Grendel once materialized, in the distance beneath mist-covered hills ("under misthleoþum," 710). Indeed,

37 See Julia Kristeva, *New Maladies of the Soul*, trans. Ross Guberman (New York: Columbia University Press, 1995), 218.

as Hugh Magennis avers, the mises en scene of the film are characterized by "muted colors and an atmospheric use of the perpetual mixture of mist, darkness, and rain."[38] In a sympathetic discussion of the film's genetic and commercial adventures, Elizabeth S. Sklar similarly notes its "gloomy, dark-hued *mis-en-scène*" (sic).[39] Yet these tentative observations on the look of the film leave too much unsaid, obscuring the function of obscurity in the film through approaches that fail to strike a balance between dialogue and moving pictures. What troubles the word-heavy approaches of Magennis and Sklar is precisely their difficulty in accounting for why they, as scholars of the original poem, still find the film so compelling. I suggest that the answer lies chiefly with visual strategies in *The Thirteenth Warrior* that resonate with both our experience of the poem and its scholarly tradition.

IV

Jas Elsner has recently suggested that the discipline of art history is essentially a form of *ekphrasis*, that is, the description of an artwork, which translates plastic forms into words. The approach has much to recommend it.[40] Obviously, film criticism represents a more complex instance of ekphrastic discourse than writing about painting or sculpture, not only because films are made of images that appear to move, but also because they are also composed of words, music, sound effects, and, increasingly, many other things as well. Yet, with these reservations the insight still holds true for film criticism. It encourages us to explore the interrelationships between textual strategies designed to evoke visual images in the minds of readers/listeners and films attempting to translate such word-pictures into the mixed media of moving, talking pictures. On one hand, we can say that film adaptations of written texts, especially with the new resources provided by CGI and other techniques, can (and perhaps should) respond more assiduously to visual cues within their source texts. If filmmakers pursued such a strategy, their adaptations might well meet with less resistance from audiences already familiar with the poem, play, or novel, however much they truncate or consolidate plot elements, add love interests, or tack on happy endings. Brief examples

38 Hugh Magennis, "Michael Crichton, Ibn Fadlan, Fantasy Cinema: *Beowulf* at the Movies," *Old English Newsletter* 35:1 (2001): 34–38 (37).

39 Elizabeth S. Sklar, "Call of the Wild: Culture Shock and Viking Masculinities in *The Thirteenth Warrior* (1999)," in *The Vikings on Film: Essays on Depictions of the Nordic Middle Ages*, ed. Kevin J. Harty (Jefferson, NC: McFarland, 2011), 121–34.

40 Jas Elsner, "Art History as Ekphrasis," *Art History* 33:1 (2010): 10–27: "The reason such accounts are ekphrasis, and hence the bedrock of art history, is that all these descriptions conspire to translate the visual and sensual nature of a work of art into a linguistic formulation capable of being voiced in a discursive argument. The act of translation is central" (12).

of this kind of attention to such visual cues in Jackson's *The Lord of the Rings*, Graham Baker's *Beowulf*, and McTiernan's *The Thirteenth Warrior* were described in this essay. On the other hand (and closer to home), scholars of movie medievalism cannot simply reduce the sources of a film to language or plot elements in their work on film adaptations. First and most extensively, their work – whether they want it to be or not – is a form of *ekphrasis* which should account for how the visual styles of source texts are adapted in films. This constitutes more than a call for authentic period costumes, wooden instead of metal shields, or leather scabbards, however. It is a call to recognize that sister arts comparisons have been an integral part of *Beowulf* studies for a long time now and that by placing interrelationships between media more toward the center of our concerns, we create a space where medieval studies and medievalism can productively interact.

Red Days, Black Knights: Medieval-themed Comic Books in American Containment Culture

Peter W. Lee

In 1961, a teenage Supergirl journeyed to the thirtieth century in an effort to join the Legion of Superheroes, a team consisting of teenagers from across the universe. In order to prove herself worthy, Supergirl unearths millennial-old objects. "Here you are," she beams, "Curios of the great past!" The artifacts include King Arthur's sword, Achilles' helmet, and Richard the Lionheart's shield. The retrieval of these ancient relics impresses the band of history-savvy young aliens – despite their human appearances, none of them are originally from Earth – and they bestow membership upon her.[1]

The Middle Ages, as depicted in American popular culture during the 1950s, confirm the merits of Supergirl's deeds. Despite the composition of the intergalactic club she was applying for, Supergirl deduces that the curios from the Earth's distant past would satisfy the Legion's initiation rites. The Legion had more than a historic interest in the relics from ancient antiquity and medieval England: they recognized the armaments as possessions of predecessors who shared the same goals. The Legion safeguarded interstellar freedom and democracy from world conquerors and saboteurs, just as they believed King Arthur and Richard Cœur de Lion had done in previous eras. While the historical accuracy of this inference may be suspect, for readers in 1961 the meaning was clear. Just as the thirtieth-century heroes identified strongly with medieval England, so did Cold War America. The "special relationship" between the US and the UK was a wartime necessity to cement the

1 Jerry Siegel and Jim Mooney, "Supergirl's Three Super Girl-Friends!," *Action Comics* 276 (May 1961) (New York: DC Comics).

transatlantic alliance through a shared heritage, and the relationship survived as a metaphor for the Free World after the Iron Curtain descended. Several American media initiated medieval "cycles" through the "special relationship" as patriotic and profitable vehicles to demonstrate solidarity with Cold War orthodoxy. The Middle Ages became Americanized as venues of popular culture, such as comic books, and a closely related medium that offers a comparison, motion pictures, showcased the longevity of American values by highlighting such ideals in a medieval past. Medieval-themed media were more about the modern United States than the Middle Ages. Quality Comics' *Robin Hood Tales* upheld Plantagenet England as a proto-democracy threatened from within and Dell Comics' Prince Valiant stories – a tie-in to the film *Prince Valiant* (1954) – safeguarded Christianity from eastern heathens. Might may not make right, but, in this context, antiquity made for authority.

Although some historians, such as H. C. Allen, argued that Anglo-Americanism would triumph over communism,[2] the prevalence of hyper-patriotic stories suggests doubts that an American victory was inevitable. The historian Robert M. Hathaway has shown that the Anglo-American political "special relationship" waxed and waned throughout the early Cold War,[3] and there were hints of dissent even in the comics. Like the movie industry, comic-book publishers had encountered public and political scrutiny as "containment culture," which the scholar Alan Nadel characterizes as the "privileged American narrative" that contributed to the political containment of communism espoused in the Truman Doctrine in 1948.[4] As fears of communism led to a Red Scare during the 1950s, containment culture applied to threats both foreign and domestic: both comic books and movies faced Congressional hearings for threatening to undermine American values. While many producers and publishers subscribed to Cold War ideology to showcase their loyalties and remain solvent, an undercurrent of resistance could be read in their products. Although censors and critics did not pick up on any potential subversion, the Americanization of the Middle Ages, England's in particular, was never complete.

2 H. C. Allen, *The Anglo-American Relationship since 1783* (London: Adam & Charles Black, 1959).

3 Robert M. Hathaway, *Great Britain and the United States: Special Relations since World War II* (Boston: Twayne Publishers, 1990).

4 Alan Nadel, *Containment Culture: American Narratives, Postmodernism, and the Atomic Age* (Durham, NC: Duke University Press, 1995), 2–3.

Errant Knights: Richard and Robin

Considered lowbrow by contemporaries and critics, comic books followed the footsteps established by motion pictures, especially the resurging medieval-themed movies and westerns.[5] Film scholars have examined the medieval genre as a loyalty oath for Hollywood's Cold Warriors struggling to escape the inquisitive glare of the House Committee on Un-American Activities (HUAC).[6] In addition to HUAC's political power, studios were reeling from the explosion of television ownership in newly emerged suburbs. In order to entice audiences, the Middle Ages became an apt genre to show that the movies were better than ever. Many films utilized then state-of-the-art widescreen: "At Last! The Magic of Cinemascope (You See It Without Special Glasses)" *Prince Valiant*'s trailer declared, trading the 3D craze for another technological gimmick. Studios lavished Technicolor, stereophonic sound, and thousands of extras on extravagant depictions of warfare: none could be effectively reproduced on the grainy black-and-white sets, but could be copied in comics.

Equipped with high-tech marvels, *Prince Valiant* found comrades-in-arms in *King Richard and the Crusaders* (1953), *Knights of the Round Table* (1953), *The Black Knight* (1954), and *The Black Shield of Falworth* (1954). *The Motion Picture Daily* summarized the genre in its review of *The Black Shield of Falworth* as a "fast-moving narrative about a young man who doesn't know his august ancestry until it suits story purposes for him to find out, and who undergoes a full course of training for knighthood, together with incidental strife and adventure, in time to engage in armored conflict to the death with his noble ancestry."[7] *The Hollywood Reporter*'s Jack Moffitt picked up on the theme of these coming-of-age sagas of defenders of king and country. He added, "Like all good costume pictures, this one emphasizes how similar our

5 Film critic Kevin J. Harty sees Hollywood's Cold War knights as little more than chain-armored cowboys galloping across medieval versions of the Old West. See Kevin J. Harty, "The Arthurian Legends on Film," in *Cinema Arthuriana: Essays on Arthurian Film*, ed. Kevin J. Harty (New York: Garland Publishing, 1991), 3–28. Stanley Corkin explores 1950s westerns in *Cowboys as Cold Warriors: The Western and U.S. History* (Philadelphia, PA: Temple University Press, 2004).

6 Scott Allen Nollen, *Robin Hood: A Cinematic History of the English Outlaw and His Scottish Counterparts* (Jefferson, NC: McFarland, 2008); Veronica Ortenberg, *In Search of the Holy Grail: The Quest for the Middle Ages* (New York: Hambledon Continuum, 2006); Laurie A. Finke and Martin B. Schichtman, *Cinematic Illuminations: The Middle Ages on Film* (Baltimore, MD: Johns Hopkins University Press, 2010); Susan Aronstein, *Hollywood Knights: Arthurian Cinema and the Politics of Nostalgia* (New York: Palgrave Macmillan, 2005), 64–98.

7 William R. Weaver, Review, *The Motion Picture Daily*, 3 August 1954. "The Black Shield of Falworth" Motion Picture Association of America. Production Code Administration records, Margaret Herrick Library, Academy of Motion Picture Arts and Sciences.

ancestors were to modern man, not how different."[8] Moffitt made the same observation about *Quentin Durward* (1955): "Without ever preaching, the scripters, while talking about France in the fifteenth century, make profound and pertinent comments on our own age." Gunpowder "had filled the world with the same cynical fear that the atom and hydrogen bombs have created today."[9] With such concerns about the present, Moffitt found understanding and escapism in the past.

Comic-book publishers had long shared the same general public with the cinema. By the 1950s, comics and the cinema were linked in Congressional eyes as contributors to not only communism, but also juvenile delinquency.[10] Movies had been subjected to increasing censorship since their inception due to their propensity for showcasing foul play and foreplay.[11] By the 1950s, Hollywood was again under scrutiny for its perceived role as a safe harbor for fellow travelers to turn red-blooded Americans into parlor pinks.[12] Concurrently, a civic outcry blamed comic books for the perceived rise of juvenile delinquency, leading to arguments for banning crime and horror titles and encouraging public comic-book burnings.[13] The child psychologist Fredric

8 Jack Moffitt, Review, *The Hollywood Reporter*, 3 August 1954. "The Black Shield of Falworth" Motion Picture Association of America. Production Code Administration records, Margaret Herrick Library, Academy of Motion Picture Arts and Sciences.

9 Jack Moffitt, Review, *The Hollywood Reporter*, 15 October 1955. "Quentin Durward" Motion Picture Association of America. Production Code Administration records, Margaret Herrick Library, Academy of Motion Picture Arts and Sciences.

10 James Gilbert, *A Cycle of Outrage: America's Reaction to the Juvenile Delinquent in the 1950s* (New York: Oxford University Press, 1986); United States Congress, *Juvenile Delinquency: Comic Books, Motion Pictures, Obscene and Pornographic Materials, Television Programs* (1955–56; repr. New York: Greenwood Press, 1969).

11 Kevin Brownlow, *Behind the Mask of Innocence: The Social Problem Films of the Silent Era* (New York: Alfred A. Knopf, 1990); Leonard J. Leff and Jerold L. Simmons, *The Dame in the Kimono: Hollywood, Censorship, and the Production Code* (Trafalgar Square, 1990; repr. Lexington: University of Kentucky Press, 2001); Gregory D. Black, *Hollywood Censored: Morality Codes, Catholics, and the Movies* (Cambridge: Cambridge University Press, 1996); Thomas Doherty, *Pre-Code Hollywood: Sex, Immorality, and Insurrection in American Cinema, 1930–1934* (New York: Columbia University Press, 1999).

12 See Victor S. Navasky, *Naming Names* (New York: The Viking Press, 1980; repr. New York: Hill and Wang, 2003).

13 William W. Savage, *Comic Books and America: 1945–1954* (Hanover, NH: Wesleyan University Press, 1998; repr. as *Commies, Cowboys, and Jungle Queens: Comic Books and America, 1945–1954* [Middletown, CT: Wesleyan University Press, 1998]); Amy Kiste Nyberg, *Seal of Approval: History of the Comics Code* (Jackson: The University Press of Mississippi, 1998); Bradford Wright, *Comic Book Nation: The Transformation of Youth Culture in America* (Baltimore, MD: Johns Hopkins University Press, 2001); David Hajdu, *The Ten Cent Plague: The Great Comic-Book Scare and How It Changed America* (New York: Farrar, Straus, and Giroux, 2008); Fredrik Strömberg, *Comic Art Propaganda: A Graphic History* (New York: St. Martin's Griffin, 2010).

Wertham's influential *Seduction of the Innocent* (1954) fanned the flames with his take on comic books' portrayal of America: "the world of the strong, the ruthless, the bluffer, the shrewd deceiver, the torturer and the thief. All the emphasis is on the exploits where somebody takes advantage of somebody else violently, sexually or threateningly," themes that he saw in titles including *Hopalong Cassidy*, *Howdy Doody*, and *Bugs Bunny*.[14] Like-minded critics agreed that such comics instructed impressionable children to emulate the depicted deviancy. A Senate subcommittee responded by enforcing a self-censorship body for the industry, the Comics Code Authority, to ensure that written narratives and artwork conformed to the rigid norms of containment culture.[15]

To deflect governmental and public scrutiny, studios and publishers demonstrated their loyalty by redirecting some titles to feature the noncontroversial Middle Ages. By playing to the Cold War ideology, publishers hoped to avoid controversy and boost sales with Code-approved titles. EC Comics, which had promoted hard-hitting tales of crime and horror, turned their attention to psychologists, air aces, and knights of valor. Dell, known for its licensed franchises such as *Tom and Jerry*, was spared the necessity of the Code's seal as it maintained an esteemed reputation for its kid-friendly titles. In its adaptations of *King Richard and the Crusaders* and *Prince Valiant*, Dell displayed its editorial policy that "eliminates entirely, rather than regulates, objectionable material [. . .] when your child buys a Dell Comic, you can be sure it contains only good fun. '*Dell Comics are Good Comics*' is our only credo and constant goal."[16] DC also flooded the newsstands with time-traveling heroes to lend helping hands, such as Batman inspiring the Magna Carta.[17] In *Superboy* no. 103 (March 1963), Superboy helps Arthur pull Excalibur from the stone, and Merlin remarks: "*You*, when you are a man, will look very much like King Arthur! You will give all his qualities . . . courage, heroism, and goodness!"[18] (In a separate issue, Superboy's dog, Krypto, fetches Excalibur from its resting place; DC was unconcerned with

14 Fredric Wertham, *Seduction of the Innocent* (New York: Rhinehart & Company, Inc., 1954; repr. New York: Main Road Books, Inc., 2004), 94, 308–9.

15 The comic-book industry had adopted a code as early as 1948. It was largely symbolic but moviemakers took satisfaction in seeing a competing media take its lumps: see Terry Ramsaye, "Code for Comics," *Motion Picture Herald* (31 July 1948), 7.

16 "A Pledge to the Parents," *Four Color* 650 (September 1955) (New York: Dell Comics).

17 Win Mortimer and Don Cameron, "The Rescue of Robin Hood!," *Detective Comics* 116 (October 1946) (New York: DC Comics).

18 Edmond Hamilton and Curt Swan, "The Secret of the Black Knight!," *Superboy* 103 (March 1963) (New York: DC Comics).

such inconsistencies.[19]) In another plot, in order to defeat weapons from 3000 years hence, the American bowman Green Arrow decides to "match this ancient arrow from the Battle of Hastings against that super-arrow from the future!" The combined might of Anglo-Americanism proves more than a match for the future.[20]

With superheroes mingling in the Middle Ages, several publishers combined the masked vigilantes and a medieval setting to create Robin Hood titles. Despite the wide range of titles, the central motifs were all similar. On one level, the combined adaptations reflected the rich literary history of Robin Hood. As Allan W. Wright has shown, Quality drew their stories from the Robin Hood gests and ballads.[21] The medieval sources aside, Quality's audience was probably more familiar with Howard Pyle's popular historical novel *The Adventures of Robin Hood* and the 1938 Errol Flynn motion picture of the same name. In addition, Robin Hood experienced a revival on television with the Richard Greene series and in movie houses, including Columbia's *The Sword of Sherwood Forest* (1946), *The Prince of Thieves* (1948), *Rogues of Sherwood Forest* (1950), and Disney's *The Adventures of Robin Hood and his Merrie Men* (1952). In utilizing these texts, both old and new, Robin Hood's Sherwood band emphasized facets of American containment culture. In Quality's rendition of the Sherwood outlaw, Robin was especially aware of foreign subversive elements, embodied by England's legendary exemplum of misrule, Prince John, who threatened the legitimate and democratic Plantagenets led by Richard the Lionheart.

Despite the varied tales and time settings for Robin Hood – some historians have placed the Middle English ballad *Geste of Robyn Hood*'s setting well into the fourteenth century[22] – all the American versions take place during the Third Crusade of the twelfth century. Quality Comics was content to continue the saga in its cover blurb: "This is a gallant story that has rung down the ages!"[23] The story is a familiar one: King Richard nobly ventures to liberate the Holy Land from the Saracens, leaving Prince John in charge. The Disney film summarizes the Americanization of Richard's rule as safe-

19 Otto Binder and George Papp, "How Krypto Made History!," *Superboy* 75 (September 1959) (New York: DC Comics).

20 Frances Herron and Jack Kirby, "The Case of the Super Arrows!," *Adventure Comics* 251 (August 1958) (New York: DC Comics).

21 Allen W. Wright, "*Robin Hood Tales* 1956–1958," *Robin Hood: Spotlight of the Month* www.boldoutlaw.com/robspot/0199.html, accessed 18 March 2012;

22 Stephen Knight, *Robin Hood: A Complete Study of the English Outlaw* (Oxford: Wiley-Blackwell, 1994); *The Poems of Laurence Minot, 1333–1352*, ed. Richard Osbert (Kalamazoo, MI: Medieval Institute Publications, 1996).

23 "The Rescue of Maid Marian," *Robin Hood Tales* no. 2. April 1956 (Stamford, CT: Quality Comics).

guarding the unwritten rules of democracy: "The strength of England stands from the well-being of her humblest peasant. The yeoman must be preserved and protected." John, living up to his epithet as "Lackland," quickly imports foreign Norman thugs, especially the usual Nottingham sheriff, and they oppress the Saxon people.[24] When Richard hears of England's suffering, he is in a dilemma. In Quality Comics' *Robin Hood Tales* no. 2, Richard learns that John has usurped the throne and he laments, "I shudder for the plight of England under his cruel fist!" Richard cannot give up the Crusade, so the Earl of Huntington, Robert Fitzooth, volunteers to go back, claiming, "I can organize Saxon and loyal Norman alike to stand against the usurper and preserve liberty until you return!"[25] The main narrative follows Fitzooth, but Richard is not forgotten. The king had a backup feature in which he forms alliances with the beleaguered peoples outside the future Iron Curtain ("Advance seemed hopeless until his Greek allies showed Richard how to build Engines of War!" one story claimed).[26]

The majority of the *Robin Hood Tales*, of course, focused on the titular hero. The series made clear that Robin Hood's opposition to John was not an act of subversion. Although Robin's men worked outside the law, he was "an outlaw in name only because he fought against the tyranny of cruel Prince John's agent, the Sheriff of Nottingham." The usurper was not Fitzooth, but John, "a tyrant as cruel and oppressive as Richard had been just and gentle!" Robin Hood is a restorer of liberty whose "crime had been defense of human rights!" Just as Batman had inspired the Magna Carta for DC Comics, Quality's Robin served a similar purpose: "It was men like Robin Hood and his band of merry outlaws of Sherwood Forest who eventually gave England her love of justice that produced Magna Charta [sic], the document that first made all men free!"[27]

Robin Hood must operate outside the confines of law and order. Quality is adamant that Robin's reputation as an outlaw was erroneously based on the assertion of an oppressive authoritarian state. Fitzooth is a nobleman and loyal supporter of the true head of state, Richard, rather than the faux rule of Prince John. The comic's revelation that John is a "half brother" dilutes his lineage to Richard's bloodline and, by connotation, his legitimacy

24 Ortenberg, *In Search of the Holy Grail*, 201–4.

25 "The Rescue of Maid Marian," *Robin Hood Tales* 2 (April 1956) (Stamford, CT: Quality Comics).

26 "Engines of War," *Robin Hood Tales* 1 (February 1956) (Stamford, CT: Quality Comics).

27 Ogden Whitney, "The Trapping of Robin Hood," *Robin Hood Tales* 1 (February 1956) (Stamford, CT: Quality Comics).

to uphold the crown.[28] In contrast, Fitzooth's faithfulness to Richard and England makes him a self-made man of the people: in addition to being a marksman, Robin Hood's ingenious disguises enable him to mingle with the Saxon commoners – his stance as a loyalist to the genuine crown in opposition to John removes him from any implication for the reader as a subversive element plotting against a legitimate government. Robin's Merry Men share their leader's passion for liberty through their individualization, if only by appearance and attire: Friar Tuck dons his monk's robes and is never without various foodstuffs, and Will Scarlet is clad in his namesake color. All are English, but they have the appearance of freedom of choice. Maid Marian eagerly joins them as the group's sole female and is no less dedicated: "The blood of free Englishmen flows through my veins! Tyranny in any form does not daunt me!"[29] In contrast, the heavyset sheriff and his tax-collecting stooges are uniform in appearance, with fat jowls, uncouth manners, and many plates of roasted drumsticks, pastries, or moneybags, all ripe for Robin's taking.

Robin Hood's status as a champion of the people was not confined to Sherwood outlaws. Other comics, such as Dell's *Four Color* no. 788, taught readers that the American Dream had a medieval precedent. In a celebration of the self-made-man motif (women excluded) prevalent in American coming-of-age stories, the comic's "Steps to Knighthood" detailed the "strict period of training from seven years of age until he reached twenty" as boys progressed from lowly pages to mounted knights.[30] In *Robin Hood Tales* no. 3, social mobility was possible for any stalwart lad. King Richard's servant, Jatho, aspires to knighthood, but the king harbors grave doubts about his skills as a fighter: "For the thousandth time, no! Keep your minds on your duties as my servant, lad! Leave fighting to the knights! [. . .] and let's hear

28 Richard acknowledges that John's corruption was innate: "John was ever greedy and cold of heart!" "The Rescue of Maid Marian," *Robin Hood Tales* 2 (April 1956) (Stamford, CT: Quality Comics). Another of Richard's men, Lord Fenwick, had his position usurped by an imposter, his "half-brother Gerald" who "seized my properties while I was away on the Crusade!" See Ogden Whitney, "The Knight in Red Armor," *Robin Hood Tales* 3 (June 1956) (Stamford, CT: Quality Comics). At one point, Quality places one episode in the court of Richard's father, Henry II, who was manipulated by a troublesome cousin, the Duke of Tedford. Queen Eleanor of Aquitaine aids Robin in eliminating this treacherous nobleman. "Menace of the Royal Assassins," *Robin Hood Tales* 5 (October 1956) (Stamford, CT: Quality Comics).

29 "Ambush of the Merry Men," *Robin Hood Tales* 4 (August 1956) (Stamford, CT: Quality Comics).

30 Bob Fujitani, "Steps in Knighthood," *Four Color* 788 (April 1957) (New York: Dell Comics).

no more prattle about swinging a sword!"[31] When Richard's horse stumbles and the king falls prey to a Saracen dueler, Jatho comes to the rescue. The young servant maintains the letter of his liege's law and does not touch a sword. Instead, he relies on his cunning, pulling down the tent on the Saracens. Richard realizes his error, and the grateful king dubs him a knight, "to serve me only with your sword and your brave heart!" The king ignores social strata and familial connections in knighting his former servant. Jatho's own ingenuity overcomes the obstacles of his low-born origins. In comparison to the Saracens' luck that enabled them to capture Richard, the narrator suggests that Jatho's social ascent was typical of the American Way, made possible in a land of the free: "Jatho's dreams came true in a ceremony to stir the hearts of men of courage everywhere!"

A similar story occurs in *Battlefield* no. 10, where the blue-eyed, "noble, gracious, and strong" Richard battles Saladin in a duel. Richard fares badly until his trusty squire, the prepubescent Robert, hands him a sword at the critical moment, and Richard makes Saladin see stars. Seeing Robert take an arrow for the cause, the lion-hearted king places the injured boy on his own horse and parades him down the ranks. "I, who was the least and humble of all the crusaders, was now honored by my king!"[32] To lend authenticity to this tale, the editor claims that the story was based on "an ancient manuscript found in the Holy Land and signed 'Robert of the Sword!'"

Whether fighting a monolithic ethnic other in the Middle East or combating a tyrannical usurper at home, *Robin Hood Tales*, like *Superboy* and *Batman*, highlight the spandex-clad heroes as defenders of an Anglo-Saxon heritage. As preservers of liberty and human rights, Robin Hood and his time-traveling superhero cohorts become forerunners of American values in medieval England that will carry into the twentieth century. Just as Robin Hood defeats the Norman barons who have oppressed the good citizens, Americans would rout the fellow travelers lurking in modern-day America. While Robin Hood safeguarded the Americanized realm, King Richard attempted to liberate the Holy Land for Christendom. Richard's Crusade is a failure in historical fact and omitted in comic-book fiction. Rather, the mantle of Christianity is taken up under a more successful leader of men, Prince Valiant.

31 Matt Baker, "The Rescue of King Richard," *Robin Hood Tales* 3 (June 1956) (Stamford, CT: Quality Comics).

32 Bill Benulis and Jack Abel, "The Crusader," *Battlefield* 10 (April 1953) (New York: Marvel Comics).

Prince Valiant: Cold Warrior Crusader

In early 1947, *Life* detailed daily life in the Middle Ages. The magazine introduced medieval faith with a parallel for the reading public: "As the American knows that all things are possible to science, medieval man knew that all things are possible to faith."[33] The link between science and spirituality was apt for the Americans. Science had introduced the nuclear age and the space race; faith helped to cope with the potential pitfalls of the hydrogen bomb and Sputnik. In 1959, the historian Jack Finegan stated that what Americans "need very much and indeed more than ever is the really new age which was begun by Jesus Christ."[34] As the historian Jason W. Stevens points out, Cold Warriors "asserted that America's democratic character had its foundations in biblical revelation [and] could not survive without recognizing the centrality of faith to its purpose."[35] The increasing menace of a godless communist regime induced Americans to showcase their solidarity with Christianity as a hallmark of American normalcy. According to the historian Jonathan P. Herzog, the mass promotion of religious fervor was necessary lest the material wants of Americans generate a spiritual bankruptcy.[36] In 1953 the first National Prayer Breakfast was held; in 1954 "under God" was placed in the Pledge of Allegiance; and in 1956 the same phrase became the national motto.[37] The evangelist Billy Graham preached in 1949 that communism "has decided against God, against Christ, against the Bible and against all religion [. . .] Communism is a religion that is inspired, directed and motivated by the Devil himself."[38] Dwight Eisenhower, who befriended Graham in his own spiritual renewal, was baptized in the Oval Office.[39]

The demonstrations of American spirituality permeated genres of popular culture. Spurred by the wrath of the Catholic Legion of Decency, which had helped give teeth to the Production Code Administration in 1934, Hollywood paid its respects to Christianity. The Code's chief, Joseph Breen, himself a devout Catholic, quashed any dirt that besmirched the church on the silver

33 "The Middle Ages," *Life Magazine* (7 April 1947), 67–85 (67).

34 Jack Finegan, *Space, Atoms, and God: Christian Faith and the Nuclear-Space Age* (Bloomington, MN: The Bethany Press, 1959), 21.

35 Jason W. Stevens, *God-Fearing and Free: A Spiritual History of America's Cold War* (Cambridge, MA: Harvard University Press, 2010), 73.

36 Jonathan P. Herzog, *The Spiritual-Industrial Complex: America's Religious Battle against Communism in the Early Cold War* (New York: Oxford University Press, 2011), 16.

37 Stephen Whitfield, *The Culture of the Cold War* (Baltimore, MD: Johns Hopkins University Press, 1991), 89.

38 Nancy Gibbs and Michael Duffy, *The Preacher and the Presidents: Billy Graham in the White House* (New York: Center Street, 2007), 7.

39 Stevens, *God-Fearing and Free*, 72.

screen.[40] Like the biblical epics sweeping across Cinemascope screens, medieval movies were shadowed by Christ.[41] In his novel *The Talisman*, Sir Walter Scott has no love for the Templars, describing them as a "singular body, to whom the Order was everything and individuality nothing."[42] For the film version of Scott's *Ivanhoe*, Breen saw otherwise. He instructed MGM's Louis B. Mayer:

> We call your attention to the fact that the Templars, who are the villains in the story, are indicated as being a religious order, and are frequently referred to as "monks." In this connection, you will bear in mind the Code clause which states: "Ministers of religion in their characters should not be used as comic characters or as villains."[43]

With such imperatives mandated by the censors, the Templars are replaced by the standby of sinister sovereigns, Prince John. Similarly, in *King Richard and the Crusaders*, Templars morph into the "Castlers," a sect unknown to history.

Twentieth Century Fox's *Prince Valiant* (1954) has no qualms highlighting the religious stakes between the virtuous Christians and the pagan adversaries. The theatrical trailer highlighted the "Christians' Revolt against the Infidels" as one of the climaxes of the film. As the film scholar Alan Lupack has noted, critics savaged *Prince Valiant* as an artless juvenile picture, even though the film vehemently upheld a clean-cut Christian morality against the horned, bearded pagans.[44] The storyline, having little to do with Hal Foster's original comic strip, is simple.[45] The evil Sligon has stolen the "Singing Sword" with his "sullied hands," thereby driving the Viking royal family from their home-

40 Thomas Doherty, *Hollywood's Censor: Joseph I. Breen and the Production Code Administration* (New York: Columbia University Press, 2007).

41 Cecil B. DeMille, director of the biblical epic *The Ten Commandments* (Paramount, 1956), penned an endorsement for a children's text of the same name. "Only under The Ten Commandments can men live together. That is why I feel that there has never been a better time than now to reaffirm The Ten Commandments for the young people of today." The book's editors repaid the favor: the illustrations of Moses are "based on Charlton Heston's portrayal in Cecil B. DeMille's production of *The Ten Commandments.*" *The Ten Commandments for Children*, ed. Mary Alice Jones (New York: Rand McNally, 1956).

42 Walter Scott, *The Talisman* (Norwalk, CT: Eastman Press, 1976), 114.

43 Joseph Breen to Louis B. Mayer, "Ivanhoe," 14 February 1950. Motion Picture Association of America. Production Code Administration records, Margaret Herrick Library, Academy of Motion Picture Arts and Sciences.

44 Alan Lupack, "Valiant and Villainous Vikings," in *The Vikings on Film: Essays on Depictions of the Nordic Middle Ages*, ed. Kevin J. Harty (Jefferson, NC: McFarland, 2011), 46–54.

45 Fred Shreiber, "An Interview with Hal Foster," *Prince Valiant*, vol. 1: *1937–1938* (Seattle: Fantagraphics Books, 2009), n.p.

land of Scandia ("Thule" in the comics). King Arthur gives them refuge and young Prince Valiant, played by Robert Wagner, enlists in the Round Table. Valiant finds a mentor, Sir Gawain; a close ally of Arthur's, Sir Brack, turns out to be in cahoots with Sligon; and Arthur's daughter, the beauteous and jealous Aleta of Ord, inspires heroism and heartbreak in Valiant. Brack captures everyone, and Sligon demands that Valiant confirm the religious affiliations of Christian subversives on a master list. The hero refuses and Sligon engages in Cold War rhetoric:

> Sligon: "You'll talk or die on the cross!"
> Valiant: "The cross is our salvation! You'll burn in hell!"

Valiant breaks free, inspires the people to revolt, rescues the Singing Sword, and kills the traitor Brack in front of a cross situated near Arthur's Round Table.

Unlike Breen's strong religious convictions, the Comics Code had only one line concerning religion: "Ridicule or attack on any religious or racial group is never permissible."[46] Although not affiliated with the Code, Dell Comics' adaptation of *Prince Valiant* left out many religious references, but did include a few that were not in the film. Dell's creed claimed that "Dell Comics are good comics" and maintaining the spirit of the Cold War orthodox was crucial to maintaining censor approval. In one early scene in the comic but not in the film, Boltar visits the exiled and delivers news from home: "All bad! Sligon grows more of a tyrant! He calls himself the sacred son of the pagan Viking God, Odin, and woe to any who still speaks of [Valiant's father, King] Aguar there!"[47] The news of Sligon's allegiance to Odin is enough to spur the Christian Valiant to beseech his father's approval to "cross the sea against the pagan traitor!"

Valiant's royal family's religious affiliation to Christianity complicates the narrative's depiction of Viking social ranking beyond good and evil. Boltar and Valiant use Norse religion in derogatory terms: the references to Sligon usurping Aguar's throne in Odin's name fills Valiant with indignation. In later stories, Dell clarifies that followers of Odin were not necessarily evil: despite Boltar's language regarding the "pagan Sligon," comics confirm that Boltar believes in Asgard, and frequently swears by Odin's name when trouble arises.[48] Religion differentiates social status in Thule: Aguar's household comprises ardent Christians whose religion connotes peerage with King

46 Reprinted in Nyberg, *Seal of Approval*, 166–69.

47 Dudley Nichols, Paul S. Newman, and Bob Fujitani, "Prince Valiant," *Four Color* 567 (June 1954) (New York: Dell Comics).

48 Valiant swears "By Odin!" at least once, but never invokes Christ. See Paul S. Newman

Arthur's elite Round Table. Boltar, despite his loyalty to Valiant, maintains a second-class status, symbolized by his faith in Norse mythology and his stereotyped Viking appearance: a horned helmet, a braided, flowing beard, and animal furs for clothes, which contrasts with Valiant's demeanor and chain-mail garb. At one moment, Valiant saves Boltar from deadly peril, quipping, "I promised myself that *you* would return to plague Thule with your boastful tales and heathen oaths!"[49] Valiant values Boltar as a worthy companion, but he is not above mocking his faith. Despite Boltar consistently invoking Odin's name, the Asgardians never come to his aid. Christianity in Dell's *Prince Valiant* tales categorizes non-Christians as second-class others. In challenging the throne's religious affiliation, usurpers like Sligon challenge all of Cold War Christendom.

In *Four Colors* no. 849's "Quest for the Grail," Dryor, a desert hermit, comes to Camelot from Jerusalem. He regales Arthur's Round Table with stories of Chroses, an invader from the East. "All fled before his warriors, who pulled down many a church to celebrate their pagan victory," he informs the stunned knights. In doing so, Chroses uncovers a "glowing, sliver chalice," presumably the Holy Grail. When Dryor begs to purchase the chalice from the Asiatic king, Chroses says no; he plans to keep the Grail "for *my own uses* to show my *defiance* of you Christians!" The comic never shows the pagan drinking from the cup, but an enraged Arthur sends Gawain, Boltar, and Valiant "to journey to the Holy Land and claim this precious cup for Christendom!"[50]

Along the way, Valiant's religious fervor is piqued. When he sees a seasick Gawain bent over the side of the boat, Valiant jokes that his comrade is making a "tribute to sea-gods." Boltar remains silent at Valiant's wisecracks, but he is undeterred from calling Odin or Thor to aid him. As in previous issues, the Norse gods do not answer, and Valiant and Gawain ignore their companion's oaths. Unlike the pagan hordes from the East, Boltar's loyalty to Aguar renders his heathenism harmless. When the heroes are lost in the desert at one moment, a discouraged Boltar muses that "the Viking Gods must be punishing me for going on this Christian quest!" Immediately, nature responds in the next panel when a crocodile slaps Boltar with its tail. Valiant realizes that "that must mean there *must* be *water* nearby!" Even

and Bob Fujitani, "Hostage to Treachery," *Four Color* 650 (September 1955) (New York: Dell Comics).

49 Paul S. Newman and Bob Fujitani, "Trial By Arms!," *Four Color* 788 (April 1957) (New York: Dell Comics).

50 Bob Fujitani, "Quest for the Grail!," *Four Color* 849 (December 1957) (New York: Dell Comics).

if the Viking gods are punishing Boltar, a higher power provides a sign of encouragement for the Christian quest.

After some harrowing adventures in Africa and the Middle East, Valiant finally meets Chroses and offers to buy the chalice, reasoning, "You have *many* chalices of gold and silver! To you it is but another cup – to us a *sacred relic*!" Chroses declines and takes Valiant captive for ransom. After the usual battle, a victorious Valiant sees the cup. He kneels before the chalice, but he discovers a stamped seal from the Roman emperor Trajan. Valiant deduces, "He lived some eighty years *after* Jesus! Our people would never have let the Romans defile the *true* grail!" To prove his point, Valiant melts the cup into slag, explaining, "This act will *show* the heathens that it is not the true Grail! And our disdain for the silver will prove how highly we value the real relic!" The quest ends in failure, but Arthur consoles that "your bold quest has shown the pagans that if they ever find the real Holy Grail, they cannot hold it against Christendom's mighty champions – Sir Gawain and Prince Valiant!"

Despite Valiant's disappointment, the comic ends with an affirmation of Christianity. Arthur declares that Valiant succeeded since "you found the very chalice you set out for – though it was not the Holy Grail!" As the creators assert, the Anglo-American Arthurian forces will hold together as they battle against racial and religious Others from Africa and the Middle East. Valiant trusts no one save his own countrymen, including the pagan, but loyal, Boltar and other good Vikings. A darker reading of the legendary relic's enduring elusiveness may suggest that ultimate victory in retrieving the emblem of Christianity – and western superiority – may prove unattainable. Boltar serves as a reminder of the viability of faiths, even if the creators subject the portly Viking to mockery. When the Christians encounter their final failure, Boltar disappears from the pages. He is conspicuously absent in the climax when Valiant uncovers the cup's falsehood, and Arthur's concluding statements to Gawain and Valiant omit Boltar, who is not among the knights in the panel.

Arthur's advice to his men to keep stiff upper lips, and that they, as Christians, will prevail may not have seemed so farfetched for readers. One history primer asserts that the Europeans were motivated to rescue the Holy Land from the "infidel" Turks, who "disliked and sometimes even hated the Christians."[51] For adults who did not read schoolbooks, or the kids who glossed over them, Dell's comic adaptation of the film *King Richard and the*

51 Philip J. Furlong, Helen M. Ganey, and Francis Downing, *Our Country Begins* (New York: W. H. Sadlier, 1939), 11–12. Study-questions tested students with inquiries such as "Were the Turks Christians?" or "Did the Turks love the Christians?" "Did the crusaders wear a red cross to remind them that they were fighting for a noble cause?"

Crusaders left little doubt which side to cheer: "the Christian kingdom in Palestine is short-lived" due to "Saladin, wisest and boldest of the Sultans." Standing against Saladin is "a man of courageous deed and remarkable valor . . . King Richard of England – Richard the Lion heart."[52] Richard's crusade ended badly, but comics did not dwell on his misfortunes abroad. Instead, the inside back cover of Prince Valiant's "Quest for the Grail" contains a "Pilgrimage" feature that describes how medieval sojourners traveled to various locations to honor relics or find cures. The text notes some popular spots for sojourners, such as Edward the Confessor's tomb in Westminster. The text points out that "the ultimate destination of every devout pilgrim was distant, hard-to-reach Jerusalem," as Valiant's adventure illustrated.[53] Although Valiant failed to recover the cup, the idea of venerating objects remained strong, and not even "infidels from the east" like Chroses could stop pilgrimages. As the Cold War continued without a definite Anglo-American victory, the Middle Ages began to break free of its inflexible containment culture, indicating that an American Renaissance following the medieval period may not be on the horizon.

Cracks in the Consensus: Making Mirth of the Medieval

The deluge of medieval-themed comics after the implementation of the Comics Code was the publishers' attempt to conform to the Cold War rhetoric of containment culture. Yet signs suggested that the Americanization of the Middle Ages was not without critics. In comparing *The Black Shield of Falworth* to other medieval-themed films for *The Hollywood Reporter*, screenwriter Jack Moffitt described the picture as a "delightful tale of youth." However, he cautioned that "after so many dull movies of knights-in-armor, the exhibitor should be careful how he sells it."[54] As the 1950s progressed, there were strains in the "special relationship" between Great Britain and the United States, stemming from causes that ranged from nuclear proliferation to the United States' role in the fading British Empire. While the medieval representation of the Anglo-American relationship survived, undercurrents of dissent in the medieval-themed comics challenged the Cold War orthodoxy.

Quality's *Robin Hood Tales* ostensibly opposes traitorous and foreign elements that conspire and oppress the democracy-loving Saxons, but

52 Matt Baker, "King Richard and the Crusaders," *Four Color* 588 (October 1954) (New York: Dell Comics).
53 Bob Fujitani, "Pilgrimages," *Four Color* 849 (December 1957) (New York: Dell Comics).
54 Jack Moffitt, Review, *The Hollywood Reporter*, 3 August 1954. "The Black Shield of Falworth" Motion Picture Association of America. Production Code Administration records, Margaret Herrick Library, Academy of Motion Picture Arts and Sciences.

the series' premise also provides a veiled warning against the Red Scare's curtailing of civil liberties at home.[55] Like those under Congressional investigation, Fitzooth finds himself persecuted by a government body that has restrained constitutional rights. In Quality's version of the origin of Robin Hood, Prince John demands that Fitzooth sign a loyalty oath that dissolves his allegiance to Richard. For John, swearing fealty is an all-or-nothing enterprise: "Sign this oath of allegiance to me and you go free! Serve me well and you will be richly rewarded! Refuse and you hang!" Fitzooth refuses and cities a higher authority than John's half-brother kinship: "Sire, my loyalty is to Richard and England! Compared to serving your evil designs, hanging would be pleasant!"[56] Stripped of his rightful fiefs and holdings, Fitzooth has no recourse but to go underground and help restore the Magna Carta, the celebrated proto-Constitution that had guaranteed human rights for the Saxons now held "in misery and bondage."[57] *Robin Hood Tales* thus reads as a critique of the Red Scare: Fitzooth thwarts a faux loyalty oath demanded by a zealous would-be tyrant and is forced to become an underground outlaw. As a freedom fighter, Robin Hood seemingly subverts royal authority, but he represents the true values of a democratic state and battles to dethrone a usurper. Just as John has abused the trust and duties of kingship, his fanatical twentieth-century counterparts, Senator Joseph McCarthy and other red-baiters in Congress, have done the same to the American people.

Quality does not emphasize the similarities between Fitzooth's unhappy losses and McCarthyism. The series bore the seal of approval from the Comics Code Authority, the regulatory body that emerged from the Senate hearings investigating childhood delinquency, which cleared the issues for public consumption, and thus shielded any Cold War critique. To pass censorship, Fitzooth must follow Cold War convention and eschew John's odious oath for a genuine pledge of fealty under the rightful king, Richard, as a demonstration of solidarity against illegitimate, un-American outsiders. John becomes the true subversive element rather than a stand-in for McCarthy. The Comics Code would have rejected any other reading for failing to meet the specification that "policemen, judges, government officials, and respected institutions shall never be presented in such a way as to create disrespect for

55 The television series *Robin Hood* (1955–60) was also a "delicious opportunity to create scripts about taking from the rich to give to the poor." The series, produced in England and broadcasted in the United States, gave voice to several blacklisted screenwriters of the Hollywood Ten. See Ronald Radosh and Allis Radosh, *Red Star Over Hollywood: The Film Colony's Long Romance with the Left* (San Francisco, CA: Encounter Books, 2006), 211.

56 "The Rescue of Maid Marian," *Robin Hood Tales* 2 (April 1956) (Stamford, CT: Quality Comics).

57 Ogden Whitney, "The Black Knight of Castle Fury," *Robin Hood Tales* 1 (February 1956) (Stamford, CT: Quality Comics).

established authority," all categories that did not apply to a false king like John.[58] For writers who felt unfairly persecuted, Fitzooth's experience may have had private meanings as they encountered public stigmatization and suffered a loss of creative freedom and revenue as the industry struggled to redefine itself. That writers generally did not sign their work – not wanting to be associated with low-brow literature, leaving historians to puzzle over their identities – provided a release valve to express their frustrations. The protest against corrupt misrule in *Robin Hood Tales* might have been recognized as a veiled critique against the rigidity of American containment culture. The historian Richard M. Fried notes that an Indiana woman led a public crusade against the Sherwood outlaw for corrupting capitalism: he robbed from the rich and gave to the poor, a clear redistributor of wealth.[59]

A more damaging critique of Cold War ideology is the readers' ultimate rejection of the series. EC publisher Bill Gaines remembers that bundles of his post-Code comics, such as *Valor*, returned unopened from the newsstands.[60] In Gaines's case, the industry may have blacklisted the publisher for his role in the Comics Code Authority's formation and the resulting economic slump. Although circulation figures do not survive, *Robin Hood Tales* lasted a mere six issues before Quality quit the comics business.[61] The cinematic medieval cycle was well worn and deflating among consumers: several Middle Ages-themed pictures, *Prince Valiant* included, met with mediocre box-office receipts.[62]

If the orthodoxy was not selling well, a more serious blow for Cold Warriors was the capitalization of the Cold War as comedy. *Mad Magazine*'s "Prince Violent" creates a parody of chivalry in general and the 1954 film in particular. The Arthurian kingdom of the prince, who is known as Viol, maintains its medieval opulence, although Arthur's world is inverted, as the Round Table is used to play cards and a joust consists of thumb wrestling. Nevertheless, Viol's Americanism remains unchallenged, even if clothed in jest: "Young Violent of Drule who aspireth to becometh a knighteth at-eth Kingeth Arthureth Routh . . . Rath . . . thooth . . . ptooey! . . . King Arthur's Round Table, whiles away the time in great fun at the sport of

58 Nyberg, *Seal of Approval*, 166.

59 Richard M. Fried, *Nightmare in Red: The McCarthy Era in Perspective* (New York: Oxford University Press, 1990), 34.

60 Hajdu, *The Ten Cent Plague*, 321.

61 The robber-of-the-rich did not generate enough profits to sustain Quality, which folded in 1956, but, in Robin Hood fashion, Fitzooth defied death, as DC Comics took over the defunct title. *Robin Hood Tales* continued for two years before the Sherwood outlaw succumbed.

62 Aronstein, *Hollywood Knights*, 65.

mock combat!"[63] Despite the mocking tone, Violent's ascension into the knightly ranks is affirmed in the climactic duel: "Due to Viol's clean living, 100% Americanism, and he doesn't bite his nails, he doth get a grip that his enemy cannot breaketh and Viol wins the thumb wrestle!" Such mock chivalry found favor with Violent's sovereign: the story ends with Viol entering knighthood. Furthermore, he sprouts his first chest hair, a sign of maturity and virility that Robert Wagner's screen incarnation had yet to develop. Princess Alota – whose name is indicative of her own ample tresses – is impressed, rids Violent of his page-boy bob for a buzz cut ("Now I see you are a man!"), and Violent's Americanization is complete.

Although Viol's "100% Americanism" helped Viol ascend to knighthood and win the princess's hand, a deepening pessimism that the Cold War might end in a hot mushroom cloud slowly crept into medieval Americana. Nevertheless, Code-approved comics also saw silver linings in a nuclear apocalypse. In 1960, DC's *Strange Adventures* predicted a medieval solution to an atomic war prophesied for 29 October 1986. In this futuristic Dark Age, "there is no more government, and the prevailing law is *Might Makes Right*!"[64] Fortunately, a band of Americans learns that centuries-old suits of armor have "hardened into a peculiar molecular structure capable of acting as a shield against nuclear radiation!" The group raids a museum for protective medieval gear. In the first installment, they storm a castle and, in Robin Hood-fashion, redistribute resources that a "black baron" has horded from an impoverished people. Afterwards, the heroes convene at a table (hexagon-shaped for the six knights). "We must not relax our vigilance!" the leader proclaims. "I propose we form a band . . . and call ourselves the *Atomic Knights*!" The others agree that they must "help right wrongs and undo evil – like the *knights of old*" because "*someone* has to represent *law and order* and the forces of *justice* in these terrible times – and it looks like the job is ours!"

Conclusion

While the Atomic Knights adopt a cheery determination to restore American values in the midst of a nuclear holocaust, the comic's creators crafted a double-edged sword. Like the medieval armor they don, the Knights' concepts of justice and democracy prove timeless, even though the United States itself perishes in the Cold War. Medieval-themed comic books, and

63 Harvey Kurtzman and Wally Wood, "Prince Violent!," *Mad Magazine* 13 (July 1954) (New York: EC Comics).

64 John Broome and Murphy Anderson, "The Rise of the Atomic Knights," *Strange Adventures* 117 (June 1960) (New York: DC Comics).

their related popular medium in motion pictures, supported the Cold War ideology by transposing the fight against communism into the medieval era, specifically Robin Hood's Plantagenet England and Valiant's Thule/Camelot. Both industries were rebounding from then-recent public and governmental scrutiny, and utilized the Middle Ages as a means of cementing solidarity with the Cold War consensus in a noncontroversial genre. Creator efforts generated mixed results, as undesirable elements managed to permeate the censored products.

Quality's *Robin Hood Tales* was an inversion on subversion, providing a dual message criticizing McCarthyism while simultaneously warning readers of foreign interlopers. Not only did Prince John and his henchmen undermine Richard's legitimate rule and oppress the Saxon peasantry, the hero, Fitzooth, must go underground to thwart this usurper to the English crown. In issue nine, a peasant cries out to an unjust tax-collector, "'Tis not my gold! But hard-earned coin freely given by poor peasants for good king Richard who needs money to carry on the crusades!"[65] Robin Hood quickly puts right this situation and ensures that the misappropriated funds will support Richard's efforts. Robin's undermining of an illegitimate ruler also creates a parallel with McCarthyism: Prince John's demands that Fitzooth adhere to a faux fealty is reminiscent of private and public requirements for loyalty oaths in the height of the Red Scare. In a later story in that same issue, Robin himself becomes a dictator of a town to save it from a greater tyranny of the Nottingham sheriff: "I, *Robin Hood*, lay claim upon this village and dub it *Robin Hood Town*!"[66] Robin surrenders the town back to its villagers by the issue's end after restoring the peace, and the grateful villagers maintain the name Fitzooth bestowed upon it. Robin, like those subpoenaed by HUAC and who refused to name names, faced stigmatization as an outlaw, yet he sacrificed his livelihood for a greater cause. The Comics Code ensured happy endings for *Robin Hood Tales*, yet the undercurrent criticizing Cold War orthodoxy remained undetected.

Danger also surrounded Prince Valiant's efforts to protect Christianity from pagan Others. In *Four Color* 719 King Aguar tells his son, Thule's neighbors, the Stonehenge-worshipping "Picts," pose an ideological and physical threat. To prepare Valiant for a tournament, Aguar says they must "show the pagan northlanders the prowess of Christian champions! That should impress them that a man who takes the cross does not do so out of

65 Bill Finger, Ross Andru, and Mike Esposito, "The Strange Vow of Robin Hood," *Robin Hood Tales* 9 (May–June 1957) (New York: DC Comics).

66 Bill Finger, Ross Andru, and Mike Esposito, "The Siege of Robin Hood Town," *Robin Hood Tales* 9 (May–June 1957 (New York: DC Comics).

weakness!"[67] When Valiant succeeds, the non-Christian Boltar tells his king, "There's a newfound respect in those pagan raiders' eyes! They'll steer clear of Arthur's shores and keep Thule well off their bows!" The Picts are subdued, but Thule and Camelot will encounter deadly peril as heathens endanger Christianity time and again. The Sherwood outlaw and Prince Valiant fought the Cold War by utilizing their medieval heritage to continue the never-ending battle for truth, justice, and the American way.

67 Paul S. Newman, "The Peril of the Round Table!," *Four Color* 719 (August 1956) (New York: Dell Comics).

Contributors

AIDA AUDEH is Associate Professor of Art History and Chair of the Department of Studio Arts & Art History at Hamline University (St. Paul, Minnesota). She is co-editor of *Dante in the Long Nineteenth Century: Nationality, Identity, and Appropriation*, contributing author to *Dante in the Nineteenth Century: Reception, Portrayal, Popularization*, and author of numerous articles on artists' interest in Dante in the nineteenth century which have appeared in journals including *Dante Studies*, *Studies in Medievalism*, and *Annali d'Italianistica*.

ELIZABETH EMERY is Professor of French at Montclair State University where she teaches courses on medieval, nineteenth-, and twentieth-century French literature and culture and serves as Graduate Coordinator. She has published articles, books, and essay anthologies pertaining to nineteenth-century French and American medievalism, most recently a monograph entitled *Photojournalism and the Origins of the Author House Museum* (1881–1914). She serves as joint editor of the journal *Romance Studies*.

KATIE GARNER is currently completing her Ph.D. in English Literature at Cardiff University. Her doctoral research examines popular and scholarly appropriations of the Arthurian legend by British women writers between 1775 and 1845.

NICKOLAS HAYDOCK, Professor of English at the University of Puerto Rico (Mayagüez Campus), teaches courses on medieval and early modern literature, medievalism, film, theory, and pedagogy. He has published two books, *Movie Medievalism: The Imaginary Middle Ages* and *Situational Poetics in Robert Henryson's "Testament of Cresseid"*. He has also co-edited, with E. L. Risden, *Hollywood in the Holy Land*. Another book on *Beowulf* films, co-written with Risden, is forthcoming. Haydock serves as the series editor for *Cambria Studies in Classicism, Orientalism, and Medievalism*.

AMY S. KAUFMAN is Assistant Professor of English at Middle Tennessee State University, where she teaches early European literature, medieval British literature, and feminist theory. She regularly publishes on both medieval Arthurian legend and medievalism in American culture and is chair of the Medievalism in Popular Culture area for the National Popular and American Culture Associations.

PETER W. LEE is a history Ph.D. candidate at Drew University, specializing in modern American culture and youth culture. His scholarship focuses on the visual arts. Among his publications are contributions to *Americana: The Journal of American Culture*, *The Bright Lights Film Journal*, *Thymos: The Journal of Boyhood Studies*, and the *Critical Surveys of Graphic Novels: Heroes and Superheroes* reference set. He is currently at working on a project concerning children in post-World War II cinema.

PATRICK J. MURPHY is Associate Professor of English at Miami University, where he teaches courses in medieval literature and the history of the English language. He is the author of *Unriddling the Exeter Riddles*. He is currently collaborating with Professor Fred Porcheddu of Denison University on a study of the medievalist fiction of Montague Rhodes James.

FRED PORCHEDDU is Viola Kleindienst Professor at Denison University (Granville, Ohio), where he teaches and writes about medieval and early modern literature and fantasy and Gothic fiction.

CLARE A. SIMMONS is a Professor of English at The Ohio State University. She is the author of *Reversing the Conquest: History and Myth in Nineteenth-Century British Literature*; *Eyes Across the Channel: French Revolutions, Party History, and British Writing 1830–1882*; and numerous essays on nineteenth-century British literature, especially medievalism. The editor of *Prose Studies*, she also edited the essay collection *Medievalism and the Quest for the "Real" Middle Ages* and Charlotte Mary Yonge's novel *The Clever Woman of the Family*. Her most recent book is *Popular Medievalism in Romantic-Era Britain*.

MARK B. SPENCER is Professor of English and Humanities at Southeastern Oklahoma State University. He holds doctorates in both medieval history and comparative literature, which he brings to bear in his study of medieval historiography and modern historical novels set during the Middle Ages and Renaissance. He is the author of *Thomas Basin (1412–1490): The History of Charles VII and Louis XI*, and his most recently published articles include studies of Sigrid Undset's *Kristin Lavransdatter* and *Quentin Durward* by Sir Walter Scott.

RICHARD UTZ is Professor and Chair in the School of Literature, Media, and Communication at the Georgia Institute of Technology. His research centers on the reception of medieval culture in postmedieval times, with an emphasis on identity, memory, nationalism, technology, and temporality, and on providing humanistic perspectives on a technological world.

Previously published volumes

Volume I

1. Medievalism in England
Edited by Leslie J. Workman. Spring 1979

2. Medievalism in America
Edited by Leslie J. Workman. Spring 1982

Volume II

1. Twentieth-Century Medievalism
Edited by Jane Chance. Fall 1982

2. Medievalism in France
Edited by Heather Arden. Spring 1983

3. Dante in the Modern World
Edited by Kathleen Verduin. Summer 1983

4. Modern Arthurian Literature
Edited by Veronica M. S. Kennedy and Kathleen Verduin. Fall 1983

Volume III

1. Medievalism in France 1500-1750
Edited by Heather Arden. Fall 1987

2. Architecture and Design
Edited by John R. Zukowsky. Fall 1990

3. Inklings and Others
Edited by Jane Chance. Winter 1991

4. German Medievalism
Edited by Francis G. Gentry. Spring 1991

Note: Volume III, Numbers 3 and 4, are bound together.

IV. Medievalism in England
Edited by Leslie Workman. 1992

V. Medievalism in Europe
Edited by Leslie Workman. 1993

VI. Medievalism in North America
Edited by Kathleen Verduin. 1994

VII. Medievalism in England II
Edited by Leslie J. Workman and Kathleen Verduin. 1995

VIII. Medievalism in Europe II
Edited by Leslie J. Workman and Kathleen Verduin. 1996

IX. Medievalism and the Academy I
Edited by Leslie J. Workman, Kathleen Verduin, and David D. Metzger. 1997

X. Medievalism and the Academy II
Edited by David Metzger. 1998

XI. Appropriating the Middle Ages: Scholarship, Politics, Fraud
Edited by Tom Shippey and Martin Arnold. 2001

XII. Film and Fiction: Reviewing the Middle Ages
Edited by Tom Shippey and Martin Arnold. 2002

XIII. Postmodern Medievalisms
Edited by Richard Utz and Jesse G. Swan. 2004

XIV. Correspondences: Medievalism in Scholarship and the Arts
Edited by Tom Shippey and Martin Arnold. 2005

XV. Memory and Medievalism
Edited by Karl Fugelso. 2006

XVI. Medievalism in Technology Old and New
Edited by Karl Fugelso with Carol L. Robinson. 2007

XVII. Defining Medievalism(s)
Edited by Karl Fugelso. 2009

XVIII. Defining Medievalism(s) II
Edited by Karl Fugelso. 2010

XIX. Defining Neomedievalism(s)
Edited by Karl Fugelso. 2010

XX. Defining Neomedievalism(s) II
Edited by Karl Fugelso. 2011

XXI. Corporate Medievalism
Edited by Karl Fugelso. 2012